5 STEPS TO A 5™

AP Macroeconomics

AP Macroeconomics

Eric R. Dodge, PhD

Front Cover: Peshkova/Shutterstock

1 2 3 4 5 6 7 8 9 LON 28 27 26 25 24

ISBN 978-1-266-71095-7
MHID 1-266-71095-7

The series editor was Grace Freedson, and the project editor was Del Franz. Series design by Jane Tenenbaum.

CONTENTS

PREFACE

So, you've decided to bite the bullet and invest your time in a book designed to help you earn a 5 on your AP Macroeconomics exam. Congratulations! You have taken the first of many small steps toward this goal. An important question remains: Why this book?

Priority number one, both for your AP course and for this book, is to prepare you to do well enough on the AP Macroeconomics exam to earn college credit. I firmly believe that this book has a comparative advantage over your other options. First, I have written this text with a certain conversational approach, rather than a flurry of formulas and diagrams that you must remember. Sure, some memorization is required for any standardized test, but a memorizer of formulas is in deep trouble when asked to analyze the relative success of several possible economic policies or to draw fine distinctions between competing economic theories. Using this book to supplement and reinforce your understanding of the theories and relationships in economics allows you to apply your analytical skills to the exam, and this gives you a significant advantage over the formula-memorizing exam taker. If you spend less time memorizing formulas and take the extra time to understand the basics, you will get along just fine with this book, and you will do extremely well on the AP Macroeconomics exam.

Second, as a college professor who has taught economics to thousands of students, I have a strong understanding of where the learning happens and where the mistakes are made.

Third, as a reader and writer of AP exams, I can tell you where points are lost and where a 5 is made on the free-response questions. Most important, I am a realist. You want to know what it takes to earn a 5 and not necessarily the finer points of the Federal Reserve System, the Sherman Antitrust Act, or the NAFTA.

Take the time to read the first four chapters of this book, which are designed to help you understand the challenge that lies ahead and to provide you with tips for success on the exam.

Take the diagnostic exam to see where you stand before beginning your review. The bulk of this book is a comprehensive review of macroeconomics with practice questions at the end of each chapter. These questions are designed to quickly test your understanding of the material presented in each chapter, not necessarily to mirror the AP exam. For exam questions that are more typical of what you will experience in May, I have provided you with two practice exams in macroeconomics, complete with essay questions, sample responses, and scoring guidelines.

Since the first edition of the book, several updates have been made to adapt to changes in the AP Macroeconomics exams. As the curriculum has changed, the text has adapted, either by adding new content or modifying existing. When the test developers have incorporated new ways of testing or scoring questions, 5 Steps has kept pace so that students are not left behind. With each new edition, multiple-choice and free-response questions are edited and updated to give you the best chance at scoring the 5.

In other big news, since 2023 AP Macroeconomics test takers have been allowed to use four-function calculators. Students should be prepared to see more mathematical problems. At the time, I wrote that I anticipated changes would soon be made to the official course description to reflect current monetary policy tools; in June 2022, those changes were announced. The 2024 edition overhauled the chapter on monetary policy to reflect the ample reserves framework used by the Federal Reserve and other central banks. It is highly likely that the next couple of years will see more testing of the ample reserves framework and free-response scoring will evolve. This is a period of transition for the AP Macroeconomics approach to monetary policy, so there may be some holdover questions that test you on the traditional fractional (or limited) reserve monetary policy. Given that, and that some nations may still have a central bank that continues to have reserve requirements, I have maintained an abbreviated section that covers these traditional tools, while shifting the primary focus to the ample reserves tool.

I do not see any reason to continue talking about the book when we could just dive in. I hope that you enjoy this book and that you find it a useful resource. Good luck!

ACKNOWLEDGMENTS

As always, this book is dedicated to my wife, Dr. Melanie Fox, and our three sons, Eli, Max, and Theo. You all make life so much more fun. Thank you.

NOTE FOR THE EDUCATORS

Dear Teacher, thank you for taking on the challenge of teaching AP Microeconomics and/or Macroeconomics to your students. The content in these subjects is not always easy to teach, but the rewards from watching your students succeed are incredible! It is critical that our students understand the economic world in which they live.

As you probably know, in recent years the College Board has made some revisions to both the Microeconomics and Macroeconomics curricula, and has published an updated "Course and Exam Description" for both. I'm quite sure that you have received plenty of information from the College Board about these changes and about the new course framework. Throughout the semester you will be teaching your students the material, while emphasizing four "Course Skills" and four "Big Ideas" as you go. This *5 Steps to a 5* book incorporates those skills and ideas in the chapters and in the practice exams, and should provide your students an excellent supplement to all the work that you are doing in the classroom.

Again, thank you for all that you do in the role of economic educator, role model, and mentor for the students. May you have a wonderful academic year!

ABOUT THE AUTHOR

Eric R. Dodge was born in Portland, Oregon, and attended high school in Tigard, Oregon. He received a bachelor's degree in business administration from the University of Puget Sound in Tacoma, Washington, before attending the University of Oregon for his master's and doctoral degrees in economics. While at the University of Oregon, he received two graduate student awards for teaching and became a die-hard fan of the Ducks. Since 1995, he has been teaching economics at Hanover College in Hanover, Indiana, the oldest private college in the state. The author is the Zeddies Chair in Economics and teaches principles of microeconomics and macroeconomics, intermediate microeconomic theory, labor economics, environmental economics, industrial organization, statistics, econometrics, introduction to sustainability, and the economics of dams.

Since 2000, Eric Dodge has served as a faculty consultant for the AP economics program and has been a reader and writer of free-response questions, table leader, and question leader at the annual AP Economics Reading. With coauthor Melanie Fox, he has also written three recently published books: *Economics Demystified, 500 Microeconomics Questions: Ace Your College Exams*, and *500 Macroeconomics Questions: Ace Your College Exams*. He splits his time between historic Madison, Indiana, and West Lafayette, Indiana, with his wife, Melanie; sons Eli, Max, and Theo; and Eliza, a neurotic, rain-fearing dog.

INTRODUCTION: THE FIVE-STEP PROGRAM

The Basics

Not too long ago, you agreed to enroll in AP Macroeconomics. Maybe you saw a flyer and the allure of economic knowledge was just too much to resist, or maybe a respected teacher encouraged you to challenge yourself and you took the bait. Either way, you find yourself here, flipping through a book that promises to help you culminate this life-changing experience with the highest of honors, a 5 in AP Macroeconomics. Can it be done without this book? Sure, there are many excellent teachers of AP Macroeconomics out there who teach, coax, and cajole their students into a 5 every year. But for the majority of students in your shoes, the marginal benefits of buying this book far outweigh the marginal costs.

Introducing the Five-Step Preparation Program

This book is organized as a five-step program to prepare you for success on the exams. These steps are designed to provide you with the skills and strategies vital to the exam and the practice that can lead you to that perfect 5. Each of the five steps provides you with the opportunity to get closer and closer to that prize trophy 5.

Following are the five steps:

Step 1: Set Up Your Study Program

In this step, you'll read a brief overview of the AP Macroeconomics exam, including an outline of topics and the approximate percentage of the exam that will test knowledge of each topic. You will also follow a process to help determine which of the following preparation programs is right for you:

- Full school year: September through May.
- One semester: January through May.
- Six weeks: Basic training for the exam.

Step 2: Determine Your Test Readiness

In this step, you'll take a diagnostic exam in macroeconomics. This pretest should give you an idea of how prepared you are to take the real exam before beginning to study for it.

- Go through the diagnostic exam step-by-step and question-by-question to build your confidence level.
- Review the correct answers and explanations so that you see what you do and do not yet fully understand.

Step 3: Develop Strategies for Success

In this step, you'll learn strategies to help you do your best on the exam. These strategies cover both the multiple-choice and free-response sections of the exam. Some of these tips are based on my understanding of how the questions are designed, and others have been gleaned from my years of experience reading (grading) the AP exams.

- Learn to read multiple-choice questions.
- Learn how to answer multiple-choice questions, including whether or not to guess.
- Learn how to plan and write the free-response questions.

Step 4: Review the Knowledge You Need to Score High

In this step, you'll review the material you need to know for the test. This review section takes up the bulk of this book. It contains a comprehensive review of macroeconomics.

There is a lot of material here, enough to summarize a yearlong experience in AP Macroeconomics and highlight the, well, highlights. Some AP courses will have covered more material than yours; some will have covered less. The bottom line is that if you thoroughly review this material, you will have studied all that is tested on the exam, and you will significantly increase your chances of scoring well. Recent editions gave new emphasis to some areas of macroeconomics to bring your review more in line with recent exams. For example, there is more coverage of how the economy can adjust from the short run to the long run in the macroeconomics review, and modifications to the discussion of monetary policy in recent years.

Step 5: Build Your Test-Taking Confidence

In this step, you'll complete your preparation by testing yourself on practice exams. This section contains two complete exams in macroeconomics, solutions, and, sometimes more importantly, advice on how to avoid the common mistakes. Be aware that these practice exams are *not* reproduced questions from actual AP Macroeconomics exams, but they mirror both the material tested by AP and the way in which it is tested.

Lastly, at the back of this book you'll find additional resources to aid your preparation. These include the following:

- A brief bibliography
- A list of websites related to AP Macroeconomics
- A glossary of terms related to the AP Macroeconomics exam
- A summary of formulas related to the AP Macroeconomics exam

Introduction to the Graphics Used in This Book

To emphasize particular skills and strategies, several icons appear in the margins, alerting you to pay particular attention to the accompanying text:

This icon indicates a very important concept or fact that you should not pass over.

This icon calls your attention to a strategy that you might want to try.

This icon alerts you to a tip that you might find useful.

Boldfaced words indicate terms that are included in the glossary. Throughout the book you will also find marginal notes, boxes, and starred areas. Pay close attention to these areas because they can provide tips, hints, strategies, and further explanations to help you reach your full potential.

5 STEPS TO A 5
AP Macroeconomics

Set Up Your Study Program

What You Need to Know About the AP Macroeconomics Exam

IN THIS CHAPTER

Summary: Learn what topics are tested, how the test is scored, and basic test-taking information.

Key Ideas

- Most colleges will award credit for a score of 4 or 5.
- Multiple-choice questions account for two-thirds of your final score.
- Free-response questions account for one-third of your final score.
- Your composite score on the two test sections is converted to a score on the 1-to-5 scale.

Background Information

The AP Economics exams that you are taking were first offered by the College Board in 1989. Since then, the number of students taking the tests has grown rapidly. In 1989, 3,198 students took the Macroeconomics exam, and by 2023 that number had increased to 148,836.

Frequently Asked Questions About the AP Economics Exams

Why Take the AP Economics Exams?

Although there might be some altruistic motivators, let's face it: most of you take the AP Economics exams because you are seeking college credit. The majority of colleges and universities will accept a 4 or 5 as acceptable credit for their Principles of Microeconomics or Macroeconomics courses. Many private colleges will give you credit if you take both exams and receive a combined score of a 9 or 10. A number of schools will even accept a 3 on an exam. This means you are one or two courses closer to graduation before you even begin working on the "freshman 15." Even if you do not score high enough to earn college credit, the fact that you elected to enroll in AP courses tells admission committees that you are a high achiever and serious about your education. In 2019 close to 60 percent of students scored a 3 or higher on the AP Macroeconomics exam.

What Is the Format of the Exams?

Table 1.1 Summarizing the format of the AP Macro and Micro exams

AP MACROECONOMICS		
Section	*Number of Questions*	*Time Limit*
I. Multiple-Choice Questions	60	1 hour and 10 minutes
II. Free-Response Questions	3	Planning time: 10 minutes Writing time: 50 minutes

AP MICROECONOMICS		
Section	*Number of Questions*	*Time Limit*
I. Multiple-Choice Questions	60	1 hour and 10 minutes
II. Free-Response Questions	3	Planning time: 10 minutes Writing time: 50 minutes

Who Writes the AP Economics Exams?

Development of each AP exam is a multiyear effort that involves many education and testing professionals and students. At the heart of the effort is the AP Macroeconomics Development Committee, a group of college and high school economics teachers who are typically asked to serve for three years. The committee and other college professors create a large pool of multiple-choice questions. With the help of the testing experts at Educational Testing Service (ETS), these questions are then pretested with college students enrolled in Principles of Microeconomics and Macroeconomics for accuracy, appropriateness, clarity, and assurance that there is only one possible answer. The results of this pretesting allow each question to be categorized by degree of difficulty. Several more months of development and refinement later, Section I of the exam is ready to be administered.

The free-response essay questions that make up Section II go through a similar process of creation, modification, pretesting, and final refinement so that the questions cover the necessary areas of material and are at an appropriate level of difficulty and clarity. The committee also makes a great effort to construct a free-response exam that allows for clear and equitable grading by the AP readers.

At the conclusion of each AP reading and scoring of exams, the exam itself and the results are thoroughly evaluated by the committee and by ETS. In this way, the College Board can use the results to make suggestions for course development in high schools and to plan future exams.

What Topics Appear on the Exams?

The College Board, after consulting with teachers of economics, develops a curriculum that covers material that college professors expect to cover in their first-year classes. This curriculum has recently undergone a revision, and the new outline for the Macroeconomics course is provided. Based upon this outline of topics, the multiple-choice exams are written such that those topics are covered in proportion to their importance to the expected economics understanding of the student. If you find this confusing, think of it this way: Suppose that faculty consultants agree that foreign currency markets are important to the Macroeconomics curriculum, maybe to the tune of 10 percent. So if 10 percent of the curriculum in your AP Macroeconomics course is devoted to foreign currency markets, you can expect roughly 10 percent of the multiple-choice exam to address this topic. Remember, this is just a guide, and each year the percentages differ slightly.

Unit 1: Basic Economic Concepts

The course begins with an introduction to economic concepts, principles, and models that will serve as a foundation for studying macroeconomics.

<u>Topics:</u>

Scarcity
Opportunity cost and the Production Possibilities Curve
Comparative advantage and gains from trade
Supply and demand
Market equilibrium, disequilibrium, and changes in equilibrium

Exam Coverage

5%–10%

Unit 2: Economic Indicators and the Business Cycle

This unit describes how economic phenomena such as employment and inflation are measured.

<u>Topics:</u>

The circular flow and GDP
Unemployment
Price indices and inflation
Real vs. nominal GDP
Business cycles

Exam Coverage

12%–17%

Unit 3: National Income and Price Determination

This unit explores how changes in aggregate spending and production, economic fluctuations, and policy actions affect national income, unemployment, and inflation.

Topics:

Aggregate demand
Short-run and long-run aggregate supply
Equilibrium and changes in the Aggregate Demand–Aggregate Supply Model
Fiscal policy

Exam Coverage
17%–27%

Unit 4: Financial Sector
This unit examines the financial sector and explains how monetary policy is implemented and transmitted through the banking system.

Topics:

Financial assets
Definition, measurement, and functions of money
Banking and the expansion of the money supply
Monetary policy

Exam Coverage
18%–23%

Unit 5: Long-Run Consequences of Stabilization Policies
This unit explores the long-run effects of fiscal and monetary policy actions and examines the concept of economic growth.

Topics:

The Phillips Curve
Money growth and inflation
Government deficits and national debt
Crowding out
Economic growth

Exam Coverage
20%–30%

Unit 6: Open Economy—International Trade and Finance
This unit covers the concept of an open economy in which a country interacts with the rest of the world through product and financial markets.

Topics:

Balance of payments accounts
Exchange rates and the foreign exchange market
Effects of changes in policies and economic conditions on the foreign exchange market
Changes in the foreign exchange market and net exports
Real interest rates and international capital flows

Exam Coverage
10%–13%

My Teacher (and the Syllabus) Keeps Talking About "Big Ideas" and "Skill Categories." What Are These?

Most of the new curricular revision was a big-picture way of describing, and teaching, the key concepts in the AP Macroeconomics course. While these are critical to your teacher's preparation, and fundamentally guide the way in which your teacher structures the course, as a student preparing for the exam you probably don't need to have a deep understanding of what is happening behind the scenes. In other words, your course will be new and improved because of these revisions, but your fantastic teacher is doing the heavy lifting on making sure these are woven throughout the course.

But in case you're still curious, there are four skill categories that identify important skills that an AP Macro student should master throughout the course. The following table provides a brief summary.

	TITLE	AN EXAMPLE
Category 1	Principles of Models: Define economic principles and models.	Can you describe how comparative advantage and specialization create opportunities for nations to gain from trade?
Category 2	Interpretation: Explain given economic outcomes.	If unemployment rates begin to rise, can you prescribe a policy to address this problem?
Category 3	Manipulation: Determine outcomes of specific economic situations.	If the government engages in deficit spending, how is this likely to affect interest rates and the exchange rate between the dollar and other foreign currencies?
Category 4	Graphing and Visuals: Model economic situations using graphs or visual representations.	Can you draw an accurately labeled AD/AS graph that shows the impact of expansionary fiscal policy?

There are also four Big Ideas that will appear throughout your course. These are intended to reinforce common concepts that are key to a deep understanding of macroeconomics. The four Big Ideas are:

1. Economic Measurements
2. Markets
3. Macroeconomic Models
4. Macroeconomic Policies

Much more detail on these Big Ideas, and the Skill Categories, can be found in the "AP Macroeconomics Course and Exam Description" that is found at https://apcentral.collegeboard.org/media/pdf/ap-macroeconomics-course-and-exam-description.pdf.

Who Grades My AP Economics Exam?

From confidential sources, I can tell you that more than 100,000 free-response essay booklets are dropped from a three-story building, and those that fall into a small cardboard box are given a 5, those that fall into a slightly larger box are given a 4, and so on until those that fall into a dumpster receive a 1. It's really quite scientific!

Okay, that's not really how it's done. Instead, every June a group of economics teachers gather for a week to assign grades to your hard work. Each of these "Faculty Consultants," or "Readers," spends a day or so getting trained on one question and one question only. Because each reader becomes an expert on that question, and because each exam book is anonymous, this process provides a very consistent and unbiased scoring of that question. During a typical day of grading, a random sample of each reader's scores is selected and cross-checked by other experienced "Table Leaders" to ensure that the consistency is maintained throughout the day and the week. Each reader's scores on a given question are also statistically analyzed to make sure that they are not giving scores that are significantly higher or lower than the mean scores given by other readers of that question. All measures are taken to maintain consistency and fairness for your benefit.

Will My Exam Remain Anonymous?

Absolutely. Even if your high school teacher happens to randomly read your booklet, there is virtually no way they will know it is you. To the reader, each student is a number, and to the computer, each student is a bar code.

What About That Permission Box on the Back?

The College Board uses some exams to help train high school teachers so that they can help the next generation of economics students to avoid common mistakes. If you check this box, you simply give permission to use your exam in this way. Even if you give permission, your anonymity is maintained.

How Is My Multiple-Choice Exam Scored?

The multiple-choice section of each Economics exam is 60 questions and is worth two-thirds of your final score. Your answer sheet is run through the computer, which adds up your correct responses. The total scores on the multiple-choice sections are based on the number of questions answered correctly. The "guessing penalty" has been eliminated, and points are no longer deducted for incorrect answers. As always, no points are awarded for unanswered questions. The formula looks something like this:

$$\text{Section I Raw Score} = N_{\text{right}}$$

How Is My Free-Response Exam Scored?

Your performance on the free-response section is worth one-third of your final score and consists of three questions. Another change to the exam is that the first question will always be scored out of 10 points, and the second and third questions will each be scored out of 5 points. Because the first question is longer than the other two, and therefore scored on a higher scale, it is given a different weight in the raw score. If you use the following sample formula as a rough guide, you'll be able to gauge your approximate score on the practice questions.

$$\text{Section II Raw Score} = (1.50 \times \text{Score 1}) + (1.50 \times \text{Score 2}) + (1.50 \times \text{Score 3})$$

So How Is My Final Grade Determined and What Does It Mean?

With a total composite score of 90 points, and 60 being determined on Section I, the remaining 30 must be divided among the three essay questions in Section II. The total composite score is then a weighted sum of the multiple-choice and the free-response sections. In the end, when all the numbers have been crunched, the Chief Faculty Consultant converts the range of composite scores to the 5-point scale of the AP grades.

Table 1.2 gives you a very rough example of a conversion, and as you complete the practice exam, you may use this table to give yourself a hypothetical grade, keeping in mind that every year the conversion changes slightly to adjust for the difficulty of the questions from year to year. You should receive your grade in early July.

Table 1.2 Sample Score Conversion

MACROECONOMICS

Score Range	*AP Grade*	*Composite Interpretation*
71–90	5	Extremely well qualified for college credit
53–70	4	Well qualified
43–52	3	Qualified
31–42	2	Possibly qualified
0–30	1	No recommendation

Example:

In Section I, you receive 50 correct and 10 incorrect responses on the macroeconomics practice exam. In Section II, your scores are 7/10, 4/5, and 5/5.

$$\text{Weighted Section I} = 50$$

$$\text{Weighted Section II} = (1.50 \times 7) + (1.50 \times 4) + (1.50 \times 5)$$
$$= 10.50 + 6 + 7.5 = 24$$

Composite Score $= 50 + 24 = 74$, which would be assigned a 5.

How Do I Register and How Much Does It Cost?

If you are enrolled in AP Macroeconomics in your high school, your teacher is going to provide all these details, but a quick summary wouldn't hurt. After all, you do not have to enroll in the AP course to register for and complete the AP exam. When in doubt, the best source of information is the College Board's Website: www.collegeboard.com.

In 2024, the fee for taking an AP exam in the U.S. was $98 for each exam. If you are taking the exam outside of the United States or Canada, the exam fee is $127. Students who demonstrate financial need may receive a partial refund to help offset the cost of testing. The fee and the amount refunded to students demonstrating financial need vary from year to year, so check the College Board Website for the latest information. There are also several *optional* fees that *can* be paid if you want your scores rushed to you or if you wish to receive multiple grade reports.

The coordinator of the AP program at your school will inform you where and when you will take the exam. If you live in a small community, your exam might not be administered at your school, so be sure to get this information.

What If My School Only Offered AP Macroeconomics and Not AP Microeconomics, or Vice Versa?

Because of budget and personnel constraints, some high schools cannot offer both Microeconomics and Macroeconomics. The majority of these schools choose the macro side of the AP program, but some choose the micro side. This puts students at a significant disadvantage when they sit down for the Microeconomics exam without having taken the course. Likewise, Macroeconomics test takers have a rough time when they have not taken the Macroeconomics course. If you are in this situation, and you put in the necessary effort, I assure you that buying this book will give you more than a fighting chance on the Macroeconomics exam even if your school did not offer that course.

What Should I Bring to the Exam?

On exam day, I suggest bringing the following items:

- The BIG news in recent years is that AP Macroeconomics test takers are now allowed to use four-function calculators. Be sure to ask whether your school will provide calculators or if you should bring your own.
- Two sharpened number 2 pencils and an eraser that doesn't leave smudges.
- Two black or blue-colored pens for the free-response section. Some students like to use two colors to make their graphs stand out for the reader.
- Your College Board SSD Accommodations Letter if you are taking an exam with approved testing accommodations.
- A watch so that you can monitor your time. You never know whether the exam room will have a clock on the wall. You cannot have a watch that accesses the Internet, and make sure you turn off any beep that goes off on the hour.
- Your school code.
- Your photo identification and social security number.
- Tissues.
- Your quiet confidence that you are prepared!

What Should I *Not* Bring to the Exam?

It's probably a good idea to leave the following items at home:

- A scientific or graphing calculator.
- Mechanical pencils, number three pencils, or colored pencils.
- A cell phone, smart watch, camera, tablet, ear buds or plugs, laptop computer, or walkie-talkie.
- Books, a dictionary, study notes, flash cards, highlighting pens, correction fluid, a ruler, or any other office supplies.
- Portable music of any kind.
- Food or drink.
- Clothing with any economics on it.
- Panic or fear. It's natural to be nervous, but you can comfort yourself that you have used this book well and that there is no room for fear on your exam.

How to Plan Your Time

IN THIS CHAPTER

Summary: The right preparation plan depends on your study habits and the amount of time you have before the test.

Key Idea

✪ Choose the study plan that's right for you.

Three Approaches to Preparing for AP Exams

What kind of preparation program for the AP exam should you use? Should you carefully follow every step, or are there perhaps some steps you can bypass? That depends not only on how much time you have but also on what kind of student you are. No one knows your study habits, likes, and dislikes better than you do. So you are the only one who can decide which approach to use. This chapter presents three possible study plans, labeled A, B, and C. Look at the brief profiles that follow. These will help you determine which plan is right for you. Table 2.1 summarizes each study plan, with a suggested timetable for each.

You're a **full-school-year prep student** if:

1. You are the kind of person who likes to plan for everything very far in advance.
2. You buy your best friend a gift two months before their birthday because you know exactly what to choose, where you will buy it, and how much you will pay for it.
3. You like detailed planning and everything in its place.
4. You feel that you must be thoroughly prepared.
5. You hate surprises.

If you fit this profile, consider **Plan A.**

You're a **one-semester prep student** if:

1. You buy your best friend a gift one week before their birthday because it sort of snuck up on you, yet you have a clear idea of exactly what you will be purchasing.
2. You are willing to plan ahead to feel comfortable in stressful situations but are okay with skipping some details.
3. You feel more comfortable when you know what to expect, but a surprise or two is cool.
4. You're always on time for appointments.

If you fit this profile, consider **Plan B.**

You're a **6-week prep student** if:

1. You buy your best friend a gift for their birthday, but you need to include a belated card because you missed it by a couple of days.
2. You work best under pressure and tight deadlines.
3. You feel very confident with the skills and background you've learned in your AP Economics classes.
4. You decided late in the year to take the exam.
5. You like surprises.
6. You feel okay if you arrive 10 to 15 minutes late for an appointment.

If you fit this profile, consider **Plan C.**

Table 2.1 Three Different Study Schedules

MONTH	PLAN A: FULL SCHOOL YEAR	PLAN B: ONE SEMESTER	PLAN C: 6 WEEKS
September to October	Introduction; Chapters 1 to 4	—	—
November	Chapters 5 to 6	—	—
December	Chapters 7 to 8	—	—
January	Chapter 9	Chapters 1 to 4	—
February	Chapter 10	Chapters 5 to 7	—
March	Chapter 11	Chapters 8 to 10	—
April	Chapter 12; Practice Exam 1	Chapters 11 to 12; Practice Exam 1	Skim Chapters 1 to 9; all rapid reviews; take Practice Exam 1
May	Review everything; take Practice Exam 2	Review everything; take Practice Exam 2	Skim Chapters 10 to 12; take Practice Exam 2

Calendar for Each Plan

Plan A: You Have a Full School Year to Prepare

Use this plan to organize your study during the coming school year.

SEPTEMBER–OCTOBER (Check off the activities as you complete them.)

_____ Determine the student mode (A, B, or C) that applies to you.
_____ Carefully read Chapters 1 to 4 of this book.
_____ Take the diagnostic exam.
_____ Pay close attention to your walk-through of the diagnostic exam.
_____ Get on the web and take a look at the AP website(s).
_____ Skim the review chapters in Step 4 of this book. (Reviewing the topics covered in this section will be part of your yearlong preparation.)
_____ Buy a few color highlighters.
_____ Flip through the entire book. Break the book in. Write in it. Toss it around a little bit . . . highlight it.
_____ Get a clear picture of your own school's AP Economics curriculum.
_____ Begin to use this book as a resource to supplement the classroom learning.

NOVEMBER (the first 10 weeks have elapsed)

_____ Read and study Chapter 5, "Fundamentals of Economic Analysis."
_____ Read and study Chapter 6, "Demand, Supply, Market Equilibrium, and Welfare Analysis."

DECEMBER

_____ Read and study Chapter 7, "Macroeconomic Measures of Performance."
_____ Read and study Chapter 8, "Consumption, Saving, Investment, and the Multiplier."
_____ Review and study Chapters 5 to 8.

JANUARY

_____ Read and study Chapter 9, "Aggregate Demand and Aggregate Supply."
_____ Review Chapters 5 to 9.

FEBRUARY

_____ Read and study Chapter 10, "Fiscal Policy, Economic Growth, and Productivity."
_____ Review and study Chapters 5 to 10.

MARCH

_____ Read and study Chapter 11, "Money, Banking, and Monetary Policy."
_____ Review and study Chapters 5 to 11.

APRIL

_____ Read and study Chapter 12, "International Trade."
_____ Review Chapters 5 to 12.
_____ Take Practice Exam 1 in the last week of April.
_____ Evaluate your Macro strengths and weaknesses.
_____ Study appropriate chapters to correct your Macro weaknesses.

MAY (first two weeks) (THIS IS IT!)

_____ Review Chapters 5 to 12—all the material!
_____ Take Practice Exam 2.
_____ Score yourself.
_____ Get a good night's sleep before the exam. Fall asleep knowing that you are well prepared.

GOOD LUCK ON THE TEST!

Plan B: You Have One Semester to Prepare

If you have already completed one semester of economic studies, the following plan will help you use those skills you've been practicing to prepare for the May exam.

JANUARY–FEBRUARY

_____ Carefully read Chapters 1 to 4 of this book.
_____ Take the diagnostic exam.
_____ Pay close attention to your walk-through of the diagnostic exam.
_____ Read and study Chapter 5, "Fundamentals of Economic Analysis."
_____ Read and study Chapter 6, "Demand, Supply, Market Equilibrium, and Welfare Analysis."
_____ Read and study Chapter 7, "Macroeconomic Measures of Performance."

MARCH (10 weeks to go)

_____ Read and study Chapter 8, "Consumption, Saving, Investment, and the Multiplier."
_____ Read and study Chapter 9, "Aggregate Demand and Aggregate Supply."
_____ Read and study Chapter 10, "Fiscal Policy."
_____ Review Chapters 5 to 10.

APRIL

_____ Read and study Chapter 11, "Money, Banking, and Monetary Policy."
_____ Read and study Chapter 12, "International Trade."
_____ Take Practice Exam 1 in the last week of April.
_____ Evaluate your Macro strengths and weaknesses.
_____ Study appropriate chapters to correct your Macro weaknesses.
_____ Review Chapters 5 to 12.

MAY (first two weeks) (THIS IS IT!)

_____ Review Chapters 5 to 12—all the material!
_____ Take Practice Exam 2.
_____ Score yourself.
_____ Get a good night's sleep before the exam. Fall asleep knowing that you are well prepared.

GOOD LUCK ON THE TEST!

Plan C: You Have Six Weeks to Prepare

Use this plan if you have been studying economics for six months or more and intend to use this book primarily as a specific guide to the AP Macroeconomics exam. If you have only six weeks to prepare, now is not the time to try to learn everything. Focus instead on the essential points you need to know for the test.

APRIL 1–15

_____ Skim Chapters 1 to 4 of this book.
_____ Skim Chapters 5 to 9.
_____ Carefully go over the Rapid Review sections of Chapters 5 to 9.
_____ Skim and highlight the Glossary at the end of the book.

APRIL 15–MAY 1

_____ Skim Chapters 10 to 12.
_____ Carefully go over the Rapid Review sections of Chapters 10 to 12.
_____ Complete the Macroeconomics Practice Exam 1.
_____ Score yourself and analyze your errors.
_____ Continue to skim and highlight the Glossary at the end of the book.

MAY (first two weeks) (THIS IS IT!)

_____ Carefully go over the Rapid Review sections of Chapters 5 to 12.
_____ Take Practice Exam 2.
_____ Score yourself and analyze your errors.
_____ Get a good night's sleep before the exam. Fall asleep knowing that you are well prepared.

GOOD LUCK ON THE TEST!

Determine Your Test Readiness

Take the Diagnostic Exam

IN THIS CHAPTER

Summary: This chapter includes a diagnostic exam for macroeconomics. It is intended to give you an idea of where you stand with your preparation. The questions have been written to approximate the coverage of material that you will see on the AP exam and are similar to the review questions that you see at the end of each chapter in this book. Once you are done with the exam, check your work against the given answers, which also indicate where you can find the corresponding material in this book. Also provided is a way to convert your score to a rough AP score.

Key Ideas

- Practice the kind of multiple-choice and free-response questions you will be asked on the real exam.
- Answer questions that approximate the coverage of topics on the real exam.
- Check your work against the given answers.
- Determine your areas of strength and weakness.
- Earmark the pages that you must give special attention.

Diagnostic Exam

MACROECONOMICS—SECTION I

ANSWER SHEET

Record your responses to the exam in the spaces below.

1 Ⓐ Ⓑ Ⓒ Ⓓ Ⓔ	21 Ⓐ Ⓑ Ⓒ Ⓓ Ⓔ	41 Ⓐ Ⓑ Ⓒ Ⓓ Ⓔ
2 Ⓐ Ⓑ Ⓒ Ⓓ Ⓔ	22 Ⓐ Ⓑ Ⓒ Ⓓ Ⓔ	42 Ⓐ Ⓑ Ⓒ Ⓓ Ⓔ
3 Ⓐ Ⓑ Ⓒ Ⓓ Ⓔ	23 Ⓐ Ⓑ Ⓒ Ⓓ Ⓔ	43 Ⓐ Ⓑ Ⓒ Ⓓ Ⓔ
4 Ⓐ Ⓑ Ⓒ Ⓓ Ⓔ	24 Ⓐ Ⓑ Ⓒ Ⓓ Ⓔ	44 Ⓐ Ⓑ Ⓒ Ⓓ Ⓔ
5 Ⓐ Ⓑ Ⓒ Ⓓ Ⓔ	25 Ⓐ Ⓑ Ⓒ Ⓓ Ⓔ	45 Ⓐ Ⓑ Ⓒ Ⓓ Ⓔ
6 Ⓐ Ⓑ Ⓒ Ⓓ Ⓔ	26 Ⓐ Ⓑ Ⓒ Ⓓ Ⓔ	46 Ⓐ Ⓑ Ⓒ Ⓓ Ⓔ
7 Ⓐ Ⓑ Ⓒ Ⓓ Ⓔ	27 Ⓐ Ⓑ Ⓒ Ⓓ Ⓔ	47 Ⓐ Ⓑ Ⓒ Ⓓ Ⓔ
8 Ⓐ Ⓑ Ⓒ Ⓓ Ⓔ	28 Ⓐ Ⓑ Ⓒ Ⓓ Ⓔ	48 Ⓐ Ⓑ Ⓒ Ⓓ Ⓔ
9 Ⓐ Ⓑ Ⓒ Ⓓ Ⓔ	29 Ⓐ Ⓑ Ⓒ Ⓓ Ⓔ	49 Ⓐ Ⓑ Ⓒ Ⓓ Ⓔ
10 Ⓐ Ⓑ Ⓒ Ⓓ Ⓔ	30 Ⓐ Ⓑ Ⓒ Ⓓ Ⓔ	50 Ⓐ Ⓑ Ⓒ Ⓓ Ⓔ
11 Ⓐ Ⓑ Ⓒ Ⓓ Ⓔ	31 Ⓐ Ⓑ Ⓒ Ⓓ Ⓔ	51 Ⓐ Ⓑ Ⓒ Ⓓ Ⓔ
12 Ⓐ Ⓑ Ⓒ Ⓓ Ⓔ	32 Ⓐ Ⓑ Ⓒ Ⓓ Ⓔ	52 Ⓐ Ⓑ Ⓒ Ⓓ Ⓔ
13 Ⓐ Ⓑ Ⓒ Ⓓ Ⓔ	33 Ⓐ Ⓑ Ⓒ Ⓓ Ⓔ	53 Ⓐ Ⓑ Ⓒ Ⓓ Ⓔ
14 Ⓐ Ⓑ Ⓒ Ⓓ Ⓔ	34 Ⓐ Ⓑ Ⓒ Ⓓ Ⓔ	54 Ⓐ Ⓑ Ⓒ Ⓓ Ⓔ
15 Ⓐ Ⓑ Ⓒ Ⓓ Ⓔ	35 Ⓐ Ⓑ Ⓒ Ⓓ Ⓔ	55 Ⓐ Ⓑ Ⓒ Ⓓ Ⓔ
16 Ⓐ Ⓑ Ⓒ Ⓓ Ⓔ	36 Ⓐ Ⓑ Ⓒ Ⓓ Ⓔ	56 Ⓐ Ⓑ Ⓒ Ⓓ Ⓔ
17 Ⓐ Ⓑ Ⓒ Ⓓ Ⓔ	37 Ⓐ Ⓑ Ⓒ Ⓓ Ⓔ	57 Ⓐ Ⓑ Ⓒ Ⓓ Ⓔ
18 Ⓐ Ⓑ Ⓒ Ⓓ Ⓔ	38 Ⓐ Ⓑ Ⓒ Ⓓ Ⓔ	58 Ⓐ Ⓑ Ⓒ Ⓓ Ⓔ
19 Ⓐ Ⓑ Ⓒ Ⓓ Ⓔ	39 Ⓐ Ⓑ Ⓒ Ⓓ Ⓔ	59 Ⓐ Ⓑ Ⓒ Ⓓ Ⓔ
20 Ⓐ Ⓑ Ⓒ Ⓓ Ⓔ	40 Ⓐ Ⓑ Ⓒ Ⓓ Ⓔ	60 Ⓐ Ⓑ Ⓒ Ⓓ Ⓔ

Diagnostic Exam: AP Macroeconomics

SECTION I

Time—70 Minutes

60 Questions

For the following multiple-choice questions, select the best answer choice and record your choice on the answer sheet provided.

1. Which of the following is an example of capital as an economic resource?

   (A) A cement mixer
   (B) A barrel of crude oil
   (C) A registered nurse
   (D) A share of corporate stock
   (E) A bachelor's degree

Question 2 is based on the production possibilities of two nations that can produce both crepes and paper.

NATION X		NATION Y	
Crepes	Paper	Crepes	Paper
0	3	0	5
9	0	5	0

2. Which of the following statements is true of these production possibilities?

   (A) Nation X has comparative advantage in paper production and should trade paper to Nation Y in exchange for crepes.
   (B) Nation X has comparative advantage in crepe production and should trade crepes to Nation Y in exchange for paper.
   (C) Nation X has absolute advantage in paper production, and Nation Y has absolute advantage in crepe production. No trade is possible.
   (D) Nation Y has absolute advantage in paper production, and Nation X has absolute advantage in crepe production. No trade is possible.
   (E) Nation Y has comparative advantage in crepe production and should trade paper to Nation X in exchange for crepes.

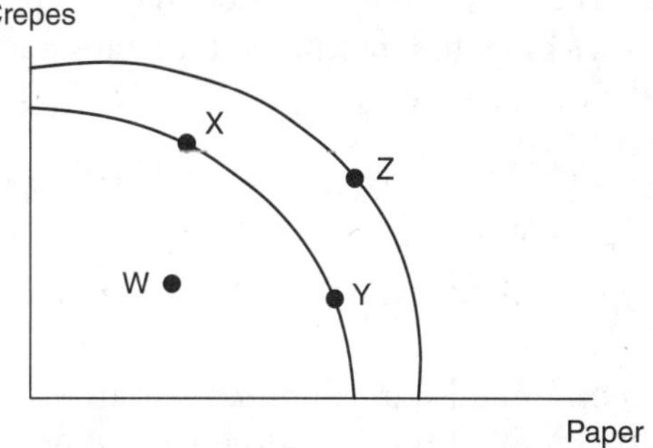

Figure D.1

3. Using Figure D.1, which of the following movements would be described as economic growth?

   (A) W to X
   (B) X to Y
   (C) W to Y
   (D) Z to W
   (E) X to Z

4. Suppose smartphones are a normal good and are exchanged in a competitive market. All else equal, an increase in household income will

   (A) increase the equilibrium quantity and increase the price.
   (B) decrease the equilibrium quantity and increase the price.
   (C) increase the equilibrium price, but the change in quantity is ambiguous.
   (D) decrease the equilibrium quantity and decrease the price.
   (E) increase the equilibrium quantity but the change in price is ambiguous.

5. You observe that the price of tomato sauce has fallen, and more tomato sauce is being exchanged in the market. What could explain this?
   (A) Income has risen, and tomato sauce is an inferior good.
   (B) The price of pizza crusts, a complementary good with tomato sauce, has fallen.
   (C) There are fewer sellers of tomato sauce in the market.
   (D) The price of raw tomatoes has fallen.
   (E) Income has fallen, and tomato sauce is a normal good.

6. Economic scarcity is the imbalance between _____ and _____.
   (A) unlimited wants; unlimited resources
   (B) unlimited wants; limited profits
   (C) unlimited wants; limited resources
   (D) unlimited consumption; limited production
   (E) limited wants; limited resources

7. An American firm moves a manufacturing plant from the United States to Brazil. How will this affect gross domestic product (GDP) in the United States and in Brazil?
   (A) U.S. GDP falls and Brazil's GDP falls.
   (B) U.S. GDP rises and Brazil's GDP falls.
   (C) U.S. GDP falls and Brazil's GDP remains constant.
   (D) U.S. GDP falls and Brazil's GDP rises.
   (E) U.S. GDP remains constant and Brazil's GDP rises.

8. For years you work as a grocery checker at a supermarket, and one day you are replaced by self-serve checkout stations. What type of unemployment is this?
   (A) Cyclical
   (B) Structural
   (C) Seasonal
   (D) Frictional
   (E) Discouraged

9. Fernanda is 20 years old and has a part-time job at a bookstore. Last week she had a job interview for an open position at the bakery. Fernanda's status in the labor market would be
   (A) unemployed.
   (B) out of the labor force.
   (C) a discouraged worker.
   (D) employed.
   (E) marginally attached.

Use the following table for Questions 10 and 11.

Total Population of Heatherton	4,000
Population 16 years and older	3,000
Employed	1,500
Unemployed	500
Out of the labor force	1,000

10. In the city of Heatherton, the labor force participation rate is _____, and the unemployment rate is _____.
    (A) 50%; 25%
    (B) 67%; 25%
    (C) 50%; 33%
    (D) 25%; 25%
    (E) 25%; 50%

11. Due to a lack of customers, Glene's Bar and Grill goes out of business in Heatherton. Glene's 50 employees are now without jobs, but they are all seeking employment in Heatherton. How does the closing of Glene's business affect the labor force participation rate and the unemployment rate in Heatherton?

	LABOR FORCE PARTICIPATION RATE	UNEMPLOYMENT RATE
(A)	Decreases	Increases
(B)	No change	No change
(C)	Decreases	No change
(D)	Increases	Increases
(E)	No change	Increases

12. The inflation rate is calculated as
    (A) the percentage change in the gross domestic product.
    (B) the percentage change in the labor force.
    (C) the percentage change in the consumer price index.
    (D) the percentage change in the federal funds rate.
    (E) the percentage change in the producer price index.

13. In a typical business cycle, what immediately follows the peak?
    (A) Recession
    (B) Trough
    (C) Growth
    (D) Expansion
    (E) Production

14. When a new apartment complex is built, it counts toward _____ in GDP calculations.

(A) rent
(B) consumption
(C) exports
(D) investment
(E) profits

15. If the consumer price index (CPI) increases by 2 percent and your nominal income increases by 8 percent, your real income has approximately

(A) increased by 4 percent.
(B) decreased by 4 percent.
(C) increased by 6 percent.
(D) decreased by 6 percent.
(E) increased by 10 percent.

16. To deflate nominal gross domestic product (GDP), you must

(A) divide nominal GDP by the price index (in hundreds).
(B) multiply real GDP by the price index.
(C) divide real GDP by the price index (in hundreds).
(D) multiply nominal GDP by the price index (in hundreds).
(E) divide nominal GDP by real GDP.

17. A stronger stock market is likely to cause which of the following changes in the consumption function and aggregate demand?

	CONSUMPTION FUNCTION	AGGREGATE DEMAND
(A)	Increase	Decrease
(B)	No change	No change
(C)	Increase	No change
(D)	Increase	Increase
(E)	Decrease	Decrease

18. An increase in corporate optimism will have which of the following effects in the market for loanable funds?

(A) An increase in supply, lowering the interest rate.
(B) A decrease in demand, increasing the interest rate.
(C) An increase in both supply and demand, and an ambiguous change in interest rates.
(D) A decrease in supply, decreasing the interest rate.
(E) An increase in demand, increasing the interest rate.

19. The marginal propensity to consume in Jamesburg is equal to .80. If government spending in Jamesburg decreases by $500, how will this ultimately affect national income?

(A) Decreases by $500
(B) Increases by $1,500
(C) Decreases by $2,500
(D) No change
(E) Decreases by $5,000

20. If the marginal propensity to save in Foxlandia is equal to .10, and the government decreases taxes by $1 billion, national income in Foxlandia will eventually

(A) stay unchanged.
(B) decrease by $10 billion
(C) increase by $1 billion.
(D) increase by $9 billion.
(E) increase by $10 billion.

21. If a nation's economy is at full employment, which of the following is likely to create a recessionary gap?

(A) Investor optimism is improving.
(B) Government spending rises and income taxes fall.
(C) Household wealth is rising.
(D) Energy prices are falling.
(E) The trade deficit is rising.

22. A nation is experiencing growth in real GDP and rising rates of inflation. What has likely caused these changes to the economy?

(A) Short-run aggregate supply has increased.
(B) Aggregate demand has increased.
(C) Short-run aggregate supply has decreased.
(D) Aggregate demand has decreased.
(E) Long-run aggregate supply has increased.

23. The unemployment rate and inflation rate in Maxland are both rising. What has happened to the economy of Maxland?

(A) Short-run aggregate supply has increased.
(B) Aggregate demand has increased.
(C) Short-run aggregate supply has decreased.
(D) Aggregate demand has decreased.
(E) Long-run aggregate supply has increased.

24. Suppose an economy is at full employment. An inflationary gap could be caused by
   (A) rising investor pessimism.
   (B) falling real interest rates.
   (C) higher income taxes.
   (D) rising trade deficits with other nations.
   (E) falling consumer wealth.

25. If the economy is operating below full employment, which of the following has the greatest positive impact on real gross domestic product?
   (A) The government decreases spending with no change in taxes.
   (B) The government increases spending with no change in taxes.
   (C) The government decreases spending and matches it with a decrease in taxes.
   (D) The government holds spending constant while decreasing taxes.
   (E) The government increases spending and matches it with an increase in taxes.

26. Suppose the economy is operating beyond full employment. Which of the following is true at this point?
   (A) The short-run aggregate supply curve is horizontal.
   (B) Further increases in aggregate demand will result in a lower price level.
   (C) A decrease in aggregate demand will result in a lower price level if prices are sticky.
   (D) Further increases in aggregate demand will not lower the unemployment rate but will create inflation.
   (E) The unemployment rate is higher than the natural rate of unemployment.

27. When government uses expansionary fiscal policy, the spending multiplier is often smaller than predicted because of
   (A) lower taxes.
   (B) increasing net exports.
   (C) falling unemployment.
   (D) lower interest rates.
   (E) rising price levels.

28. The best example of a negative supply shock to the economy would be
   (A) a decrease in government spending.
   (B) a decrease in the real interest rate.
   (C) an increase in the money supply.
   (D) unexpectedly higher resource prices.
   (E) technological improvements.

29. The Phillips curve represents the relationship between
   (A) inflation and the money supply.
   (B) unemployment and the money supply.
   (C) the money supply and the real interest rate.
   (D) inflation and unemployment.
   (E) investment and the real interest rate.

30. If the economy is experiencing a recession, how will a plan to decrease taxes for consumers and increase spending on government purchases affect real gross domestic product (GDP) and the price level?
   (A) Real GDP rises and the price level falls.
   (B) Real GDP falls and the price level rises.
   (C) Real GDP rises and the price level rises.
   (D) Real GDP falls and the price level falls.
   (E) Real GDP stays the same and the price level rises.

31. Of the following choices, the one most likely to be preferred by supply-side economists would be
   (A) increased government spending.
   (B) higher tariffs on imported goods.
   (C) lower taxes on household income.
   (D) higher welfare payments.
   (E) a tax credit on capital investment.

32. Automatic stabilizers in the economy serve an important role in
   (A) increasing the length of the business cycle.
   (B) balancing the budget.
   (C) increasing a budget surplus in a recession.
   (D) decreasing net tax revenue during economic growth.
   (E) lessening the impact of a recession.

33. The "crowding-out" effect is the result of
   (A) decreasing interest rates from contractionary fiscal policy.
   (B) increasing interest rates from expansionary fiscal policy.
   (C) increasing interest rates from expansionary monetary policy.
   (D) increasing unemployment rates from expansionary monetary policy.
   (E) a depreciating dollar versus other currencies.

34. In a recession, expansionary monetary policy is designed to

(A) decrease aggregate demand so that real prices will decrease, which is good for the economy.
(B) increase aggregate demand, which will increase real output and increase employment.
(C) increase unemployment, but low prices negate this effect.
(D) keep interest rates high, which attracts foreign investment.
(E) boost the value of the dollar in foreign currency markets.

35. A contractionary monetary policy will cause the nominal interest rate, aggregate demand, output, and the price level to change in which of the following ways?

	NOMINAL INTEREST RATE	AGGREGATE DEMAND	OUTPUT	PRICE LEVEL
(A)	Decrease	Increase	Increase	Increase
(B)	Decrease	Decrease	Decrease	Increase
(C)	Increase	Decrease	Decrease	Increase
(D)	Increase	Decrease	Decrease	Decrease
(E)	Increase	Increase	Increase	Increase

36. Suppose a nation has a limited reserve banking system. Which of the following choices would serve to increase the supply of money in the banking system?

(A) A higher interest rate paid by banks when borrowing from the central bank
(B) Buying government securities from commercial banks
(C) A higher reserve requirement
(D) A lower personal income tax rate
(E) A lower investment income tax rate

37. A financial asset that gives the holder a small percentage of ownership in a corporation is called

(A) a share of stock.
(B) a Treasury bill.
(C) fiat money.
(D) an insurance policy.
(E) a corporate bond.

38. When a firm wants to raise money without relinquishing ownership of the firm, they will most likely issue ____ to the public.

(A) a share of stock
(B) a Treasury bill
(C) mutual funds
(D) an insurance policy
(E) a corporate bond

39. A nation has a banking system with ample reserves. Which of the following monetary policies would lessen the effectiveness of expansionary fiscal policy?

(A) Decreasing the value of the domestic currency.
(B) Lowering the income tax rate.
(C) Raising the interest rate paid to commercial banks that deposit with the central bank.
(D) Lowering the policy rate.
(E) Lowering the reserve ratio.

40. Which of the following is an accurate statement of the money supply in the United States?

(A) The money supply is backed by gold reserves.
(B) The money supply is controlled by elected members of Congress.
(C) $M1$ is larger than $M2$.
(D) Paper money can be exchanged at commercial banks for an equal amount of gold.
(E) The most liquid measure of money is $M1$.

41. A nation has a banking system with limited reserves. Excess reserves in the banking system increase if

(A) the reserve ratio is increased.
(B) checking deposits increase.
(C) the discount rate is increased.
(D) the central bank sells government securities to commercial banks.
(E) income tax rates increase.

42. Suppose a nation has a limited reserve banking system. If a bank has \$1,000 in checking deposits and the bank is required to reserve \$250, what is the reserve ratio? How much does the bank have in excess reserves? What is the size of the money multiplier?

(A) 25%, \$750, $M = ¼$
(B) 75%, \$250, $M = 4$
(C) 25%, \$750, $M = 4$
(D) 75%, \$750, $M = ¼$
(E) 25%, \$250, $M = 4$

43. Suppose the reserve ratio is 10 percent and the central bank buys $1 million in government securities from commercial banks. If money demand is perfectly elastic, which of the following is likely to occur?

(A) Money supply increases by $10 million, lowering the interest rate and increasing AD.
(B) Money supply remains constant, the interest rate does not fall, and AD does not increase.
(C) Money supply increases by $10 million, the interest rate does not fall, and AD does not increase.
(D) Money supply decreases by $10 million, raising the interest rate and decreasing AD.
(E) Money supply decreases by $10 million, the interest rate does not rise, and AD does not decrease.

44. When a government engages in deficit spending, how does this affect the market for loanable funds, the real interest rate, and private investment spending?

	LOANABLE FUNDS	REAL INTEREST RATE	PRIVATE INVESTMENT SPENDING
(A)	Supply decreases	Decreases	Decreases
(B)	Demand increases	Increases	Decreases
(C)	Demand increases	Decreases	Decreases
(D)	Demand decreases	Increases	Increases
(E)	Supply increases	Decreases	Increases

45. If the velocity of money is constant, an increase in the money supply will create _____ in the long run.

(A) unemployment
(B) economic growth
(C) inflation
(D) an increase in real GDP
(E) higher interest rates

Use Figure D.2 for Questions 46 and 47.

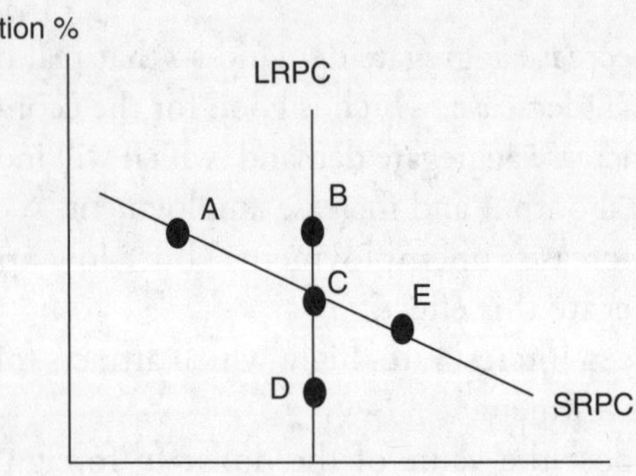

46. This nation's economy is currently in long-run equilibrium at point C. What would occur to cause the economy to move to point E?

(A) A decrease in aggregate demand
(B) A decrease in long-run aggregate supply
(C) An increase in aggregate demand
(D) A decrease in short-run aggregate supply
(E) An increase in short-run aggregate supply

47. This nation's economy is currently in long-run equilibrium at point C. What would occur to cause the economy to move to point D?

(A) A decrease in aggregate demand
(B) A decrease in long-run aggregate supply
(C) An increase in aggregate demand
(D) A decrease in short-run aggregate supply
(E) An increase in short-run aggregate supply

48. If a nation's capacity to produce more output with the same resources has improved, we call it

(A) a recession.
(B) economic growth.
(C) a depression.
(D) a peak in the business cycle.
(E) a trough in the business cycle.

49. When a nation experiences economic growth, we shift the _____ curve _____.

(A) LRAS; rightward
(B) AD; rightward
(C) SRAS; leftward
(D) SRAS; rightward
(E) AD; leftward

50. Dodgetopia's economy is currently operating at full employment output Yf with the price level of PLf. Assume the government of Dodgetopia engages in expansionary fiscal policy. What level of output and price level will the economy experience in the long run?

	OUTPUT	PRICE LEVEL
(A)	Yf	PLf
(B)	Greater than Yf	Greater than PLf
(C)	Yf	Greater than PLf
(D)	Greater than Yf	PLf
(E)	Less than Yf	Less than PLf

51. Economic output is currently below full employment. If no action is taken, how will this economy adjust in the long run?

(A) The SRAS will decrease, increasing the size of the recessionary gap.
(B) The LRAS will decrease, bringing the economy back to full employment.
(C) The AD will increase, bringing the economy back to full employment.
(D) The SRAS will increase, bringing the economy back to full employment.
(E) The AD will decrease, increasing the size of the recessionary gap.

52. Long-term economic growth is most likely under which scenario?

(A) Deficit spending to increase aggregate demand
(B) Government investment in high-tech research and development
(C) Higher resource prices
(D) Tax cuts on consumption spending
(E) Weak environmental protection and high levels of pollution

53. All else equal, economic growth should result in

(A) higher real output per worker.
(B) a decrease in demand for capital goods.
(C) a lower standard of living.
(D) a decrease in demand for labor.
(E) no change in real output per worker.

54. If the world price of copper exceeds the domestic (U.S.) price of copper, we would expect

(A) the United States to be a net exporter of copper.
(B) the United States to impose a tariff on imported copper to protect domestic producers.
(C) the demand for U.S. copper to fall.
(D) a growing trade deficit in the United States in goods and services.
(E) the dollar to depreciate relative to the currencies of other copper-producing nations.

55. Suppose the Japanese economy is suffering a prolonged recession. Lower Japanese household incomes will affect U.S. exports to Japan, demand for the dollar, and the value of the dollar relative to the yen in which of the following ways?

	EXPORTS TO JAPAN	DEMAND FOR $	VALUE OF $
(A)	Decrease	Decrease	Decrease
(B)	Decrease	Decrease	Increase
(C)	Decrease	Increase	Decrease
(D)	Increase	Decrease	Decrease
(E)	Increase	Decrease	Increase

56. Which of the following is a likely effect of a higher tariff imposed by the United States on imported automobiles?

(A) Net exports will fall and the dollar will appreciate in value.
(B) Net exports will fall and the dollar will depreciate in value.
(C) The price of automobiles in the United States will fall.
(D) Net exports will rise and the dollar will depreciate in value.
(E) Net exports will rise and the dollar will appreciate in value.

57. If the Central Bank of Hanoveria has been lowering interest rates relative to interest rates in other nations, how would this affect the balance of payments and value of Hanoveria's currency?

(A) Money would flow into the capital account, depreciating the currency.
(B) Money would flow out of the capital account, depreciating the currency.
(C) Money would flow into the current account, depreciating the currency.
(D) Money would flow out of the current account, appreciating the currency.
(E) Money would flow into the capital account, appreciating the currency.

58. When the Mexican economy is strong and real GDP is rising, what happens to the supply of the Mexican peso, the demand for the American dollar, and the value of the peso relative to the dollar?

	SUPPLY OF PESO	DEMAND FOR DOLLAR	VALUE OF PESO
(A)	Increasing	Increasing	Increasing
(B)	Decreasing	Increasing	Decreasing
(C)	Increasing	Increasing	Decreasing
(D)	Decreasing	Decreasing	Increasing
(E)	Increasing	Decreasing	Decreasing

59. Which of the following transactions would appear as a monetary inflow into the U.S. current account?

(A) An American buys a car produced in Sweden.
(B) An American bank buys stock in a Swedish firm that produces cars.
(C) A European investor buys a factory in Wisconsin.
(D) A Brazilian family sends money to a daughter attending college in Indiana.
(E) A Swedish retail store buys furniture produced in the United States.

60. Suppose real interest rates in the United States are higher than real interest rates in the European Union (EU). How will this difference in real interest rates affect currency markets and the value of the U.S. dollar relative to the European euro?

(A) Demand for the euro rises, increasing the dollar's value against the euro.
(B) Demand for the dollar rises, increasing the dollar's value against the euro.
(C) Supply of the dollar rises, decreasing the dollar's value against the euro.
(D) Supply of the euro rises, decreasing the dollar's value against the euro.
(E) Demand for the dollar rises, decreasing the dollar's value against the euro.

› Answers and Explanations

This test was designed to test you on topics that you will see on the AP Macroeconomics exam in the approximate proportions that you will see them. Chronologically they appear in the approximate order of their review in Step 4 of this book, but this is not the case on the AP exam. Topics on your practice exams will be shuffled.

Questions from Chapters 5 and 6

1. **A**—Economic capital includes machinery, like a cement mixer, used to produce goods and services. A barrel of oil is a natural resource, and a nurse is a unit of labor. A share of corporate stock is a financial instrument used to raise money so that a firm can purchase more economic resources.

2. **B**—A quick calculation of opportunity costs shows that the opportunity cost of one more paper is three crepes in Nation X and one crepe in Nation Y. The opportunity cost of one more crepe is one-third paper in Nation X and one crepe in Nation Y. Nations benefit by specializing in the goods for which they have a comparative advantage. Thus, Nation Y can specialize in paper production, and Nation X can specialize in crepe production. Nation X trades some crepes to Nation Y in exchange for paper.

3. **E**—Economic growth occurs when the production possibility frontier shifts outward. A movement from W to X or to Y is an improved allocation of unemployed resources, but the potential production has not grown for this nation.

4. **A**—If smartphones are normal goods, an increase in household income increases demand for smartphones, which increases quantity and price. Even though this is a macroeconomics exam, be prepared for simple supply and demand questions to test your understanding of markets.

5. **D**—Lower prices and higher quantities in a market are a result of an outward shift in supply. The lower price of raw tomatoes, a key input in making tomato sauce, would increase the supply of tomato sauce.

6. **C**—The basic premise of economics is that society's wants are always greater than the ability of society's resources to satisfy all of those wants.

Questions from Chapter 7

7. D—The GDP of a nation includes the value of production done within the borders of that nation, regardless of the nationality of the owners. If a U.S. factory moves to Brazil, U.S. GDP falls and it rises in Brazil.

8. B—Structural unemployment is the result of changing demand for skills, not the business cycle. Automation decreases the demand for human grocery checkers, and this trend is unlikely to reverse itself.

9. D—Although Fernanda is interviewing for a new job, the fact that she already has a job classifies her as employed.

10. B—The labor force is the sum of the employed (1,500) and unemployed (500), and the labor force participation rate is the percentage of the working-age population (3,000) that is in the labor force; LFPR = (1,500 + 500)/3,000 = 67%. The unemployment rate is the percentage of the labor force that is unemployed; UR = 500/2,000 = 25%.

11. E—Unemployed persons are already in the labor force, so when 50 people go from employed to unemployed, the labor force participation rate does not change. However, when 50 additional people become unemployed, the unemployment rate increases.

12. C—The rate of inflation is the month-to-month, or year-to-year, percentage change in the consumer price index (CPI).

13. B—The peak of the business cycle represents the height of economic activity immediately before a downturn or recession. A recession is sometimes referred to as an economic contraction.

14. D—New construction is classified as investment spending in GDP tabulations.

15. C—The percentage change in real income is approximately equal to the percentage change in nominal income minus the percentage change in the price level.

16. A—Nominal values must be adjusted to take into account rising prices. To deflate nominal values to real values, divide the nominal value by the price index (in hundredths).

Questions from Chapter 8

17. D—A strong stock market increases consumer wealth and optimism, shifting the consumption function upward. Since aggregate demand includes consumption, aggregate demand increases.

18. E—In the market for loanable funds, investment (*I*) represents demand and saving represents supply. More *$I* increases the demand for loanable funds and increases the interest rate.

19. C—The spending multiplier (M) is equal to 1/(1 – MPC). In this case, M = 1/(1 – .80) = 5, so if government spending falls by $500, eventually total spending would decrease fivefold, or $2,500.

20. D—The tax multiplier Tm is equal to MPC/MPS. In this case Tm = .90/.10 = 9, so if taxes fall by $1 billion, eventually national income would increase by $9 billion.

21. E—A recessionary gap would occur if real GDP falls below the full-employment level. A trade deficit means that net exports falls and becomes negative. Since net exports is a component of aggregate demand, a trade deficit would shift AD to the left, creating the recessionary gap.

22. B—Rising real GDP and rising price levels are consistent with a rightward shift of aggregate demand along the upward sloping short-run aggregate supply curve.

23. C—A decrease in the short-run aggregate supply curve is bad news for an economy. The price level would increase and the real GDP would decrease, causing unemployment rates to rise.

24. B—An inflationary gap would occur if the nation was producing beyond full-employment GDP, and an increase in aggregate demand would be the cause. Falling real interest rates would increase investment spending and shift aggregate demand to the right.

25. B—The spending multiplier is larger than the tax multiplier, which is larger than the balanced budget multiplier (equals 1). Of the available choices, if you want the largest increase in real GDP, you should increase government spending and leave taxes unchanged. An even larger impact would be seen if we increased spending and decreased taxes, but this is not one of your options.

Questions from Chapter 9

26. D—If the economy is beyond full employment, the short-run AS curve is nearly vertical. At this point, increasing aggregate demand cannot increase output and will only increase prices.

27. E—The full multiplier is only felt if short-run aggregate supply is horizontal. Any increase in the price level decreases the impact of the spending multiplier.

28. D—Higher resource prices shift the short-run aggregate supply (SRAS) curve to the left. All other choices either do not impact the SRAS curve or they would act as positive shocks to the SRAS curve.

29. D—The Phillips curve shows the short-run inverse relationship between the inflation rate and the unemployment rate. In the long run, this curve is vertical at the natural rate of unemployment.

Questions from Chapter 10

30. C—In the aggregate demand (AD) and aggregate supply (AS) model, lower taxes and more government spending increases AD. This rightward shift increases real GDP and begins to increase the price level.

31. E—Supply-side economists advocate increased aggregate supply through incentives for investment and productivity. These would likely come in the form of lower taxes on interest income from savings or tax credits for investment.

32. E—As a recession deepens, a progressive tax system and transfer programs like welfare assistance kick in and shorten the downturn in the business cycle. These automatic stabilizers produce recessionary deficits and inflationary surpluses.

33. B—Expansionary fiscal policy, intended to boost aggregate demand, requires borrowing increases interest rates and lessens private investment spending. The decrease in investment spending weakens the impact of expansionary fiscal policy.

Questions from Chapter 11

34. B—Increasing the money supply lowers interest rates and increases investment spending (I), aggregate demand (AD), real GDP, and employment.

35. D—A contractionary money supply increases nominal interest rates, decreases aggregate demand and real GDP, and decreases the price level.

36. A—Buying government securities (i.e., bonds) increases the money supply in a system with limited reserves. This was one of the Fed's traditional tools of monetary policy prior to the current ample reserves framework. Remember that the central bank, like the Fed, does not impact taxes, as taxes are fiscal policy made by the executive and legislative branches.

37. A—Firms can raise money by selling shares of stock, each of which represents a small percentage of ownership in the firm.

38. E—A firm can raise money by issuing corporate bonds. When people buy the bonds, they are essentially lending the firm money for operations or investments. The firm promises to repay the holder of the bonds over time, with interest included.

39. C—Central banks with ample reserves increase or decrease the interest rate paid to commercial bank deposits as a way of influencing interest rates throughout the banking system. If expansionary fiscal policy intends to increase aggregate demand, higher interest rates would lessen that impact by reducing aggregate demand. This would work counter to expansionary fiscal policy.

40. E—Nearest to cash, $M1$ is the most liquid of monetary measures. The U.S. dollar is not backed by gold. Our fiat money has value because the Fed ensures stable prices.

41. B—When more deposits are made, the bank increases required reserves by the fraction of the reserve ratio, and increased excess reserves are lent to borrowers to create more money.

42. C—When a nation has a limited reserve system, banks are required to keep a minimum fraction of deposits on reserve. The reserve ratio is required reserves divided by deposits, so $rr = 0.25$. With $250 in required reserves, excess reserves are $750. The money multiplier is equal to $1/rr = 4$. When a nation, like the U.S., has an ample reserves banking system, there is no reserve requirement and so the money multiplier does not apply.

43. C—The money multiplier is 10 because the reserve ratio is 0.10. If money demand is horizontal, a $1 million increase in excess reserves shifts the money supply curve rightward by $10 million but will not lower the nominal interest rate. If the interest rate does not fall, aggregate demand does not rise.

44. B—Government borrowing increases the demand for loanable funds, which increases the real interest rate. Higher real interest rates will discourage, or "crowd out," private investment spending.

45. C—The quantity theory of money asserts that the velocity of money is constant and that the economy naturally returns to full employment in the long run. A main implication of this theory is that any increase in the money supply will only increase the price level (inflation) in the long run.

46. A—A decrease in aggregate demand creates higher unemployment and lower inflation in the short run. Any movement along the SRPC is the result of a shift in aggregate demand.

47. E—An increase in the SRAS curve would cause a lower price level, reducing inflation rates. In the long run, the economy would return to full employment at the lower price level.

48. B—Long-run economic growth is different from an expansion in the business cycle. Think of it as an outward shift in a nation's production possibilities.

49. A—Economic growth in the long run represents a fundamental increase in a nation's full-employment level of output. An increase in AD or SRAS would increase real output but only in the short run. The rightward shift of the LRAS curve would reflect the long-run growth.

50. C—Expansionary fiscal policy would increase aggregate demand, creating a short-run inflationary gap. In the long run, nominal input prices rise and short-run aggregate supply curve shifts leftward. Eventually the level of output returns to full employment but at a higher price level.

51. D—Since the economy is operating below full employment, there is a recessionary gap. In the long run, nominal input prices fall and short-run aggregate supply shifts to the right, eliminating the recessionary gap and returning the economy to full employment.

52. B—Economic growth is more likely when a nation invests in research and technological advancements. These investments are costly in the short run but usually create long-run growth that more than compensates for that cost.

53. A—Economic growth increases a nation's productivity, so real output per worker is expected to rise. This growth should raise the nation's standard of living and increase the demand for all factors of production.

Questions from Chapter 12

54. A—Nations are net exporters of a good when the world price is greater than the domestic price. A higher world price creates a surplus in the domestic market and the surplus is exported. This situation improves the U.S. balance of trade and would not foster any U.S. protective trade policy. In currency markets, the dollar likely appreciates, as foreign consumers need dollars to buy U.S. copper.

55. A—When relative incomes are falling in Japan, fewer U.S. goods are demanded, so U.S. exports fall. The decrease in the demand for U.S. dollars causes the dollar to depreciate.

56. E—A tariff causes imports to fall, so net exports rise for the United States. With fewer consumers demanding foreign-built cars, the demand for foreign currency falls, decreasing the value of foreign currency, appreciating the value of the U.S. dollar.

57. B—Lower interest rates will cause foreign investors to pull money out of Hanoveria's capital markets and seek higher returns in other nations. This decrease in the demand for Hanoveria's investments will decrease the demand for the currency, depreciating its value.

58. C—A strong Mexican economy will cause consumers to demand more American-made products, which requires a greater supply of pesos to match the increased demand for the dollars. When the supply of pesos increases, it decreases the value of the peso, measured in dollars per peso. At the same time, stronger demand for dollars increases the value of the dollar, measured in pesos per dollar.

59. E—The current account tracks the international flow of money spent on goods and services. When a foreign retailer buys furniture made in the United States, the United States exports the goods and money flows into the U.S. current account.

60. B—Higher interest rates in the United States will attract European investment in American financial markets, increasing the demand for the U.S. dollar. Stronger demand for the dollar causes the dollar to rise in value, or appreciate, relative to the euro.

AP Macroeconomics Diagnostic Exam

SECTION II

Free-Response Questions
Planning Time—10 minutes
Writing Time—50 minutes

At the conclusion of the planning time, you have 50 minutes to respond to the following three questions. Approximately half of your time should be given to the first question, and the second half should be divided evenly between the remaining two questions. Be careful to clearly explain your reasoning and to provide clear labels to all graph axes and curves and to use arrows to show directional changes.

1. Dowindya is an open economy with a balanced budget and zero net exports. The economy is currently in an inflationary output gap.

(A) Draw a correctly labeled graph of the long-run aggregate supply, short-run aggregate supply, and aggregate demand curves, and show each of the following:
i. The current equilibrium real output and price level, labeled as Y* and PL*, respectively
ii. Full-employment output, labeled Yf

(B) Suppose the Dowindyan Economic Council (DEC) advises the nation's policymakers to do nothing to bring the economy to full employment.
i. Explain how the economy adjusts to full employment in the long run.
ii. On your graph in part (A), show how the economy adjusts to full employment in the long run.

(C) Dowindya has a limited reserve banking system. Suppose the central bank of Dowindya rejects the DEC's advice and plans monetary policy to eliminate the inflationary gap.
i. In a correctly labeled graph of the money market, show how the monetary policy will affect the equilibrium interest rate.
ii. Explain how this monetary policy will return the economy to full employment.

(D) Dowindya and the United States trade goods and services in the global economy. Based on your graph in part (C):
i. Does the value of the Dowindyan currency appreciate, depreciate, or remain the same value against the dollar?
ii. Based on your response in part (D)(i), how will this affect net exports in Dowindya? Explain.
iii. Based on your response in part (D)(ii), will this make the central bank's efforts to return the economy to full employment more difficult, less difficult, or have no impact? Explain.

2. On January 1, 2020, the economy of Dodgetopia is at full employment. Two months later, households in Dodgetopia are so concerned about a new infectious disease that they greatly reduce private consumption spending.

(A) How will this decrease in private consumption spending affect private savings in the economy?

(B) Draw a correctly labeled graph of the loanable funds market in Dodgetopia. Based on your response in part (A), indicate in the graph the change in the real interest rate.

(C) Based on your change in the real interest rate from part (B), respond to the following questions:

i. What is the short-run effect on aggregate demand? Explain.

ii. What is the long-run effect on economic growth? Explain.

3. The nation of Foxlandia produces cheese and bacon. If all resources are devoted to cheese production, 100 units of cheese can be produced. If all resources are devoted to bacon production, 400 units of bacon can be produced.

(A) With bacon on the vertical axis, draw a correctly labeled graph of Foxlandia's production possibilities curve.

(B) Use the table of labor market information to answer the following:

i. Calculate the labor force participation rate in Foxlandia. Show your work.

ii. Calculate the unemployment rate in Foxlandia. Show your work.

Employed part time	7 million
Employed full time	12 million
Unemployed and seeking a job	1 million
Out of the labor force	5 million

iii. In your graph from part (A), add a point labeled "U" that reflects the unemployment rate found in part (B)(ii).

(C) Suppose that engineers in Foxlandia develop technology that allows for maximum cheese production to double. Add a new production possibilities curve in your graph from part (A) to reflect the technological advancement in cheese production.

Free-Response Grading Rubric

Question 1 (10 points)

Part (A): 2 points

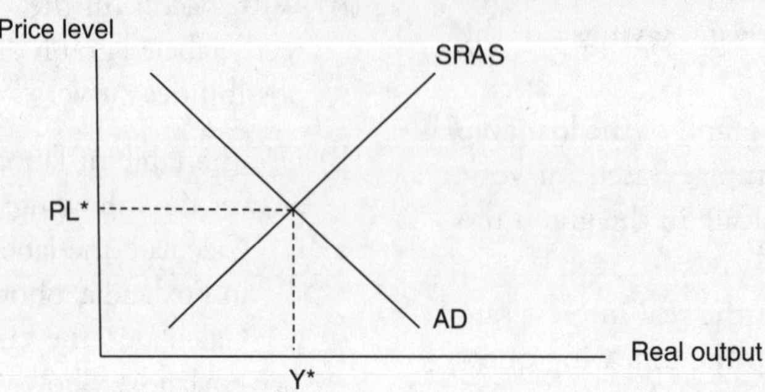

- One point is earned for drawing a correctly labeled graph showing a downward-sloping aggregate demand (AD) curve, an upward-sloping short-run aggregate supply (SRAS) curve, the equilibrium output level labeled Y*, and the equilibrium price level labeled PL*.

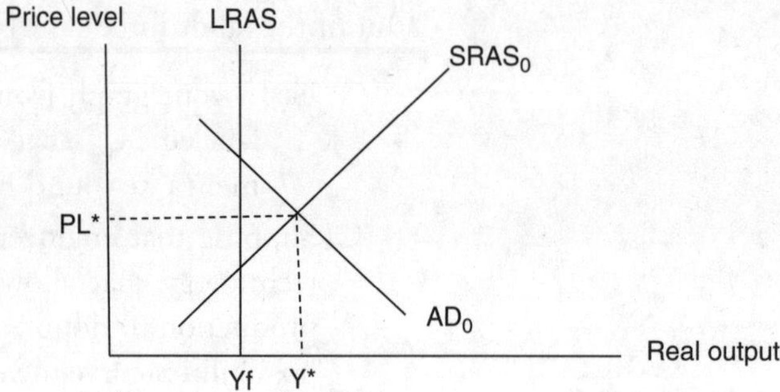

- One point is earned for drawing a correctly labeled vertical long-run aggregate supply (LRAS) curve with full-employment output labeled Yf that is less than the short-run equilibrium output level, Y*.

Part (B): 2 points

- One point is earned for stating that nominal input prices will increase, causing the SRAS to shift to the left until real output falls to Yf.
- One point is earned for drawing a leftward shift of the SRAS curve that intersects AD and LRAS at real output Yf.

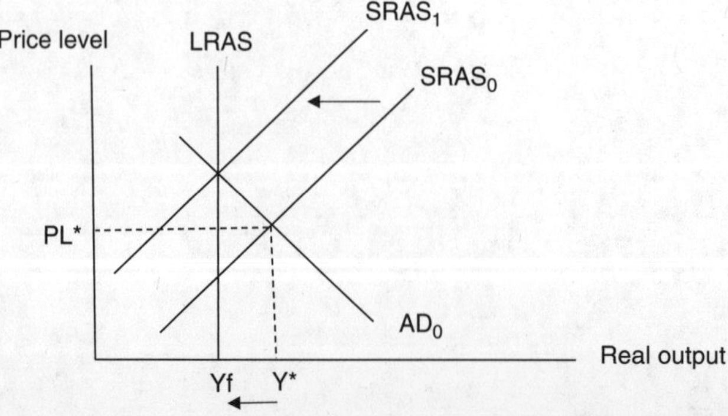

Part (C): 3 points

- One point is earned for drawing a correctly labeled graph of the money market with limited reserves.

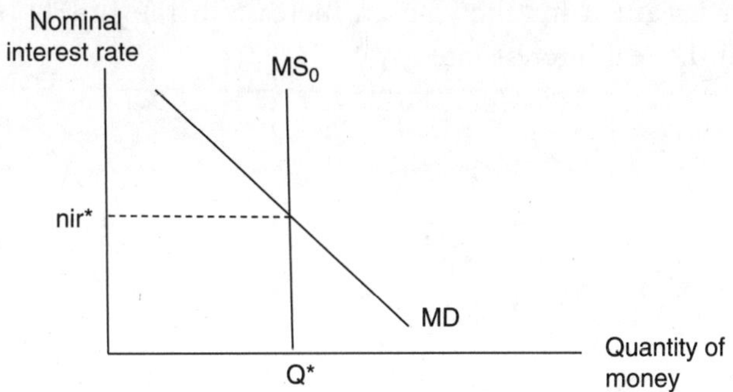

- One point is earned for showing the money supply curve shifting leftward, increasing the nominal interest rate.
- One point is earned for explaining that higher interest rates will decrease investment spending, decreasing aggregate demand and decreasing real output to full employment.

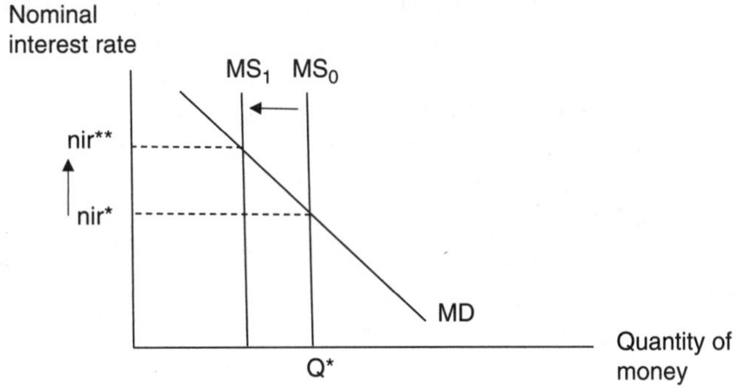

Part (D): 3 points

- One point is earned for stating that the Dowindyan currency will appreciate.
- One point is earned for explaining that next exports will decrease because Dowindya's appreciating currency makes exports more expensive to foreign consumers. Note: The appreciating currency also makes imports less expensive for Dowindya's consumers.
- One point is earned for stating that falling net exports will make the central bank's efforts less difficult because falling net exports will also decrease aggregate demand, reducing the inflationary gap.

Question 2 (5 points)

Part (A): 1 point

- One point is earned for stating that private saving will increase.

Part (B): 2 points

- One point is earned for drawing a correctly labeled graph of the market for loanable funds, with downward-sloping demand and upward-sloping supply curves.
- One point is earned for showing an increase in the supply of loanable funds and a decrease in the real interest rate.

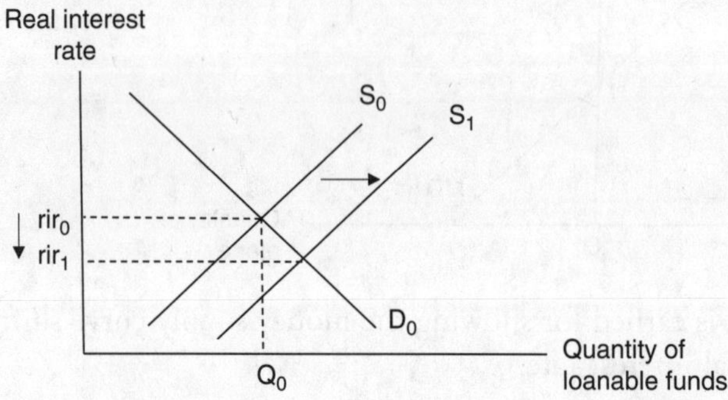

Part (C): 2 points

- One point is earned for stating that short-run aggregate demand will increase because lower interest rates will increase investment spending.
- One point is earned for stating the long-run growth will increase because higher investment spending increases a nation's stock of capital.

Question 3 (5 points)

Part A: 1 point

- One point is earned for a correctly labeled production possibilities curve with 400 units of bacon on the vertical axis and 100 units of cheese on the horizontal axis.

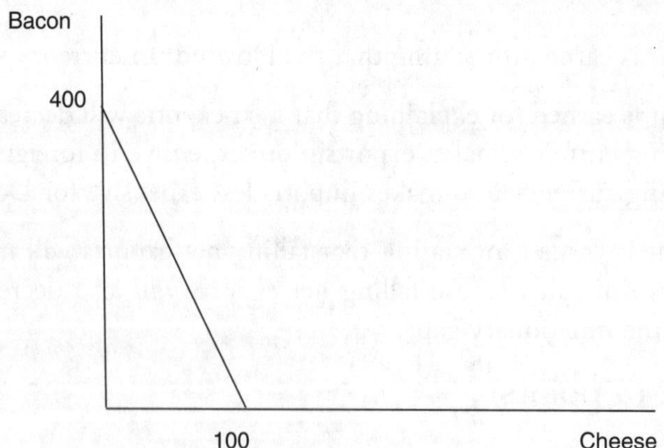

Part B: 3 points

i. One point is earned for calculating, with work shown, the labor force participation rate LFPR = (7 million + 12 million + 1 million)/25 million = .80 or 80%.

ii. One point is earned for calculating, with work shown, the unemployment rate UR = (1 million)/(7 million + 12 million + 1 million) = .05 or 5%.

iii. One point is earned for adding a point "U" to the graph that lies to the left of the PPC.

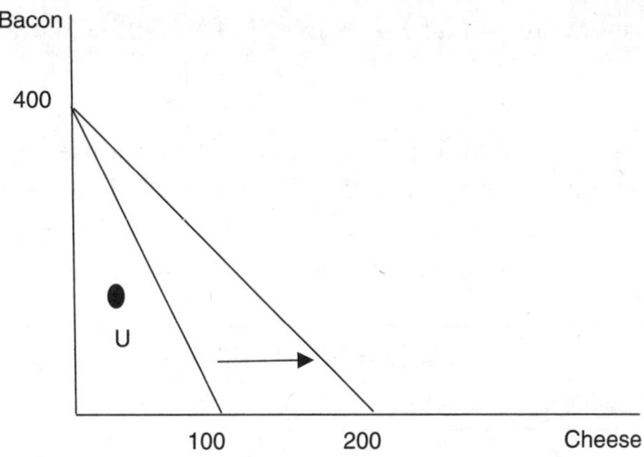

Part C: 1 point

One point is earned for adding a second PPC to the graph that intersects the vertical axis at 400 units of bacon and intersects the horizontal axis at 200 units of cheese.

Are there ever any opportunities for partial credit in FRQs?

Yes, these are often called "consistency points," and these allow you to earn points on subsequent sections of an FRQ, so long as your responses are consistent with earlier incorrect responses.

For example, let's look at Problem #1, part (A). Suppose you mistakenly drew a recessionary gap in your graph. You're definitely not going to get the second graphing point. However, in part (B) you could earn both points if you correctly described how the economy would adjust to a recessionary gap in the long run. In part (C), suppose you showed the money supply increasing and lowering the interest rate. This is not the correct way to eliminate the inflationary gap. But if your response to part (D) was that the currency would depreciate and you had a good explanation for that depreciation, you could still earn a consistency point.

So there are opportunities for partial credit in the FRQs, but you really want to shoot for earning perfect credit so you can bag the perfect 5.

Scoring and Interpretation

Now that you have completed the diagnostic exam and checked your answers, it is time to assess your knowledge and preparation. If you saw some questions that caused you to roll your eyes and mutter "What the . . . ?" then you can focus your study on those areas. If you breezed through some questions, great!

Calculate your raw score with the formula that follows. If you left any multiple-choice questions blank, there is no penalty. Take this raw score on the diagnostic exam and compare it to the table that follows to estimate where you might score at this point.

Calculate Your Score:

Multiple-Choice Questions:

______________ = ______________
(# right) MC raw score

Free-Response Questions:

Free-Response Raw Score = (1.50 × Score 1) + (1.50 × Score 2) + (1.50 × Score 3) = ________

Add the raw scores from the multiple-choice and free-response sections to obtain your total raw score for the diagnostic exam. Use the following table to determine your grade, remembering these are rough estimates using questions that are not actually from AP exams, so do not read too much into this conversion from raw score to AP score.

MACROECONOMICS	
Raw Diagnostic Score	*AP Grade*
71–90	5
53–70	4
43–52	3
31–42	2
0–30	1

No matter how you scored on the diagnostic exam, it is time to begin to review for your AP Macroeconomics exam.

Develop Strategies for Success

How to Approach Each Question Type

IN THIS CHAPTER

Summary: Use these question-answering strategies to raise your AP score.

Key Ideas

Multiple-Choice Questions

- Read the question carefully.
- Try to answer the question yourself before reading the answer choices.
- Guess if you can eliminate one or more answer choices.
- Remember that drawing a picture can help.
- Don't spend too much time on any one question.

Free-Response Questions

- Write clearly and legibly.
- Be consistent from one part of your answer to another.
- Draw a graph if one is required.
- If the question can be answered with one word or number, don't write more.
- Pay attention to the prompts.

Section I: Multiple-Choice Questions

Because you are a seasoned student accustomed to the educational testing machine, you have surely participated in more standardized tests than you care to count. You probably know some students who always seem to ace the multiple-choice questions and some students who would rather set themselves on fire than sit for another round of "bubble trouble." I hope that, with a little background and a few tips, you might improve your scores in this important component of the AP Macroeconomics exam.

First, the background. Every multiple-choice question has three important parts:

1. The **stem** is the basis for the actual question. Sometimes this comes in the form of a fill-in-the-blank statement, rather than a question.

   Example
   The value of the U.S. dollar would decrease if

   Example
   If the economy is operating below full employment, which of the following fiscal policies is most likely to decrease the unemployment rate?

2. The **correct answer option.** Obviously, this is the one selection that best completes the statement, or responds to the question in the stem. Because you have purchased this book, you will select this option many, many times.
3. **Distractor options.** Just as it sounds, these are the incorrect answers intended to distract the person who decided not to purchase this book. You can locate this person in the exam room by searching for the individual who is repeatedly smacking their forehead on the desktop.

Students who do well on multiple-choice exams are so well prepared that they can easily find the correct answer, but other students do well because they are savvy enough to identify and avoid the distractors. Much research has been done on how to best study for, and complete, multiple-choice questions. You can find some of this research by using your favorite Internet search engine, but here are a few tips that many economics students find useful.

1. *Let's be careful out there.* You must carefully read the question. This sounds pretty obvious, but you would be surprised how tricky those test developers can be. For example, rushing past and failing to see the use of a negative can throw a student.

   Example
   Which of the following is *not* true of expansionary monetary policy in a limited reserve banking system?

   A. A lower nominal interest rate increases aggregate demand.
   B. Banks see a decrease in excess reserves.
   C. Expansionary monetary policy is used to combat recessionary gaps.
   D. Lower nominal interest rates should increase real domestic output.
   E. Expansionary monetary policy is conducted by the Federal Reserve.

   A student who is going too fast and ignores the negative *not* might select option (A) because it is true of expansionary monetary policy, and it was the first option that the student saw.

2. *See the answer, be the answer.* Many people find success when they carefully read the question and, before looking at the alternatives, visualize the correct answer. This allows the person to narrow the search for the correct option and identify the distractors. Of course, this visualization tip is most useful for students who have used this book to thoroughly review the economic content.

Example

In the long run, the Phillips curve is

Before you even look at the options, you should know that the answer is "vertical." Find that option, and then quickly confirm to yourself that the others are indeed wrong.

3. *Never say never.* Words like "never" and "always" are called absolute qualifiers. If these words are used in one of the choices, it is rarely the correct choice.

Example

Which of the following is true about the level of real GDP in the short run?

A. Real GDP is always falling.
B. Real GDP is never at full-employment.

If you can think of any situation where the statements in (A) and (B) are untrue, then you have discovered distractors and can eliminate these as valid choices.

4. *Easy is as easy does.* It's exam day and you're all geared up to set this very difficult test on its ear. The first question looks like a no-brainer. Of course! The answer is 7%, choice (C). But rather than smiling at the satisfaction that you knew the answer, you doubt yourself. Could it be that easy? Sometimes they are just that easy.

5. *Sometimes a blind squirrel finds an acorn.* Should you guess? If you have no clue which choice is correct, guessing is a no-lose strategy. Even with a wild guess, you have a 20 percent chance of getting it right. If you leave it blank, you have no chance. I am sure that you can do the math.

6. *Draw it, nail it.* Many questions can be easily answered if you do a quick sketch in the margins of your test book. Hey, you paid for that test book; you might as well use it.

Example

In an economy with a vertical aggregate supply curve, a decrease in consumer confidence will cause output and the price level to change in which of the following ways?

	OUTPUT	PRICE LEVEL
(A)	No change	Increase
(B)	Decrease	Decrease
(C)	Increase	No change
(D)	No change	No change
(E)	No change	Decrease

These types of questions are particularly difficult because the answer requires two ingredients. First, it requires a very thorough understanding of the AD/AS model, and here is where your graph comes in. Second, you must be able to determine how an event like lower consumer confidence affects the AD/AS model. The first thing you should do is quickly draw the situation given to you in the question: a vertical AS curve. Show a downward-sloping AD curve shifting to the left and you can see that option (E) is correct. The graph speaks for itself.

7. *Come back, come back!* There are 60 questions, and none of these is worth more than the other. If you are struggling with a particular question, circle it in your exam book

and move on. Another question deeper into the exam might jog a memory of a theory you studied or something you learned from a practice exam in this book. You can then go back and quickly slay the beast. But if you spend a ridiculous amount of time on one question, you will feel your confidence and your time slipping away. This leads to my last tip.

8. *Timing is everything, kid.* You have about 70 seconds of time for each of the 60 questions. Keep an eye on your watch as you pass the halfway point. If you are running out of time and you have a few questions left, skim them for the easy (and quick) ones so that the rest of your scarce time can be devoted to those that need a little extra reading or thought.

   Other things to keep in mind:

   - Take the extra half of a second required to clearly fill in the bubbles.
   - Don't smudge anything with sloppy erasures. If your eraser is smudgy, ask the proctor for another.
   - Absolutely, positively check that you are bubbling the same line on the answer sheet as the question you are answering. I suggest that every time you turn the page you double-check that you are still lined up correctly.

Section II: Free-Response Questions

Your score on the FRQs amounts to one-third of your grade, and as a longtime reader of essays, I assure you there is no other way to score highly than to know your stuff. While you can guess on a multiple-choice question and have a one-in-five chance of getting the correct answer, there is no room for guessing in this section. There are, however, some tips that you can use to enhance your FRQ scores.

1. *Easy to Read = Easy to Grade.* Organize your responses around the separate parts of the question and clearly label each part of your response. In other words, do not hide your answer; make it easy to find and easy to read. It helps you, and it helps the reader see where you're going. *Trust me, helping the reader can never hurt.* This leads to a related tip: Write in English, not Sanskrit. Even the most levelheaded and unbiased reader has trouble keeping their patience while struggling to read sloppy handwriting. I have seen three readers spend almost 10 minutes using the Rosetta stone to decipher a paragraph of text that was obviously written by a time-traveling student from the Byzantine Empire.

2. *Consistently wrong can be good.* The free-response questions are written in several parts, each building upon the first. If you are looking at an eight-part question, it can be scary. However, these questions are graded so that you can salvage several points even if you do not correctly answer the first part. The key thing for you to know is that you must be consistent, even if it is consistently wrong. For example, you might be asked to draw an AD/AS graph showing how expansionary monetary policy can eliminate a recessionary gap. Following sections might ask you to show the change in the aggregate price level and real GDP—each being determined by the AD/AS graph you drew earlier. So let's say you draw your graph, but you show *contractionary* monetary policy. Obviously you are not going to receive that graphing point. But if you proceed by showing correct changes to the aggregate price level and real GDP for your *incorrect* graph, you would be surprised how forgiving the grading rubric can be.

3. *Have the last laugh with a well-drawn graph.* There are some points that require an explanation (i.e., "Describe how . . ."). Not all free-response questions require a graph, but a garbled paragraph of explanation can be saved with a perfect graph that tells the reader you know the answer to the question. This does not work in reverse.

4. *If I say draw, you better draw, Tex.* There are what readers call "graphing points," and these cannot be earned with a well-written paragraph. For example, if you are asked to draw the AD/AS scenario described above, certain points will be awarded for the graph and only the graph. A delightfully written and entirely accurate paragraph of text will not earn the graphing points. You also need to clearly label graphs. You might think that downward-sloping line is obviously an aggregate demand curve, but some of those graphing points will not be awarded if lines and points are not clearly, and accurately, identified. And please, please, draw your graph larger than a postage stamp. If the reader cannot clearly see the important aspects of the graph, you will not earn those points.

5. *Give the answer, not a dissertation.* There are some parts of a question where you are asked to simply "identify" something. For example, "Identify the equilibrium real rate of interest," or "Identify a point in the production possibility graph that reflects an inefficient use of resources." This type of question requires a quick piece of analysis that can literally be answered in one word or number. That point will be given if you provide that one word or number whether it is the only word you write or the fortieth that you write. For example, you might be given a table that shows combinations of inflation rates and unemployment rates. One part of the question asks you to identify the unemployment rate that corresponds to full employment in the economy. Suppose the correct answer is 4%. The point is given if you say "4%," "four percent," and maybe even "iv%." If you write a 500-word Magna Carta concluding with "4%," you will get the point but will have wasted precious time. This brings me to . . .

6. *Welcome to the magical kingdom.* If you surround the right answer to a question with a paragraph of economic wrongness, you will usually earn the point, so long as you say the magic word. The only exception is a direct contradiction of the right answer. For example, suppose that when asked to *identify* the unemployment rate at full employment, you spend a paragraph describing how trade agreements are unfair and therefore are subject to import quotas and that the exchange rate between the unemployed and the production possibility frontier means the answer is four percent. You will get the point! You said the unemployment rate is 4%, and "four percent" was the magic words. However, if you say that the answer is four percent but that it is also five and on Mondays it is 7%, you have contradicted yourself and the point will not be earned.

7. *Marginally speaking.* This point is made in the first two chapters of review in this book, but it bears repeating here as a valuable test-taking strategy. In economics, anything that is optimal or efficient or rational or cost minimizing or profit maximizing can be answered by telling the reader that the marginal benefits must equal the marginal costs. Depending on the situation, you might have to clarify that "marginal benefit" to the firm is "marginal revenue" or to the employer "marginal revenue product." If the question asks you *why* the answer is four, there is always a very short phrase that readers look for so that they may award the point. This answer often includes the appropriate marginal comparison.

8. *Identify, Illustrate, Define, Indicate, and Explain.* Each part of a free-response question includes a prompt that tells you what the reader will be looking for so that the points can be earned. If the question asks you to "identify" something, you may need only

one word or a short phrase to earn all the points. Writing a paragraph here will only waste your time. As mentioned, any reference to "illustrate" will require you to draw, or redraw, a graph to receive points. If the question asks you to "define" a concept, you need to devote more time to providing your best definition of that concept. If you are prompted to "indicate" something, you must simply state what is expected to happen. For example, suppose you are told that the central bank, in a system with limited reserves, has sold bonds in an open market operation and you are asked to indicate what will happen to interest rates. All you need to do to earn the point is indicate that interest rates will increase. You may also earn the point if you clearly indicate, preferably with an arrow, in a graph of the money market that interest rates are rising. The most time-intensive prompt is usually one that involves "explain." Suppose you are told that the Canadian dollar is appreciating relative to the U.S. dollar. Then you are asked to explain how this will impact domestic output and the price level in the United States. To give yourself the best chance at earning all the points, your response must provide two parts. First, give a clear statement of what exactly will happen; second, explain why it is going to happen.

Here are some other things to keep in mind:

- The free-response section begins with a 10-minute reading period. Use this time well to jot down some quick notes to yourself so that when you actually begin to respond, you will have a nice start.
- Do not write on *that* page. When you receive and open your free-response booklet, you will see that one of the very first pages says, "do not write your responses on this page because nothing on this page will be scored." Trust me here, if you write the perfect response on *that* page, you will receive nothing for it. These standardized tests are serious about following instructions!
- The first parts of the free-response questions are the easiest parts. Spend just enough time to get these points before moving on to the more difficult sections.
- The questions are written in logical order. If you find yourself explaining Part C before responding to Part B, back up and work through the logical progression of topics.
- Abbreviations are your friends. You can save time by using commonly accepted abbreviations for economic variables and graphical curves, and you will get more adept at their use as your mastery improves. For example, in macroeconomics you can save some time by using "OMO" rather than "open market operation," and in microeconomics you can use "MRP" rather than "marginal revenue product."
- *Show your work.* In recent years, the exam has included more mathematical components that allow you to demonstrate that you know a particular economic concept by computing something. Virtually all these problems include the prompt "show your work," and you will *not* earn points if you have not set up the mathematical problem correctly and shown your work clearly. For example, suppose that price inflation is 5% and your nominal salary increases by 7%; you are asked to compute how much your real salary has changed and show your work. You know that your real salary has increased by 2%, but if you simply state that the answer is 2% you will not earn the point, because you did not show your work. The simple fix for this is to write: 7% − 5% = 2%. Point earned!
- A calculator is not a substitute for knowledge and studying. It's nice that you are now allowed to use a four-function calculator, but that little device will not earn you the perfect 5. You absolutely must come into the exam with maximum preparation and knowledge. The calculator is there to facilitate the number crunching, nothing more and nothing less.

Review the Knowledge You Need to Score High

Fundamentals of Economic Analysis

IN THIS CHAPTER

Summary: If there are two concepts that you should have down pat, they are (1) scarce resources require decision makers to make decisions that involve costs and benefits and (2) these decisions are best made when the additional benefits of the action are exactly offset by the additional costs of the action. This chapter presents material that, at least on the surface, appears to be "Econ-lite." Some readers might make the mistake of simply glossing over it on the way to meatier topics. I urge you to take the time to reinforce these early concepts, for they should, like a bad earworm, stick in your subconscious throughout your preparation for the AP exam.

Key Ideas

- Scarcity
- Opportunity Cost
- Marginal Analysis
- Production Possibilities
- Functions of Economic Systems

5.1 Scarce Resources

Main Topics: *Economic Resources, Scarcity, Trade-Offs, Opportunity Cost, Marginal Analysis*

Economic Resources

Economics is the study of how people, firms, and societies use their scarce productive resources to best satisfy their unlimited material wants. Resources, or Factors of Production, are commonly separated into four groups:

- *Labor.* Human effort and talent, physical and mental. This can be augmented by education and training (human capital).
- *Land or natural resources.* Any resource created by nature. This may be arable land, mineral deposits, oil and gas reserves, or water.
- *Physical capital.* Human-made equipment like machinery as well as buildings, roads, vehicles, and computers.
- *Entrepreneurial ability.* The effort and know-how to put the other resources together in a productive venture.

Scarcity

All of the above resources are scarce, or in limited supply. Since productive resources are scarce, it makes sense that the production of goods and services must be scarce.

Example:

Sometimes it is easier to see this if you look at the production of something familiar, like the production of a term paper.

- *Labor.* Your hours of research, writing, and rewriting. As we all know, these hours are scarce, or limited to the number of waking hours in the day.
- *Land/natural resources.* Paper (trees) and electricity (rivers, coal, natural gas, wind, solar). Not only are these in scarce supply, but your ability to acquire these resources is also limited by your income, which is a result of using some of your scarce labor hours to work for a wage.
- *Capital.* Your computer, printer, desk, pens and pencils, and the library and sources within.
- *Entrepreneurial ability.* The skill that it takes to compile the research into a coherent, thoughtful, and articulate piece of academic work.

Trade-Offs

The fact that we are faced with scarce resources implies that individuals, firms, and governments are constantly faced with trade-offs.

Individuals

Consumers choose between housing arrangements (Do I rent an apartment or buy a home?), transportation options, grocery store items, and many other daily purchases. Workers and students must choose from a wide range of employment and education opportunities. (Do I pick up an extra shift? Do I pursue my MBA or PhD?)

Firms

For the firm, decisions are often centered on which good or service can be provided, how much should be produced, and how to go about producing those goods and services.

A local restaurant considers whether or not to stay open later on Saturday night. A steel company must decide whether to open a plant in Indiana or in Indonesia.

Governments

Every society, in one form or another, places many tough decisions in the hands of government, both local and national. Not surprisingly, local government is faced with issues that are likely to have an immediate impact on the lives of local citizens. (Should we use tax revenues to pave potholes in the streets or buy a new city bus?) At the national level, not all citizens might/would feel the impact immediately, but the stakes are likely much higher. (Should we open protected wilderness areas to oil and gas exploration? Should we impose a tariff on imported rice?)

Regardless of the decision maker—individual, firm, or government—the reality of scarce resources creates a trade-off between the opportunity that is taken and the opportunity that was not taken and thus forgone. The value of what was given up is called the **opportunity cost**.

Opportunity Cost

At the most basic level, the opportunity cost of doing something is all that you sacrifice to do it. In other words, if you use a scarce resource to pursue activity X, the opportunity cost of activity X is activity Y, the next best use of that resource.

Example:

You have one scarce hour to spend between studying for an exam or working at a coffee shop for $8 per hour. If you study, the opportunity cost of studying is $8.

Example:

"Pay close attention here; this is a very common mistake."
—Hillary, AP Student

You have one scarce hour to spend between studying for an exam or working at a coffee shop for $8 per hour or mowing your uncle's lawn for $10 per hour. If you choose to study, what is the opportunity cost of studying?

Be careful! A common mistake is to add up the value of *all* your other options ($18), but this misses an important point. In this scenario, and in many others, you have one hour to allocate to one activity, thus giving up the others. By choosing to study, you really only gave up one thing: mowing the lawn *or* serving cappuccinos, not both.

The opportunity cost of using your resource to do activity X is the value the resource would have in its *next best alternative use*. Therefore, the opportunity cost of studying is $10, the better of your two alternatives.

At this point, you might be wondering, "Does everything have a dollar figure attached to it? Can't we just enjoy something without slapping a price tag on it?"

This is an excellent question, and the concept can often be a difficult point to make. If you have one scarce hour and you could either work at the coffee shop for $8 or take a restful nap, the opportunity cost of working is the nap, which certainly has value. How can we place a dollar value on the nap? Maybe you are giving serious thought to taking the nap, but your employer at the coffee shop really needs you to work. Maybe your employer offers you $10 to forgo the nap and come to work. After some consideration, you still choose the nap. Surely there is a price (the wage) that would be high enough to entice you to come to work at the coffee shop. If your employer offered you just enough to compensate you for the nap you gave up, you have found the value that you placed on the nap.

Marginal Analysis

Another way of making decisions is to weigh the costs and benefits of doing, or consuming, the *next one*. You have one cup of coffee and are deciding whether to have another (the next one). You have studied five hours for an economics exam and need to decide if it is in your best interest to study another hour (the next one).

These decisions are said to be made at the margin. The next cup of coffee brings with it *additional* (or marginal) benefits to the consumer but comes at *additional* (marginal) costs. The rational consumer weighs the additional benefits against the additional costs.

Marginal analysis. This is a concept that is seen throughout economics, and throughout this book, but let's briefly look at it from a consumer's point of view.

Marginal cost (MC). The additional cost incurred from the consumption of the next unit of a good or service.

Marginal benefit (MB). The additional benefit received from the consumption of the next unit of a good or service. Another way of measuring marginal benefit is to ask yourself, "How much would I pay for the next unit of this good?"

Example:

The soda machine down the hall charges me $1.00 for every can of pop.

The decision to buy another soda is another example of marginal analysis. If I expect to receive at least $1 in additional benefit, or if I am willing to pay $1 or more to have it, buying another soda is a rational decision. This decision is shown in Figure 5.1.

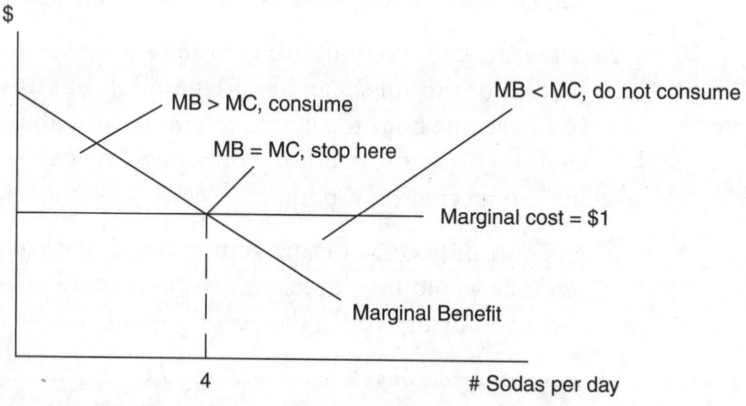

Figure 5.1

So how many sodas will I consume in a typical day? For each of the first three sodas, my MB > $1, the marginal cost of the next soda. The fourth soda provides me with exactly $1 in marginal benefit, so I find it exactly worth my while to buy it. The fifth soda is not bought because the MC > MB. Notice that my MB declines as I consume more sodas. This is a fairly predictable relationship, since I am likely to enjoy my first soda of the day more than my fifth.

Rule:

Do something if the marginal benefits ≥ marginal costs of doing it.

Stop doing something when the marginal benefits = marginal costs of doing it.

Never do something when the marginal benefits < marginal costs of doing it.

You will find this to be true in consumption, production, hiring, and many other economic decisions.

5.2 Production Possibilities

Main Topics: *Production Possibilities Curve, Resource Substitutability, Law of Increasing Costs, Comparative Advantage and Specialization, Efficiency, Growth*

Production Possibilities Curve

To examine production and opportunity cost, economists find it useful to create a simplified model of an individual, or a nation, that can choose to allocate its scarce resources between the production of two goods or services. For now we assume that those resources are being fully employed and used efficiently.

Example:

The owner of a small bakery can allocate a fixed amount of labor (the chef and her helpers), capital (mixers, pans, and ovens), natural resources (raw materials), and her entrepreneurial talent toward the production of pastries and pizza crusts.

The **production possibilities** table (Table 5.1) lists the different combinations of pastries and crusts that can be produced with a fixed quantity of scarce resources.

Table 5.1 Bakery Production Possibilities

PASTRIES	PIZZA CRUST
0	10
1	8
2	6
3	4
4	2
5	0

If the chef wishes to produce one more pastry, she must give up two pizza crusts. If she wishes one more crust, she must give up one-half of a pastry.

In other words:

The opportunity cost of a pastry is two crusts.
The opportunity cost of a pizza crust is one-half of a pastry.

We can graphically depict Table 5.1 in a **production possibility curve** (PPC). Each point on the curve represents some maximum output combination of the two products. Some refer to this curve as a **production possibility frontier** (PPF) because it reflects the outer limit of production. Any point outside the frontier (e.g., 4, 8) is currently unattainable, and any point inside the frontier (e.g., 1, 2) fails to use all the bakery's available resources in an efficient way. We talk more about efficiency at the end of this section.

So here you might wonder, "Why is there a limit to the production of these goods? In other words, why doesn't the frontier just expand to allow an unlimited amount of either?"

Over the course of time, the frontier is believed to expand. But at any given point in time, we must confront the scarcity problem again. The resources used to produce these goods are scarce, and thus, the production frontier is going to act as a binding constraint. The concept of economic growth is introduced in this chapter and also discussed in Chapter 10, but for the time being, the frontier looks like Figure 5.2.

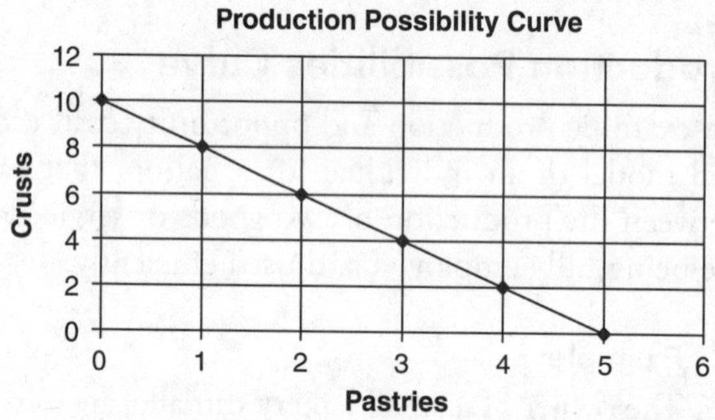

Figure 5.2

The opportunity cost of each good is also apparent in the production possibility curve itself. We ignore the fact that the curve slopes downward and simply focus on its magnitude, or absolute value.

- The slope of the curve, 2 in our case, measures the opportunity cost of the good on the x-axis.
- The inverse of the slope, ½ in our case, measures the opportunity cost of the good on the y-axis.

Notice that with a straight line, the opportunity cost of producing more of each good is always a constant. Is this realistic?

Resource Substitutability

Suppose our bakery chef is currently producing 10 pizza crusts and zero pastries. But today she decides that she should produce one pastry and eight crusts. In Figure 5.2, this decision appears fairly straightforward.

What we often forget is that resources must be reallocated from pizza crust production to pastry production. Labor, capital, and natural resources must be removed from crust production and moved into pastry production.

Perhaps some of the capital (i.e., pans) in the bakery are better suited to pizza crust production than pastry production. Certainly raw materials like chocolate and frosting are not very useful for pizza crust production but are extremely valuable to the pastry production.

The same could be said for individual laborers. Maybe the entrepreneur herself was trained as a French pastry chef and can make pizza crusts but not as well as she can make éclairs. The fact that these resources are better suited to the production of one good, and less easily adaptable to the production of the other good, gives us the concept of . . .

Law of Increasing Costs

Law of increasing costs tells us that the more of a good that is produced, the greater its opportunity cost. This reality gives us a production possibility curve that is concave to the origin, or *bowed outward*, as shown in Figure 5.3.

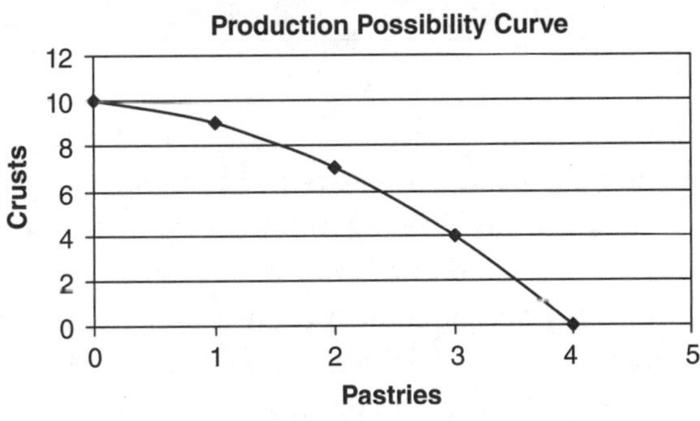

Figure 5.3

Now as the bakery produces more pastries, the opportunity cost (slope) begins to rise. Of course, the same is happening if the chef chooses to produce more crusts.

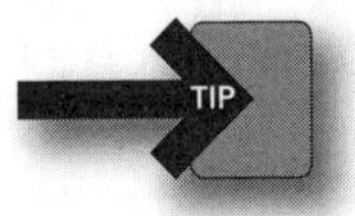

- Because resources are not perfectly adaptable to alternative uses, our production possibility curve is unlikely to be linear and will probably become steeper as production moves downward along the curve.

Comparative Advantage and Specialization

I went to the dentist's office the other day. For 30 minutes the dental hygienist took an x-ray and then cleaned and flossed my teeth. When she was done, the dentist popped in, peeked at her handiwork, studied my x-ray, and sent me on my way with a new toothbrush. Why did my dentist let the hygienist do all the cleaning and flossing when she is perfectly capable of doing the task? Because the dentist's scarce time resource is better used performing tasks like oral surgery. The opportunity cost of the dentist flossing my teeth is the revenue earned from a procedure that only she is qualified to perform. Forgoing the revenue from the oral surgery is avoided by assigning the cleaning tasks to the hygienist, whose specialty is oral hygiene but not oral surgery.

The law of increasing costs tells us that it becomes more costly to produce a good as you produce more of it. This reality prompts us to find other, less expensive ways to get our hands on additional units. The concepts of **specialization** and **comparative advantage** describe the way that individuals, nations, and societies can acquire more goods at lower cost.

Example:

Suppose our bakery, which can produce both pizza crusts and pastries, shares the local market with a pizza parlor. The pizza parlor can also produce pastries, but it might rather produce pizza crusts. Each firm would like to produce more goods at lower cost. Table 5.2 shows the production possibilities of these two firms and the opportunity costs of producing more of each good. To make things simpler, we assume that both businesses have access to the same economic resources.

Table 5.2 Production Possibilities and Opportunity Costs

BAKERY		PIZZA PARLOR	
Pastries	*Crusts*	*Pastries*	*Crusts*
10	0	5	0
0	5	0	10
OPPORTUNITY COSTS		OPPORTUNITY COSTS	
1 pastry costs	1 crust costs	1 pastry costs	1 crust costs
½ crust	2 pastries	2 crusts	½ pastry

Because the bakery can produce more pastries than the pizza parlor, the bakery has **absolute advantage** in pastry production. The pizza parlor has absolute advantage in crust production. Simply being able to produce more of a good does not mean that the firm produces that good at a lower opportunity cost.

Both producers could produce pastries, but the bakery can produce pastries at lower opportunity cost (0.5 crusts versus 2 crusts). The bakery is said to have **comparative advantage** in the production of pastries. Likewise, the table illustrates that the pizza parlor has the comparative advantage in pizza crusts (0.5 pastries versus 2 pastries). These producers can, and indeed should, **specialize** by producing only pastries at the bakery and only crusts at the pizza parlor. Because these firms are specializing and producing at lower cost, not only do they benefit by earning more profit, but consumers across town also benefit from purchasing goods at lower prices.

In microeconomics, the principle of comparative advantage explains why the pediatrician delivers the babies while the electrician wires the house and not the other way around. In macroeconomics, this principle is the basis for showing how nations can gain from free trade. We explore trade among nations in the last chapter. To see the microeconomics gains from specialization, we do a game called "before and after."

Before. Each firm devotes half of its resources to pastry production and half to crust production.

Total citywide pastry production = 5 + 2.5 = 7.5
Total citywide crust production = 2.5 + 5 = 7.5

"Know the different ways of showing comparative advantage. This is a potential free-response question."
—AP Teacher

After. Each firm specializes in the production of the good for which it has comparative advantage.

Total citywide pastry production = 10 + 0 = 10
Total citywide crust production = 0 + 10 = 10

Figure 5.4 shows both production possibility frontiers and how a combination of 10 crusts and 10 pastries (specialization) was previously unattainable and is superior to when each firm produced at the midpoint (50/50) of their individual frontiers.

- If firms and individuals produce goods based on their comparative advantage, society gains more production at lower cost.

Efficiency

If not all available resources are being used to their fullest, the economy is operating at some point inside the production possibility frontier. This is clearly inefficient. But even if the economy is operating at some point on the frontier, who is to say that it is the point that is

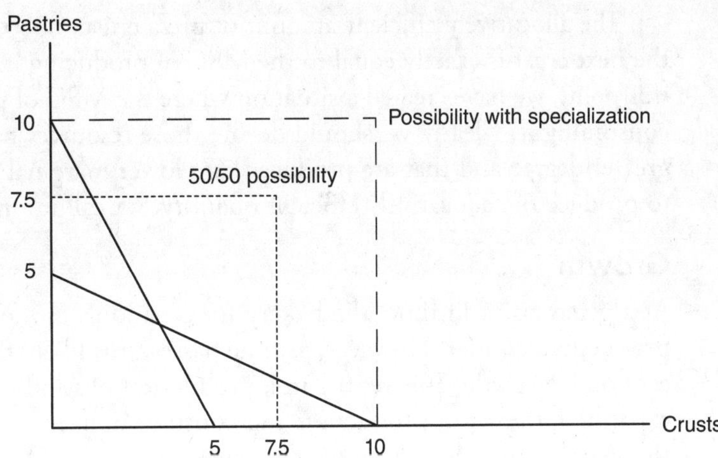

Figure 5.4

most desired by the citizens? If it does not happen to be the point that society most wants, we are also facing an inefficient situation.

In this production possibility model, there are two types of efficiency:

Productive efficiency. The economy is producing the maximum output for a given level of technology and resources. All points on the production frontier are productively efficient.

Allocative efficiency. The economy is producing the optimal mix of goods and services. By optimal, we mean that it is the combination of goods and services that provides the most net benefit to society. If society is allocatively efficient, it is operating at the best point on the frontier.

How do we determine which point is the best point? Remember how I determined the optimal number of sodas to consume every day? Suppose we could measure, society-wide, the marginal social benefit (MSB) received from the consumption of pizza crusts. Like my MB for sodas, the MSB for crusts is falling as more crusts are consumed. We already know that the marginal social cost (MSC) of producing pizza crusts increases. The marginal social cost of producing and marginal social benefit of consuming more pizza crusts are illustrated in Figure 5.5.

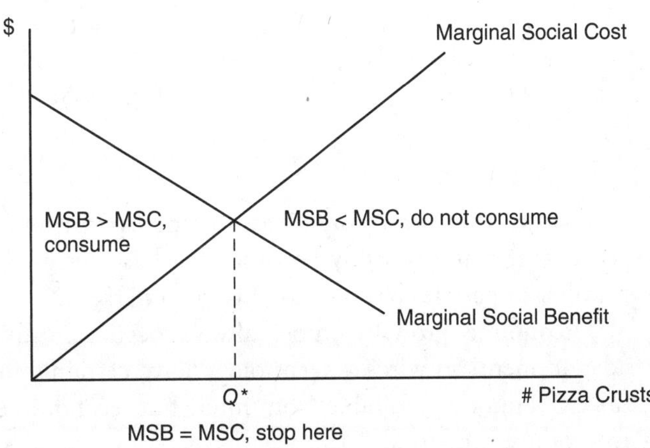

Figure 5.5

The allocatively efficient amount of pizza crusts is Q^*, the quantity where the MSB of the next crust is exactly equal to the MSC of producing it. If we produce anything beyond this point, we have created a situation where the MSC of producing it exceeds our MSB of consuming it. Clearly we should devote those resources to other goods that we desire to a greater degree and that are produced at a lower marginal social cost. When a market fails to produce the allocatively efficient quantity, we call it a **market failure.**

Growth

At a given point in time, the bakery (or a nation's economy) cannot operate beyond the production frontier. However, as time passes, it is likely that firms and nations experience economic growth. This results in a production possibilities frontier that moves outward, expanding the set of production and consumption. More discussion of growth follows in the macroeconomic section of the review.

Economic growth, the ability to produce a larger total output over time, can occur if one or all of the following occur:

- An increase in the quantity of resources. For example, the bakery acquires another oven.
- An increase in the quality of existing resources. For example, the chef acquires the best assistants in the city.
- Technological advancements in production. For example, electric mixers versus hand mixers.

Figure 5.6 illustrates economic growth for the bakery.

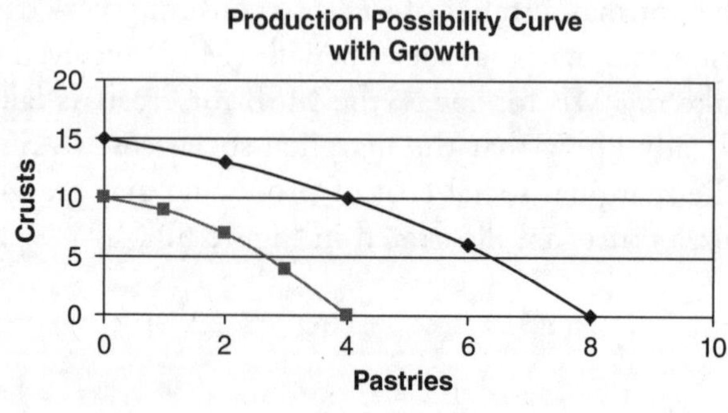

Figure 5.6

Notice that the frontier has not increased proportionally. The maximum number of crusts that could possibly be produced has increased by 50 percent, while the maximum number of pastries has increased by 100 percent.

Economic growth almost always occurs in this way. For example, technological advancements in wireless technology have certainly increased the nation's capacity to produce cell phones and tablet computers but has not likely measurably increased our capacity to produce tomatoes.

5.3 Functions of Economic Systems

Main Topic: *Market Systems*

Market Systems

"This concept, although an easy one, is a definite MC question. Don't miss it." —Adam, AP Student

In the twenty-first century, most industrially advanced nations have gravitated toward a **market economy—capitalism.**

Keys to a Market System

- *Private Property.* Individuals, not government, own most economic resources. This private ownership encourages innovation, investment, growth, and trade.

  Example:

  If the state owned the bakery ovens, mixers, and even the building itself, how much of an incentive would our entrepreneur have to maintain the equipment, the inventory, or even the quality of the product? Knowing that the state could take these resources with very little notice, our chef might just do the bare minimum, and if this situation happened all over town, the local economy would languish.

- *Freedom.* Individuals are free to acquire resources to produce goods and services and free to choose which of their resources to sell to others so that they may buy their own goods and services.

  Example:

  The bakery can freely use its resources to produce rolls, pastries, croissants, and anything else it believes leads to profitability. Of course, this freedom is limited by legal constraints. The bakery cannot sell illegal drugs from the back door, and the chef is not free to offer open-heart surgery with her bagels.

- *Self-Interest and Incentives.* Individuals are motivated by self-interest in their use of resources. Entrepreneurs seek to maximize profit, while consumers seek to maximize happiness. With these incentives, goods are sold and bought.

  Example:

  Our bakery owner, motivated by profit, seeks to offer products that appeal to her customers. Customers, seeking to maximize their happiness, consume these bakery products only if they satisfy their personal tastes and wants.

- *Competition.* Buyers and sellers, acting independently, and motivated by self-interest, freely move in and out of individual markets. Again, the issue of incentives is powerful. A new firm, eager to compete in a market, only enters that market if profits are available.

  Example:

  Competition implies that prices are determined in the marketplace and not controlled by individual sellers, buyers, or the government. Our bakery owner employs labor at the going market wage, which is determined in the competitive local labor market. She offers baked products at the going price, which is determined in the competitive local market for those goods.

- *Prices.* Prices send signals to buyers and sellers, and resource allocation decisions are made based on this information. Prices also serve to ration goods to those consumers who are most willing and able to pay those prices. Prices coordinate the decentralized economic activity of millions of individuals and firms in a way that no one central economic figure can hope to achieve. Prices, not just for goods and services but also for labor and other resources, are the delivery mechanism for the previous incentives—profit for the firm and happiness for the consumer.

Example:

As the price of labor, relative to capital, changes, the bakery chef might be motivated to readjust her employment of assistants. Changes in the relative price of her products might prompt consumers to readjust their purchasing decisions.

› Review Questions

1. Economics is best described as

(A) the study of how scarce material wants are allocated between unlimited resources.
(B) the study of how scarce labor can be replaced by unlimited capital.
(C) the study of how decision makers choose the best way to satisfy their unlimited material wants with a scarce supply of resources.
(D) the study of how unlimited material wants can best be satisfied by allocating limitless amounts of productive resources.
(E) the study of how capitalism is superior to any other economic system.

2. A student decides that, having already spent three hours studying for an exam, she should spend one more hour studying for the same exam. Which of the following is most likely true?

(A) The marginal benefit of the fourth hour is certainly less than the marginal cost of the fourth hour.
(B) The marginal benefit of the fourth hour is at least as great as the marginal cost of the fourth hour.
(C) Without knowing the student's opportunity cost of studying, we have no way of knowing whether or not her marginal benefits outweigh her marginal costs.
(D) The marginal cost of the third hour was likely greater than the marginal cost of the fourth hour.
(E) The marginal benefit of the third hour was less than the marginal cost of the third hour.

The island nation of Beckham uses economic resources to produce tea and crumpets. Use the following production possibilities frontier (PPF) for questions 3 to 4.

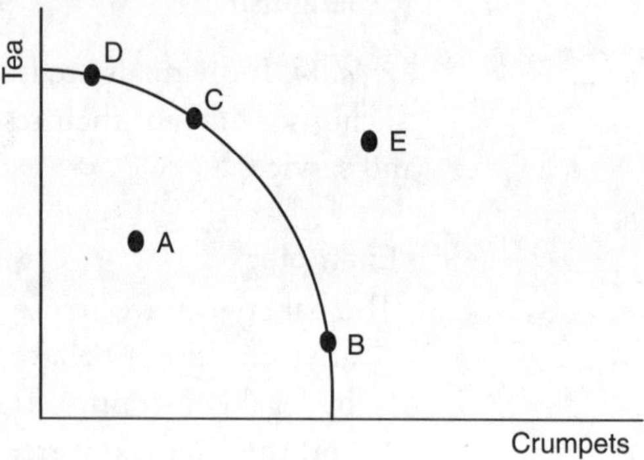

3. Economic growth is best represented by a movement from

(A) A to B.
(B) B to C.
(C) C to D.
(D) D to E.
(E) E to A.

4. The shape of this PPF tells us that

(A) economic resources are perfectly substitutable from production of tea to production of crumpets.
(B) citizens prefer that an equal amount of tea and crumpets be produced.
(C) the opportunity cost of producing crumpets rises as more crumpets are produced.
(D) the opportunity cost of producing crumpets is constant along the curve.
(E) the opportunity cost of producing tea falls as you produce more tea.

5. Ray and Dorothy can both cook and can both pull weeds in the garden on a Saturday afternoon. For every hour of cooking, Ray can pull 50 weeds and Dorothy can pull 100 weeds. Based on this information, how should they allocate their time?
   (A) Ray pulls weeds, since he has absolute advantage in cooking.
   (B) Dorothy pulls weeds, since she has absolute advantage in cooking.
   (C) Dorothy cooks, since she has comparative advantage in cooking.
   (D) Ray cooks, since he has comparative advantage in cooking.
   (E) Dorothy pulls weeds, since she has comparative advantage in cooking.

❯ Answers and Explanations

1. **C**—It is important to remember that society has a limitless desire for material wants, but satisfaction of these wants is limited by scarce economic resources. Economics studies how to solve this problem in the best possible way.

2. **B**—As she studies more hours, the marginal benefit decreases and the marginal cost increases. If we observe her studying for the fourth hour, then it must be the case that the MB ≥ MC of studying for that next hour. If we observe her putting her books away and doing something else, the opposite must be true.

3. **D**—Economic growth is an outward expansion of the entire PPF. A movement from the interior to the frontier (A to B) is not growth, it just tells us that some unemployed resources (A) are now being used to their full potential (B).

4. **C**—When the PPF is concave to the origin (or bowed outward) it is an indicator of the law of increasing costs. This is a result of economic resources not being perfectly substitutable between tea and crumpets. A baking sheet used to bake crumpets might be quite useless in producing tea leaves.

5. **D**—For Ray, the opportunity cost of cooking is 50 weeds, while Dorothy's opportunity cost of cooking is 100 unpulled weeds. Ray does not pull weeds because he has comparative advantage in cooking. Dorothy does not cook because she has comparative advantage in weed pulling.

❯ Rapid Review

Economics: The study of how people, firms, and societies use their scarce productive resources to best satisfy their unlimited material wants.

Resources: Called factors of production, these are commonly grouped into the four categories of labor, physical capital, land or natural resources, and entrepreneurial ability.

Scarcity: The imbalance between limited productive resources and unlimited human wants. Because economic resources are scarce, the goods and services a society can produce are also scarce.

Trade-offs: Scarce resources imply that individuals, firms, and governments are constantly faced with difficult choices that involve benefits and costs.

Opportunity cost: The value of the sacrifice made to pursue a course of action.

Marginal: The next unit or increment of an action.

Marginal social benefit (MSB): The additional benefit that society receives from the consumption of the next unit of a good or service.

Marginal social cost (MSC): The additional cost that society incurs from the production of the next unit of a good or service.

Marginal analysis: Making decisions based on weighing the marginal benefits and costs of that action. The rational decision maker chooses an action if the MB ≥ MC.

Production possibilities: Different quantities of goods that an economy can produce with a given amount of scarce resources. Graphically, the trade-off between the production of two goods is portrayed as a production possibility curve or frontier (PPC or PPF).

Production possibility curve or frontier (PPC or PPF): A graphical illustration that shows the maximum quantity of one good that can be produced, given the quantity of the other good being produced.

Law of increasing costs: The more of a good that is produced, the greater the opportunity cost of producing the next unit of that good.

Absolute advantage: This exists if a producer can produce more of a good with the same quantity of resources, or the same quantity of goods with fewer resources, than all other producers.

Comparative advantage: A producer has comparative advantage if it can produce a good at lower opportunity cost than all other producers.

Specialization: When firms focus their resources on production of goods for which they have comparative advantage, they are said to be specializing.

Productive efficiency: Production of maximum output for a given level of technology and resources. All points on the PPF are productively efficient.

Market failure: A market outcome for which the quantity produced is not allocatively efficient (MSB ≠ MSC) and either too many or too few units are produced.

Allocative efficiency: Production of the combination of goods and services that provides the most net benefit to society. The optimal quantity of a good is achieved when the MB = MC of the next unit. This only occurs at one point on the PPF.

Economic growth: This occurs when an economy's production possibilities increase. It can be a result of more resources, better resources, or improvements in technology.

Market economy (capitalism): An economic system based on the fundamentals of private property, freedom, self-interest, and prices.

Demand, Supply, and Market Equilibrium

IN THIS CHAPTER

Summary: A thorough understanding of the way in which the market system determines price and quantity pays dividends both in microeconomics and macroeconomics.

Key Ideas

- Demand
- Supply
- Equilibrium

6.1 Demand

Main Topics: *Law of Demand, Income and Substitution Effects, The Demand Curves, Quantity Demanded versus Demand Determinants of Demand*

For many years now, you have understood the concept of demand. On the surface, the concept is rather simple: people tend to purchase fewer items when the price is high than they do when the price is low. This is such an intuitively appealing concept that your typical consumer cares little about the rationale and still manages to live a happy life. As someone knee-deep in reviewing to take the AP Macroeconomics exam, you need to go "behind the scenes" of demand. Intuition will take you only so far; you need to know the underlying theory of what is perhaps the most widely understood, and sometimes misunderstood, economic concept.

You might be asking yourself, "Self, I'm studying for a macroeconomics exam. Why do I need to learn about demand, supply, and equilibrium in microeconomics markets?" Well, the quick answer is that this does appear on the AP Macroeconomics outline of topics, so it is fair game on the multiple-choice section of the exam. But, as you will see in the review later, demand and supply and equilibrium appear in macroeconomic models too. It is important to build a good foundation of how this simple model works so that you can apply it later and score big points on the free-response questions that are sure to appear on the AP Macroeconomics exam.

Law of Demand

Let's get this part out of the way. The **law of demand** is commonly described as follows: *Holding all else equal, when the price of a good rises, consumers decrease their quantity demanded for that good.* In other words, there is an inverse, or negative, relationship between the price and the quantity demanded of a good.

"Holding all else equal"? Economic models—demand is just one of many such models—are simplified versions of real behavior. In addition to the price, there are many factors that influence how many units of a good consumers purchase. In order to predict how consumers respond to changes in one variable (price), we must assume that all other relevant factors are held constant. Say we observed that last month the price of orange juice fell, consumer incomes rose, the price of apple juice increased, and consumers bought more orange juice. Was this increased orange juice consumption because the price fell, because incomes rose, or perhaps because apple juice became more expensive? Maybe it increased for all these reasons. Maybe for none of these reasons. It is impossible to isolate and measure the effect of one variable (i.e., orange juice prices) on the consumption of orange juice if we do not control (hold constant) these other external factors. At the heart of the law of demand is a consumer's willingness and ability to pay the going price. If the consumer becomes more willing, or more able, to consume a good, then either the price has fallen or one of these external factors has changed. We spend more time on these demand "determinants" a little later in this chapter.

Income and Substitution Effects

One of the important factors behind the scenes of the law of demand is the economic mantra "*only relative prices matter.*" I'm sure you have heard the stories from your parents or grandparents about how the price of a cup of coffee back in the good old days was just a nickel. Today you might get the same coffee for $5. These prices are simply **money** (or **absolute**, or **nominal**) **prices**, and when it comes to a demand decision, a money price alone is near useless. However, if you think about the money price in terms of (1) what other goods $5 could buy or (2) how much of your income is absorbed by $5, then you're talking **relative** (or **real**) **prices**. These are what matter. The number of units of any other good Y that must be sacrificed to acquire the first good X measures the relative price of good X.

Example:

Let's keep things simple and say that you divide your $10 daily income between apple fritters at today's prices of $1 each and chocolate chip bagels at $2 each. These are the money prices of your labor and of these two yummy snacks.

Table 6.1 Money vs. Relative Prices

	MONEY PRICE		RELATIVE PRICE		SHARE OF INCOME	
	Today	*Tomorrow*	*Today*	*Tomorrow*	*Today*	*Tomorrow*
Fritter	$1	$2	1/2 bagel	1 bagel	1/10	1/5
Bagel	$2	$2	2 fritters	1 fritter	1/5	1/5

Today at the price of $1, the relative cost of a fritter is one-half of a bagel (see Table 6.1). Relative to your income, it amounts to one-tenth of your budget.

Tomorrow, when the price doubles to $2 per fritter, two things happen to help explain, and lay the foundation for, the law of demand:

1. The relative price of a fritter has risen to one bagel, and the relative price of a bagel has fallen from two fritters to one fritter. Since fritters are now *relatively more expensive*, we would expect you to consume more bagels and fewer fritters. This is known as the ***substitution effect***.

2. Relative to your income, the price of a fritter has increased from one-tenth to one-fifth of your budget. In other words, if you were to buy only fritters, today you can purchase 10 but tomorrow the same income would only buy you 5. This lost purchasing power is known as the ***income effect***.

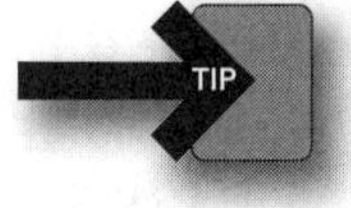

- ***Substitution effect.*** The change in quantity demanded resulting from a change in the price of one good relative to the price of other goods.
- ***Income effect.*** The change in quantity demanded resulting from a change in the consumer's purchasing power (or real income).

When the price of fritters increased, both of these effects caused our consumer (you) to decrease the quantity demanded, thus predicting a response consistent with the law of demand.

So at this point you might ask, "How would a consumer react if the prices of fritters and bagels and daily income had all doubled?"

Since the price of fritters, relative to the price of bagels, and relative to daily income, has not changed, the consumer is unlikely to alter behavior. This is why we say that only relative prices matter.

The Demand Curve

The residents of a small town love to quench their summer thirsts with lemonade. Table 6.2 summarizes the townsfolk's daily consumption of cups of lemonade at several prices, holding constant all other factors that might influence the overall demand for lemonade. This table is sometimes referred to as a **demand schedule.**

Table 6.2 Demand Schedule for Lemonade

PRICE PER CUP ($)	QUANTITY DEMANDED (CUPS PER DAY)
.25	120
.50	100
.75	80
1.00	60
1.25	40

The values in Table 6.2 reflect the law of demand: *Holding all else equal, when the price of a cup of lemonade rises, consumers decrease their quantity demanded for lemonade.* It is often quite useful to convert a demand schedule like the one above into a graphical representation, the **demand curve** (Figure 6.1).

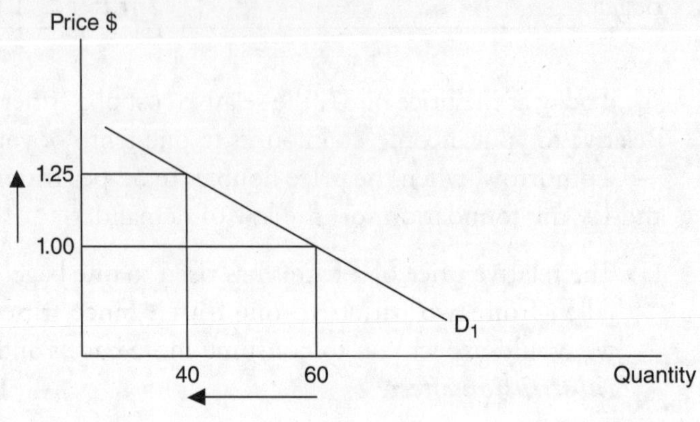

Figure 6.1

Quantity Demanded versus Demand

The law of demand predicts a downward (or negative) sloping demand curve (Figure 6.1). If the price moves from $1 to $1.25, and all other factors are held constant, we observe a decrease in the *quantity demanded* from 60 to 40 cups. It is important to place special emphasis on "quantity demanded." If the price of the good changes and all other factors remain constant, the demand curve is held constant, and we simply observe the consumer moving along the fixed demand curve. If one of the external factors changes, the entire demand curve shifts to the left or right. These external factors are referred to as determinants, or shifters, of demand.

Determinants of Demand

So, what are all of these factors that we insist on holding constant? These **determinants of demand** influence both the willingness and ability of the consumer to purchase units of the good or service. In addition to the price of the product itself, there are a number of variables that account for the total demand for a good like lemonade:

- Consumer income.
- The price of a substitute good such as iced tea.
- The price of a complementary good such as a Popsicle.
- Consumer tastes and preferences for lemonade.
- Consumer expectations about future prices of lemonade.
- Number of buyers in the market for lemonade.

- *Consumer Income*

Demand represents the consumer's willingness and ability to pay for a good. Income is a major factor in that "ability" to pay component. For most goods, when income increases, demand for the good increases. Thus, for these **normal goods**, increased income results in a graphical rightward shift in the entire demand curve. There are other

inferior goods, fewer in number, where higher levels of income produce a decrease in the demand curve.

Example:
When looking to furnish a first college apartment, many students increase their demand for used furniture at yard sales. Upon graduation and employment in their first real job, new graduates increase their demand for new furniture and decrease their demand for used furniture. For them, new furniture is a normal good, while used furniture is an inferior good.

- An *increase in demand* is viewed as a *rightward shift* in the demand curve. There are two ways to think about this shift:
  a. At all prices, the consumer is willing and able to buy more units of the good. In Figure 6.2 you can see that at the constant price of $1, the quantity demanded has risen from two to three.
  b. At all quantities, the consumer is willing and able to pay higher prices for the good.
- Of course, the opposite is true of a *decrease in demand*, or *leftward shift* of the demand curve. In Figure 6.2 you can see that at the constant price of $1, the quantity demanded has fallen from two to one.

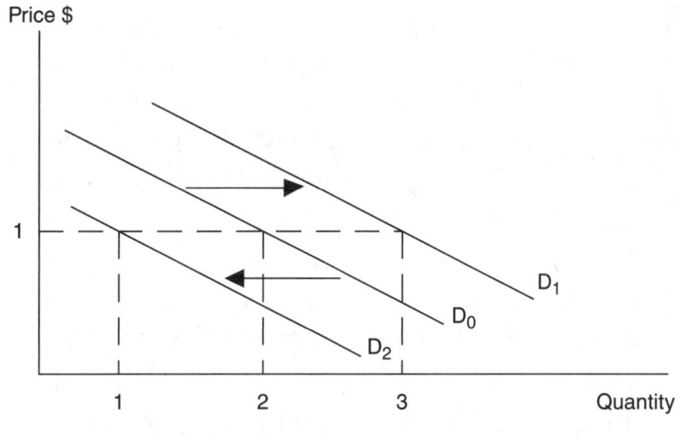

Figure 6.2

- *Price of Substitute Goods*

Two goods are substitutes if the consumer can use either one to satisfy the same essential function, therefore experiencing the same degree of happiness (utility). If the two goods are substitutes, and the price of one good X falls, the consumer demand for the substitute good Y decreases.

Example:
Ivy Vine College (IVC) and Mammoth State University (MSU) are considered substitute institutions of higher learning in the same geographical region. Ivy Vine College, shamelessly seeking to increase its reputation as an "elite" institution, increases tuition, while Mammoth State's tuition remains the same. We expect to see, holding all else constant, a decrease in quantity demanded for IVC degrees and an increase in the overall demand for MSU degrees. (See Figures 6.3 and 6.4.)

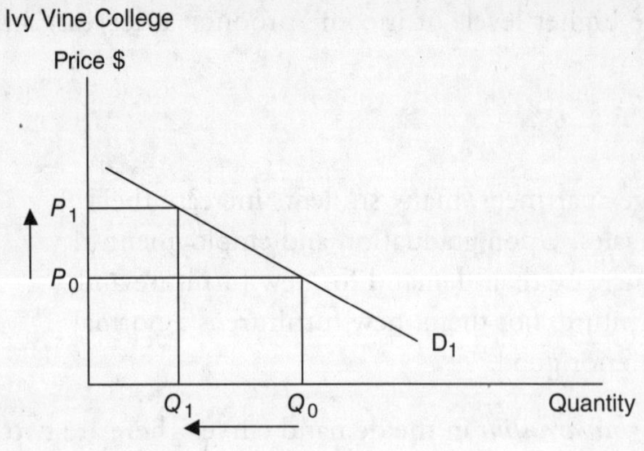

Figure 6.3

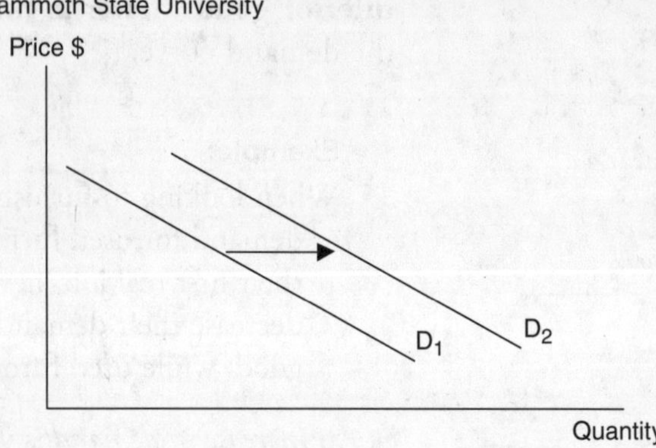

Figure 6.4

- *Price of Complementary Goods*

Two goods are complements if the consumer receives more utility from consuming them together than she would receive consuming each separately. I enjoy consuming tortilla chips by themselves, but my utility increases if I combine those chips with a complementary good like salsa or nacho cheese dip. If any two goods are complements, and the price of one good X falls, the consumer demand for the complement good Y increases.

> "Finally, something in a textbook that I can fathom!"
> —Adam, AP Student

Example:

College students love to order late-night pizza delivered to their dorm rooms. The local pizza joint decreased the price of breadsticks, a complement to the pizzas. We expect to see, holding all else constant, an increase in quantity demanded for breadsticks and an increase in the demand for pizzas.

- *Tastes and Preferences*

We have different internal tastes and preferences. Collectively, consumer tastes and preferences change with the seasons (more gloves in December, fewer lawn chairs), with fashion trends, or with advertising. A stronger preference for a good is an increase in the willingness to pay for the good, which increases demand.

- *Future Expectations*

The future expectation of a price change or an income change can cause demand to shift today. Demand can also respond to an expectation of the future availability of a good.

Example:

On a Wednesday, you have reason to believe that the price of gasoline is going to rise $0.05 per gallon by the weekend. What do you do? Many consumers, armed with this expectation, increase their demand for gasoline today. We might predict the opposite behavior, a decrease in demand today, if consumers expect the price of gasoline to fall a few days from now.

Demand can also be influenced by future expectations of an income change.

Example:

One month prior to your college graduation day, you land your first full-time job. You have signed an employment contract that guarantees a specific salary, but you will not receive your first paycheck until the end of your first month on the job. This future expectation of a sizable increase in income often prompts consumers to increase their demand for normal goods now. Maybe you would start shopping for a car, a larger apartment, or several business suits.

Example:

For years, auto producers have been promising more alternative-fuel cars, but so far these cars are relatively difficult to find on dealership lots. Suppose the major auto producers promise widespread availability of affordable electric cars in the next 12 months. This expectation of increased availability in the future will likely decrease the demand for these cars today.

- *Number of Buyers*

An increase in the number of buyers, holding other factors constant, increases the demand for a good. This is often the result of demographic changes or increased availability in more markets.

Example:

When the Soviet Union fractured and the Russian government began allowing more foreign investment, corporations such as Coca-Cola, Apple, and McDonald's found millions of new buyers for their products. Globally, the demand for colas, iPhones, and burgers increased.

Example:

As the average age of Americans has gradually increased, there are now more people above the age of 70 years old. This demographic change has caused an increase in the demand for prescription drugs, hip replacements, and other medical services.

6.2 Supply

Main Topics: *Law of Supply, Increasing Marginal Costs, The Supply Curve, Quantity Supplied versus Supply, Determinants of Supply*

If there are three words that you need to have in your arsenal for the AP exams, they are "Demand and Supply," or "Supply and Demand" if you are the rebellious type. The previous section covered the demand half of this duo, and so it stands to reason that we should spend a little time studying the other side. Unlike demand, few of us have ever had up close and personal experience as suppliers. Because you likely lack such personal experience with supply, it is helpful to put yourself in the shoes of someone who wishes to profit from the production and sale of a product. If something happens that would increase your chances of earning more profit, you increase your supply of the product. If something happens that will hurt your profit opportunities, you decrease your supply of the product.

Law of Supply

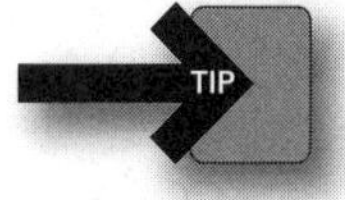

Drumroll, please. The **law of supply** is commonly described as follows: "*Holding all else equal, when the price of a good rises, suppliers increase their quantity supplied for that good.*" In other words, there is a direct, or positive, relationship between the price and the quantity supplied of a good.

Again, we insist on qualifying our law with the phrase "holding all else equal." Similar to the *demand model*, the *supply model* is a simplified version of real behavior. In addition to the price, there are several factors that influence how many units of a good producers supply. In order to predict how producers respond to fluctuations in one variable (price), we must assume that all other relevant factors are held constant. Before we talk about these external supply determinants, let's examine what is happening behind the scenes of the law of supply.

Increasing Marginal Costs

The more you do something (e.g., a physical activity), the more difficult it becomes to do the next unit of that activity. Anyone who has run laps around a track, lifted weights, or raked leaves in the yard understands this. If you were asked to rake leaves, as more hours of raking are supplied, it becomes physically more and more difficult to rake the next hour. We also include the opportunity cost of the time involved in the raking, and you surely know that time is precious to a student. If you have a paper to write or an exam to cram for, raking leaves for an hour comes at a dear cost. In terms of forgone opportunities, the marginal cost of raking leaves rises as you postpone that paper or study session.

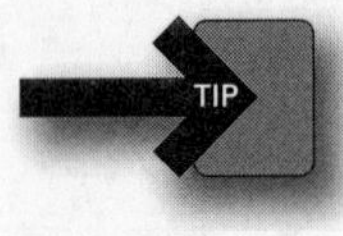

When we discussed production possibilities in Chapter 5, we addressed a key economic concept: as more of a good is produced, the greater is its marginal cost.

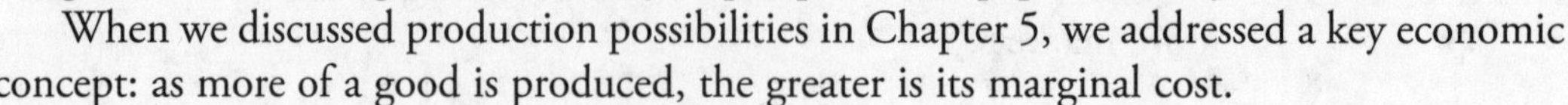

- As suppliers increase the quantity supplied of a good, they face rising marginal costs.
- As a result, they only increase the quantity supplied of that good if the price received is high enough to at least cover the higher marginal cost.

The Supply Curve

A small town has a thriving summer sidewalk lemonade stand industry. Table 6.3 summarizes the daily quantity of cups of lemonade offered for sale at several prices, holding constant all other factors that might influence the overall supply of lemonade. This table is sometimes referred to as a **supply schedule.**

Table 6.3 Supply Schedule for Lemonade

PRICE PER CUP ($)	QUANTITY SUPPLIED (CUPS PER DAY)
.25	40
.50	60
.75	80
1.00	100
1.25	120

"Make sure on the AP test to include all labels, especially arrows." —Adam, AP Student

The values in this table reflect the law of supply: "*Holding all else equal, when the price of a cup of lemonade rises, suppliers increase their quantity supplied for lemonade.*" Remember those profit opportunities? If kids can sell more cups of lemonade at a higher price, they will do so. It is often quite useful to convert a supply schedule like the one in Table 6.3 into a graphical representation: the **supply curve** (Figure 6.5).

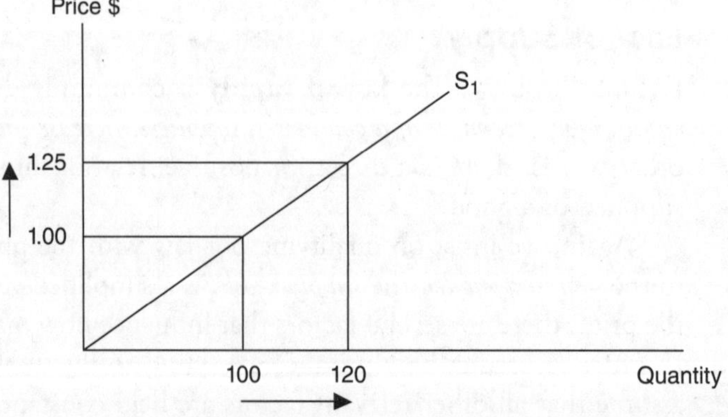

Figure 6.5

"This is an important distinction to make."
—AP Teacher

Quantity Supplied versus Supply

The law of supply predicts an upward- (or positive-) sloping supply curve (Figure 6.5). When the price moves from $1 to $1.25, and all other factors are held constant, we observe an increase in the *quantity supplied* from 100 cups to 120 cups. Just as with demand, it is important to place special emphasis on "quantity supplied." When the price of the good changes, and all other factors are held constant, the supply curve is held constant; we simply observe the producer moving along the fixed supply curve. If one of the external factors changes, the entire supply curve shifts to the left or right. These external factors are referred to as determinants, or shifters, of supply.

Determinants of Supply

Lemonade producers are willing and able to supply more lemonade if something happens that promises to increase their profit opportunities. In addition to the price of the product itself, there are a number of variables, or **determinants of supply**, that account for the total supply of a good like lemonade:

- The cost of an input (e.g., sugar) to the production of lemonade
- Technology and productivity used to produce lemonade
- Taxes or subsidies on lemonade
- Producer expectations about future prices
- The price of other goods that could be produced
- The number of lemonade stands in the industry

- *Cost of Inputs*

If the cost of sugar, a key ingredient in lemonade, unexpectedly falls, it has now become less costly to produce lemonade, and so we should expect producers all over town, seeing the profit opportunity, to increase the supply of lemonade at all prices. This results in a graphical rightward shift in the entire supply curve.

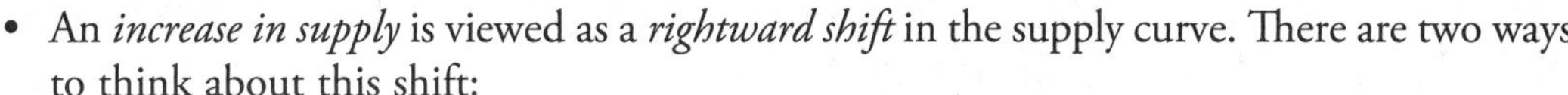

TIP

- An *increase in supply* is viewed as a *rightward shift* in the supply curve. There are two ways to think about this shift:
    1. At all prices, the producer is willing and able to supply more units of the good. In Figure 6.6 you can see that at the constant price of $1, the quantity supplied has risen from two to three.
    2. At all quantities, the marginal cost of production is lower, so producers are willing and able to accept lower prices for the good.

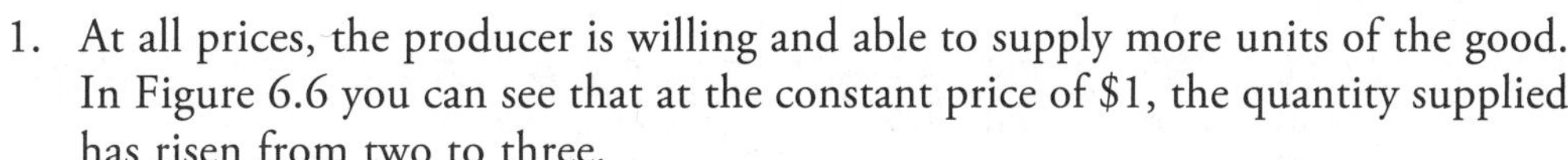

- Of course, the opposite is true of a *decrease in supply*, or *leftward shift* of the supply curve. In Figure 6.6 you can see that at the constant price of $1, the quantity supplied has fallen from two to one.

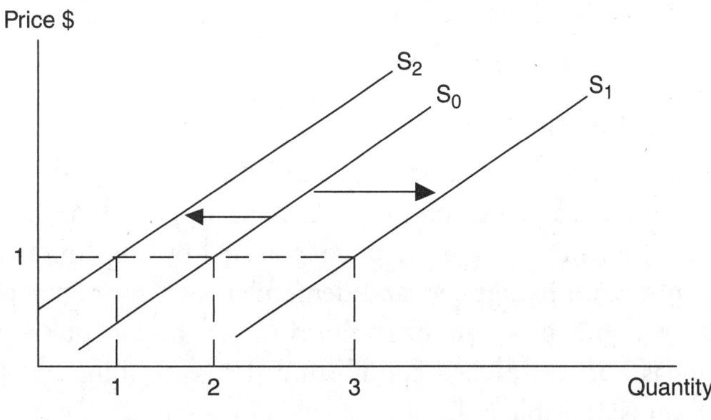

Figure 6.6

"Remember, the tax goes to the government and is NOT included in the profit."
—Hillary, AP Student

- *Technology or Productivity*

A technological improvement usually decreases the marginal cost of producing a good, thus allowing the producer to supply more units, and is reflected by a rightward shift in the supply curve. If kids all over town began using electric lemon squeezers rather than their sticky bare hands, the supply of lemonade would increase.

- *Taxes and Subsidies*

A per unit tax is treated by the firm as an additional cost of production and would therefore decrease the supply curve, or shift it leftward. Mayor McScrooge might impose a 25-cent tax on every cup of lemonade, decreasing the entire supply curve. A subsidy is essentially the anti-tax, or a per unit gift from the government because it lowers the per unit cost of production.

- *Price Expectations*

A producer's willingness to supply today might be affected by an expectation of tomorrow's price. If it were the 2nd of July and lemonade producers expected a heat wave and a 4th of July parade in two days, they might hold back some of their supply today and hope to sell it at an inflated price on the holiday. Thus, today's quantity supplied at all prices would decrease.

- *Price of Other Outputs*

Firms can use the same resources to produce different goods. If the price of a milkshake were rising and profit opportunities were improving for milkshake producers, the supply of lemonade in a small town would decrease and the quantity of milkshakes supplied would increase.

- *Number of Suppliers*

When more suppliers enter a market, we expect the supply curve to shift to the right. If several of our lemonade entrepreneurs are forced by their parents to attend summer camp, we would expect the entire supply curve to move leftward. Fewer cups of lemonade would be supplied at each and every price.

6.3 Market Equilibrium

Main Topics: *Equilibrium, Shortage, Surplus, Changes in Demand, Changes in Supply, Simultaneous Changes in Demand or Supply*

Demanders and suppliers are both motivated by prices, but from opposite camps. The consumer is a big fan of low prices; the supplier applauds high prices. If a good were available, consumers would be willing to buy more of it, but only if the price is right. Suppliers would love to accommodate more consumption by increasing production but only if justly compensated. Is there a price and a compatible quantity where both groups are content? Amazingly enough, the answer is a resounding "maybe." Discouraged? Don't be. For now we assume that the good is exchanged in a free and competitive market, and if this is the case, the answer is "yes."

Equilibrium

The market is in a state of **equilibrium** when the quantity supplied equals the quantity demanded at a given price. Another way of thinking about equilibrium is that it occurs at the quantity where the price expected by consumers is equal to the price required by suppliers. So if suppliers and demanders are, for a given quantity, content with the price, the market is in a state of equilibrium. If there is pressure on the price to change, the market has not yet reached equilibrium. Let's combine our lemonade tables from the earlier sections in Table 6.4.

Table 6.4 Combining Demand and Supply Schedules

PRICE PER CUP ($)	QUANTITY DEMANDED (CUPS PER DAY)	QUANTITY SUPPLIED (CUPS PER DAY)	$Q_d–Q_s$	SITUATION	PRICE SHOULD
.25	120	40	80	Shortage	Rise
.50	100	60	40	Shortage	Rise
.75	80	80	0	Equilibrium	Stable
1.00	60	100	−40	Surplus	Fall
1.25	40	120	−80	Surplus	Fall

At a price of 75 cents, the daily quantity demanded and quantity supplied are both equal to 80 cups of lemonade. The equilibrium (or market clearing) price is therefore 75 cents per cup. In Figure 6.7 the equilibrium price and quantity are located where the demand curve intersects the supply curve. Holding all other demand and supply variables constant, there exists no other price where $Q_d = Q_s$.

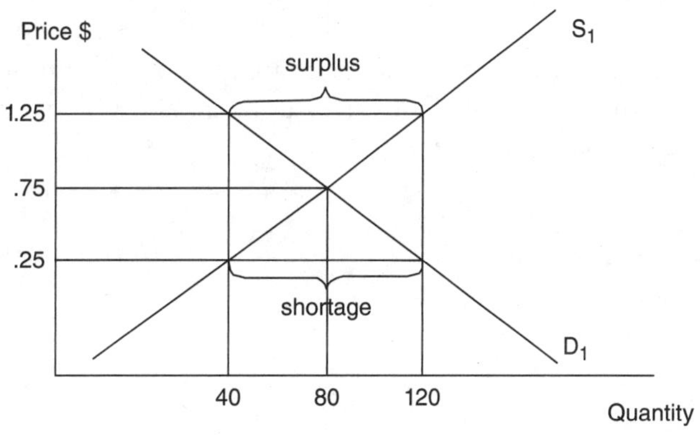

Figure 6.7

"In a free market, shortages and surpluses always return to equilibrium in the long run."
—Adam, AP Student

Shortage

A **shortage** exists at a market price when the quantity demanded exceeds the quantity supplied. This is why a shortage is also known as **excess demand**. At prices of 25 cents and 50 cents per cup, you can see the shortage in Figure 6.7. Remember that consumers love low prices, so the quantity demanded is going to be high. However, suppliers are not thrilled to see low prices and therefore decrease their quantity supplied. At prices below 75 cents per cup, lemonade buyers and sellers are in a state of **disequilibrium**. The disparity between what the buyers want at 50 cents per cup and what the suppliers want at that price should remedy itself. Thirsty demanders offer lemonade stand owners prices slightly higher than 50 cents and, receiving higher prices, suppliers accommodate them by squeezing lemons. With competition, the shortage is eliminated at a price of 75 cents per cup.

Surplus

A **surplus** exists at a market price when the quantity supplied exceeds the quantity demanded. This is why a surplus is also known as **excess supply**. At prices of $1 and $1.25 per cup, you can see the surplus in Figure 6.7. Consumers are reluctant to purchase as much lemonade as suppliers are willing to supply and, once again, the market is in disequilibrium. To entice more consumers to buy lemonade, lemonade stand owners offer slightly discounted cups of lemonade and buyers respond by increasing their quantity demanded. Again, with competition, the surplus would be eliminated at a price of 75 cents per cup.

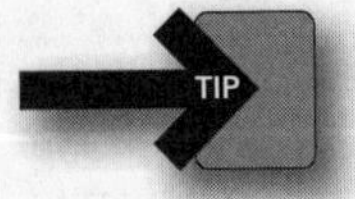

- Shortages and surpluses are relatively short-lived in a competitive market as prices rise or fall until the quantity demanded again equals the quantity supplied.

Changes in Demand

"Explain your logic every time you shift a curve, no matter what!" —Jake, AP Student

While our discussion of market equilibrium implies a certain kind of stability in both the price and quantity of a good, changing market forces disrupt equilibrium, either by shifting demand, shifting supply, or shifting both demand and supply.

Increase in Demand

About once a winter a freak blizzard hits southern states like Georgia and the Carolinas. You can bet that the national media show video of panicked southerners scrambling for bags of rock salt and bottled water. Inevitably a reporter tells us that the price of rock salt has skyrocketed to $17 per bag. What is happening here? In Figure 6.8, the market for rock salt is initially in equilibrium at a price of $2.79 per bag. With a forecast of a blizzard, consumers expect a lack of future availability for this good. This expectation results in a feverish increase in the demand for rock salt and, at the original price of $2.79, there is a shortage. The market's cure for a shortage is a higher equilibrium price. (Note: The equilibrium quantity of rock salt might not increase much, since blizzards are short-lived and the supply curve might be nearly vertical.)

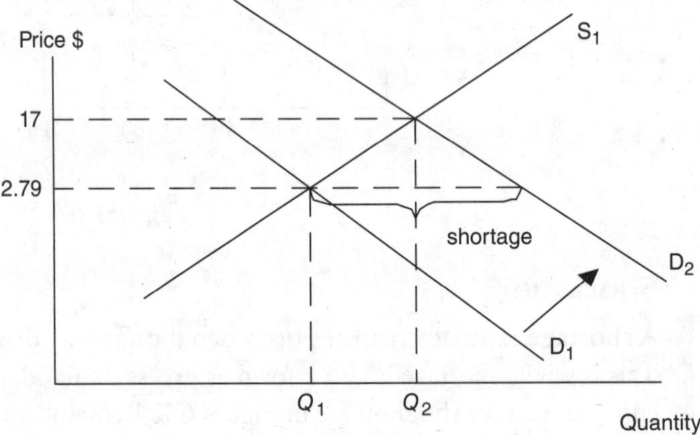

Figure 6.8

Decrease in Demand

The 2009 recession was damaging to the automobile industry. When average household incomes fell in the United States, the demand for cars, a normal good, decreased. Manufacturers began offering deeply discounted sticker prices, zero-interest financing, and other incentives to reluctant consumers so that they might purchase a new car. In Figure 6.9 you can see that the original price of a new car was at P_1. Once the demand for new cars fell, there was a surplus of cars on dealer lots at the original price. The market cure for a surplus is a lower equilibrium price; ultimately, fewer new cars were bought and sold.

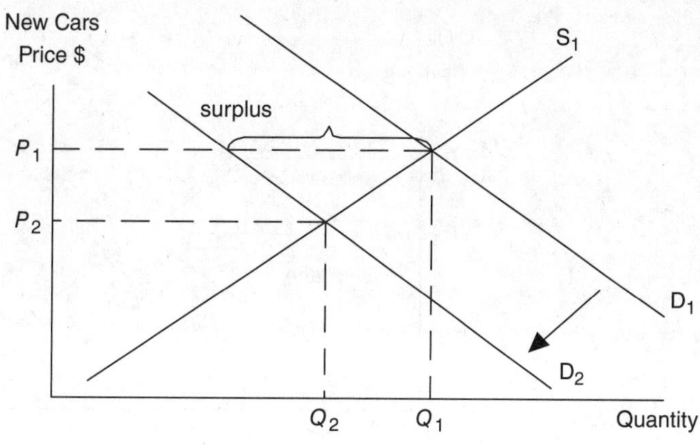

Figure 6.9

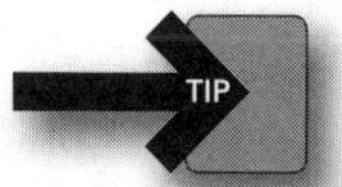

- When demand increases, equilibrium price and quantity both increase.
- When demand decreases, equilibrium price and quantity both decrease.

Changes in Supply

Increase in Supply

Advancements in computer technology and production methods have been felt in many markets. Figure 6.10 illustrates how, because of better technology, the supply of laptop computers has increased. At the original equilibrium price of P_1 there is now a surplus of laptops. To eliminate the surplus, the market price must fall to P_2 and the equilibrium quantity must rise to Q_2.

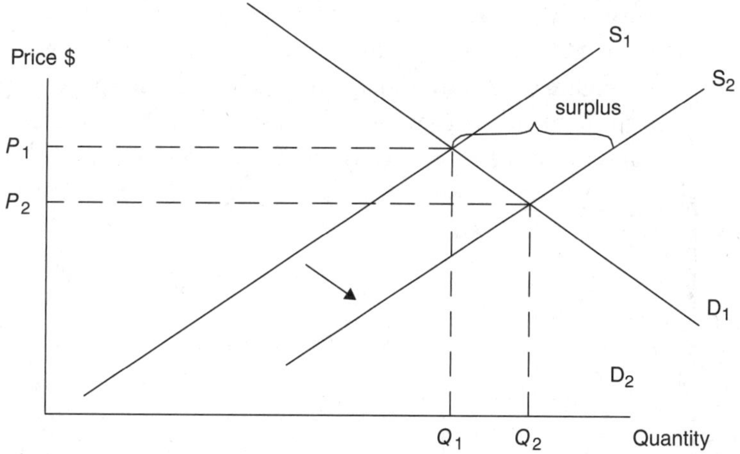

Figure 6.10

Decrease in Supply

Geopolitical conflict in the Middle East usually slows the production of crude oil. This decrease in the global supply of oil can be seen in Figure 6.11. At the original equilibrium price of P_1 per barrel, there is now a shortage of crude oil on the global market. The market eliminates this shortage through higher prices and, at least temporarily, the equilibrium quantity of crude oil falls.

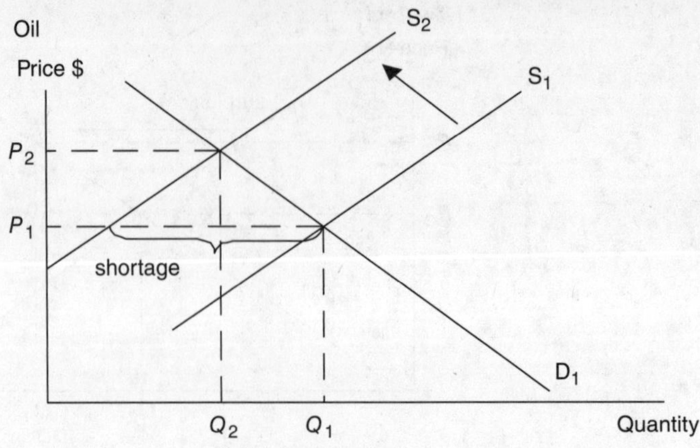

Figure 6.11

- When supply increases, equilibrium price decreases and quantity increases.
- When supply decreases, equilibrium price increases and quantity decreases.

Simultaneous Changes in Demand and Supply

When both demand and supply change at the same time, predicting changes in price and quantity becomes a little more complicated. An example should illustrate how you need to be careful.

In recent years consumers have increased their demand for eggs as a substitute for other protein products like beef. All else being equal, rising demand for eggs would increase the equilibrium price of eggs and increase the equilibrium quantity exchanged in the market.

But in 2022 and again in 2023, a deadly avian flu rapidly spread through global chicken farms, greatly reducing the number of egg-laying hens. This significant decrease in the supply of eggs, all else equal, would increase prices and reduce the quantity of eggs in the market. During this time, the price of a dozen eggs nearly doubled in the U.S. market.

Figure 6.12 shows a large decrease in the supply of eggs coupled with a modest increase in the demand for eggs. These two shifts combine to create a big increase in the equilibrium market price and a relatively small decrease in the equilibrium market quantity.

"Use different-colored pens when drawing multiple curves on a single graph. This helps keep things clear when you shift many curves at a time." —Jake, AP Student

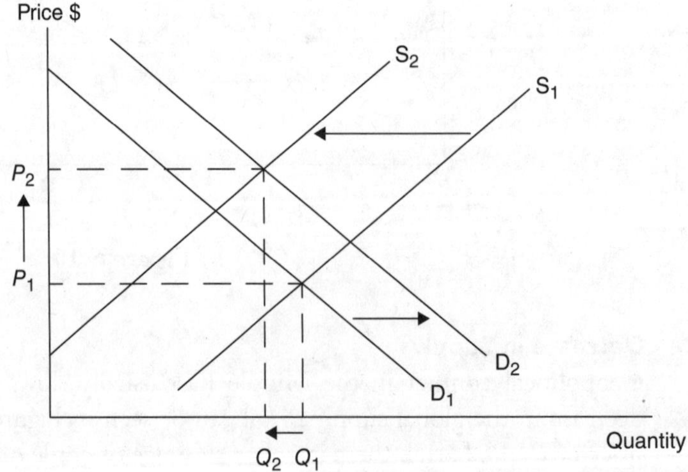

Figure 6.12

"If you don't know the answer, it is probably where the sticks cross." —Chuck, AP Student

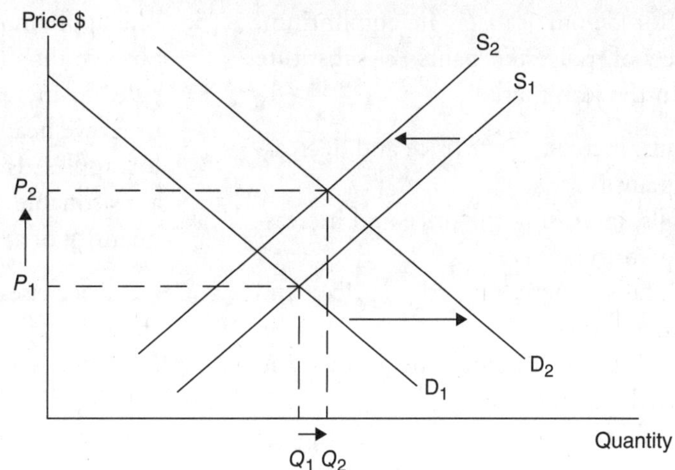

Figure 6.13

But this is just one possible outcome of these two events. Had the rightward shift in demand been larger than the leftward shift in supply, the price would still be higher than before, but the equilibrium quantity would have increased. This is shown in Figure 6.13. Without more information, this combination of events has an uncertain, or ambiguous, impact on the market quantity, but the price is going to rise.

- When both demand and supply are changing, one of the equilibrium outcomes (price or quantity) is predictable and one is ambiguous.
- Before combining the two shifting curves, predict changes in price and quantity for each shift, by itself.
- The variable that is rising in one case and falling in the other case is your ambiguous (or indeterminate) prediction.

❯ Review Questions

1. When the price of pears increases, we expect the following:

(A) Quantity demanded of pears rises.
(B) Quantity supplied of pears falls.
(C) Quantity demanded of pears falls.
(D) Demand for pears falls.
(E) Supply of pears rises.

2. If average household income rises and we observe that the demand for pork chops increases, pork chops must be

(A) an inferior good.
(B) a normal good.
(C) a surplus good.
(D) a public good.
(E) a shortage good.

3. Suppose that aluminum is a key production input in the production of bicycles. If the price of aluminum falls, and all other variables are held constant, we expect

(A) the demand for aluminum to rise.
(B) the supply of bicycles to rise.
(C) the supply of bicycles to fall.
(D) the demand for bicycles to rise.
(E) the demand for bicycles to fall.

4. The market for denim jeans is in equilibrium, and the price of polyester pants, a substitute good, rises. In the jean market
   (A) supply falls, increasing the price and decreasing the quantity.
   (B) supply falls, increasing the price and increasing the quantity.
   (C) demand falls, increasing the price and decreasing the quantity.
   (D) demand rises, increasing the price and increasing the quantity.
   (E) supply and demand both fall, causing an ambiguous change in price but a definite decrease in quantity.

5. The apple market is in equilibrium. Suppose we observe that apple growers are using more pesticides to increase apple production. At the same time, we hear that the price of pears, a substitute for apples, is rising. Which of the following is a reasonable prediction for the new price and quantity of apples?
   (A) Price rises, but quantity is ambiguous.
   (B) Price falls, but quantity is ambiguous.
   (C) Price is ambiguous, but quantity rises.
   (D) Price is ambiguous, but quantity falls.
   (E) Both price and quantity are ambiguous.

› Answers and Explanations

1. **C**—If the price of pears rises, either quantity demanded falls or quantity supplied rises. Entire demand or supply curves for pears can shift but only if an external factor, not the price of pears, changes.
2. **B**—When income increases and demand increases, the good is a normal good. Had the demand for pork chops decreased, they would be an inferior good.
3. **B**—This is a determinant of supply. If the raw material becomes less costly to acquire, the marginal cost of producing bicycles falls. Producers increase the supply of bicycles. Recognizing this as a supply determinant allows you to quickly eliminate any reference to a demand shift.
4. **D**—When a substitute good becomes more expensive, the demand for jeans rises, increasing price and quantity.
5. **C**—Increased use of pesticides increases the supply of apples because fewer apples are lost to insects. If the price of a substitute increases, the demand for apples increases. Combining these two factors predicts an increase in the quantity of apples but an ambiguous change in price. *To help you see this, draw these situations in the margin of the exam.*

› Rapid Review

Law of demand: Holding all else equal, when the price of a good rises, consumers decrease their quantity demanded for that good.

All else equal: To predict how a change in one variable affects a second, we hold all other variables constant. This is also referred to as the *ceteris paribus* assumption.

Absolute (or **money**) **prices:** The price of a good measured in units of currency.

Relative prices: The number of units of any other good Y that must be sacrificed to acquire the first good X. Only relative prices matter.

Substitution effect: The change in quantity demanded resulting from a change in the price of one good relative to the price of other goods.

Income effect: The change in quantity demanded that results from a change in the consumer's purchasing power (or real income).

Demand schedule: A table showing quantity demanded for a good at various prices.

Demand curve: A graphical depiction of the demand schedule. The demand curve is downward sloping, reflecting the law of demand.

Determinants of demand: The external factors that shift demand to the left or right.

Normal goods: A good for which higher income increases demand.

Inferior goods: A good for which higher income decreases demand.

Substitute goods: Two goods are consumer substitutes if they provide essentially the same utility to the consumer. A Honda Accord and a Toyota Camry might be substitutes for many consumers.

Complementary goods: Two goods are consumer complements if they provide more utility when consumed together than when consumed separately. Cars and gasoline are complementary goods.

Law of supply: Holding all else equal, when the price of a good rises, suppliers increase their quantity supplied for that good.

Supply schedule: A table showing quantity supplied for a good at various prices.

Supply curve: A graphical depiction of the supply schedule. The supply curve is upward sloping, reflecting the law of supply.

Determinants of supply: One of the external factors that influences supply. When these variables change, the entire supply curve shifts to the left or right.

Market equilibrium: Exists at the only price where the quantity supplied equals the quantity demanded. Or, it is the only quantity where the price consumers are willing to pay is exactly the price producers are willing to accept.

Shortage: Also known as *excess demand*, a shortage exists at a market price when the quantity demanded exceeds the quantity supplied. The price rises to eliminate a shortage.

Disequilibrium: Any price where quantity demanded is not equal to quantity supplied.

Surplus: Also known as *excess supply*, a surplus exists at a market price when the quantity supplied exceeds the quantity demanded. The price falls to eliminate a surplus.

Macroeconomic Measures of Performance

Technically, this is the first chapter in the review of macroeconomics, but both AP Microeconomics and Macroeconomics courses begin with coverage of "Basic Economic Concepts," a section that includes the following topics:

- *Scarcity*
- *Opportunity cost and the Production Possibilities Curve*
- *Comparative advantage and gains from trade*
- *Supply and demand*
- *Market equilibrium, disequilibrium, and changes in equilibrium*

IN THIS CHAPTER

Summary: Should we raise or lower interest rates? Should we cut or increase taxes? The media is always buzzing about some macroeconomic policy intended to make our lives better. What does it mean to do better? How is "better" measured in something as large and complex as the macroeconomy? In general, macroeconomic policies share the goal of stabilizing and improving the economy, and they also share reliance on statistical measures of economic performance. Though "statistics" might sound like a dirty word to you and your classmates, as AP Macroeconomics test takers, you need to understand how some important measures are, well, measured. Knowing how they are measured provides you with a much better way of responding to exam questions that ask you to use theoretical models to fix a macroeconomic problem. You cannot speak intelligently about growing the economy until you know how economic growth is measured. Likewise, if you want to perform better on the AP Macroeconomics exam, you might want to know exactly how those statistics (your grade) are compiled and study accordingly.

This chapter introduces measurement of economic production and paves the way for models of the macroeconomy and policies intended to improve this economic performance.

Key Ideas:

- ✪ The Circular Flow Model
- ✪ Gross Domestic Product
- ✪ Real versus Nominal
- ✪ Inflation and the Consumer Price Index
- ✪ Unemployment

7.1 The Circular Flow Model

Main Topic: *Circular Flow Model of a Closed Economy*

The Circular Flow Model

"What comes around goes around." If you remember nothing else about the circular flow model, remember this old phrase. The **circular flow of goods and services** (or **circular flow of economic activity**) is a model of an economy showing the interactions among households, firms, and government as they exchange goods and services and resources in markets. In other words, it is a game of "follow the dollars."

Figure 7.1 illustrates a model of a **closed economy**, where the foreign markets are not assumed (yet) to exist. Domestic households offer their resources to firms in the resource market so that those firms can produce goods and services. The households are paid competitive prices for those resources. They use that income to consume the very goods that were produced through the employment of their productive resources. Revenues from the sale of goods and services are then used to provide income to those households. In this simplified model, every dollar of income in the household ends up as revenue for the firm.

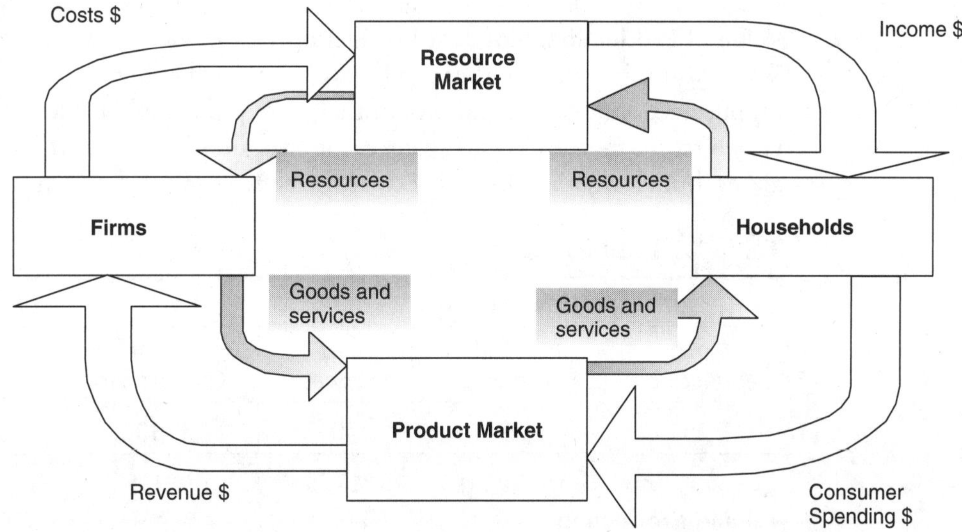

Figure 7.1

"What About the Government?"

Though not pictured in Figure 7.1, the government plays an important role in the circular flow model. The government is an employer of inputs and a producer of goods and services. The government collects taxes both from households and firms and uses the funds to pay for the inputs that they employ.

"How Much Economic Activity Is Being Generated?"

We can add up all the dollars earned as income by resource owners, or we can add up all the spending done on goods and services, or we can add up the value of all those goods and services.

"Where Does It Begin, Where Does It End?"

It doesn't matter; it's the counting of the dollars that is the important first step in measuring economic performance.

Macroeconomic Goals

Figure 7.1 implies that a steady flow of goods and dollars circulating throughout the economy is necessary or commerce ceases. The big issue is how we keep this flow strong, and how we know when it is weak. Measuring success is the focus of the sections that follow. Most modern societies maintain the fairly broad goal of keeping spending and production in the macroeconomy strong without drastically increasing prices.

7.2 Accounting for Output and Income

Main Topics: *Valuing Production, Gross Domestic Product (GDP), National Income Concepts, Real and Nominal GDP, The GDP Deflator, Business Cycles*

Valuing Production

The key here is to measure the value of the goods that are produced, not just the amount of goods that are produced. Remember the circular flow? If we need to follow the dollars to measure economic activity, we need to know prices of these goods.

Value of Production, Not Just Production

When you track the monthly production of a small coffee shop, you could sum up all the cappuccinos, café lattes, and scones that were purchased. Table 7.1 represents the output in two recent months. At first glance, the two months produced the same amount (100) of goods, but clearly the mix of goods at the coffee shop is different.

Table 7.1 Production

JANUARY			FEBRUARY		
# of Cappuccinos	*# of Café Lattes*	*# of Scones*	*# of Cappuccinos*	*# of Café Lattes*	*# of Scones*
25	25	50	30	30	40

Valuing Production

To paint a more accurate picture of production, we need to incorporate the value of these items as shown in Table 7.2.

Table 7.2

JANUARY	QUANTITY	PRICES	VALUE OF PRODUCTION
Cappuccinos	25	$3.00	$75.00
Café Lattes	25	$2.50	$62.50
Scones	50	$1.50	$75.00
Totals	100		$212.50
FEBRUARY			
Cappuccinos	30	$3.00	$90
Café Lattes	30	$2.50	$75
Scones	40	$1.50	$60
Totals	100		$225

While the total production at the coffee shop remained the same from month to month, the value of that production has increased in February. There are now more dollars circulating.

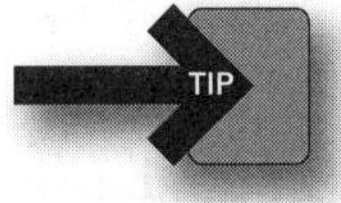

- Don't just add up the quantities; multiply by prices and add up the values.

Gross Domestic Product (GDP)

Aggregation, Not Aggravation

To move from valuing production of one firm to the entire town, to the state, or to the U.S. economy, we need to **aggregate**. Simply stated, we need to value all production of all firms and then add them up to get the value of production for the entire domestic economy. It is this aggregated measure of the total value of domestic production that allows us to calculate our first important macroeconomic statistic, **GDP**. Annual GDP is the market value of the final goods and services produced within a nation in a year. If the good or service is produced within the borders of the United States, it counts toward U.S. GDP. It does not matter if the firm is headquartered in Indonesia; so long as it is producing in Indiana, it appears in the U.S. GDP.

What's In, What's Out

Final goods are those that are ready for consumption. A bottle of ketchup at the Piggly Wiggly is counted. **Intermediate goods** are those that require further processing before they are counted as a final good. When the tomatoes used to make ketchup are purchased from a grower, they are not counted toward GDP. At least not until those tomatoes, and their value, find themselves in a bottle of ketchup and sold at the supermarket. A raw material like a tomato might be bought and sold several times before it appears as a final product. If we were to count the dollars at every stage of this process, we would be **double counting,** and this is to be avoided. Suppose the tomatoes go through three stages: harvest, processing, and retail sale as a bottle of ketchup. Along the way a pound of tomatoes is sold, bought, and altered. The pound of tomatoes was sold from the grower to the processor for 50 cents. The bottle of ketchup was sold to a grocery store for $1.50, and eventually the ketchup was sold to a consumer for $3. If we added all of these transactions, we come up with $5, which overstates the value of the good in its final use. GDP only adds the final transaction as the value of the final good produced and consumed.

Secondhand sales are not counted. This falls under the "do not double count" rule. If you buy a new Ford sedan in 2023, it would count in the GDP for 2023. If you resell it to your neighbor in 2025, it is not counted again. Final goods and services are only counted once, in the year in which they were produced.

Nonmarket transactions are not counted toward GDP. For example, if I have a clogged drain in my kitchen, I have two choices: fix it myself or call the plumber and pay to have it fixed. Doing it myself does not contribute to GDP, but paying a plumber to do it does. The same job is done, but only the latter ends up in the books. In a similar way, regular housework done at home by an unpaid member of the household is not counted, though it is very much a productive effort. This reality is sometimes cited as a criticism of GDP accounting: some valuable services are counted and others are not.

Underground economy transactions are not counted. For obvious reasons, the illegal sale of goods or services or paying someone cash "under the table" for work are not counted. Informal bartering between individuals is also not counted. You might help a friend study for economics, while she helps you study for biology, but this kind of bartering would not appear on any official ledger of production, even though it might be quite productive.

As a practical matter, official tabulation of GDP is never 100 percent accurate because the value of final goods and services is based on a survey of representative firms, not a complete census of all firms throughout the nation. Despite this methodology, economists work very hard to get a fairly accurate picture of the value of a nation's production.

Aggregate Spending

Since GDP is measured by adding up the value of the final goods and services produced in a given year, we just need to figure out from where this spending is coming. Spending on output is done by four sectors of the macroeconomy.

Consumer Spending (*C*). The largest component of GDP is the spending done by consumers. Consumers purchase services, like tax preparation or a college degree. Consumers also consume nondurable goods, like food, which are those goods that are consumed in under a year. Durable goods, like a Jet Ski, are goods expected to last a year or more.

Investment Spending (*I*). Investment is defined as current spending in order to increase output or productivity later. There are three general types of investment that are included in GDP:

- *New capital machinery purchased by firms.* Examples are a fleet of delivery trucks produced for UPS, or a new air-conditioning system at a Holiday Inn.
- *New construction for firms or consumers.* A new store built for Gap Inc. is investment spending. New residential housing (apartments or homes) is considered investment spending, since it is expected to provide housing services for years.
- *Market value of the change in unsold inventories.* If GM produces a new Cadillac in 2022, but it remains unsold on December 31, 2022, it would not be counted as consumer spending in 2022. It would appear in *I* as unsold inventory. Later, when it is eventually sold, it is added to *C* and deducted from *I*.

Government Spending (*G*). The government, at all levels, purchases final goods and services and invests in infrastructure. These include police cars, the services provided by social workers, computers for the government, or Humvees for the military. Infrastructure investments include highways, an airport, and a new county jail.

Note: Government transfer payments to citizens who qualify for government benefits (e.g., retired veterans) amount to sizable government expenditures but do not count toward GDP because these are not dollars spent on the production of goods and services.

Net Exports ($X - M$). We should add any domestically produced goods purchased by foreign consumers (exports = X) but subtract any spending by our citizens on purchases of goods made within other nations (imports = M). This way we include dollars flowing into our economy and acknowledge that some dollars flow out and land in other economies.

Most macroeconomic policies, directly or indirectly, influence GDP. Knowing the components of GDP is very useful when you are tested on policies.

Aggregate spending (GDP) = $C + I + G + (X - M)$

National Income Concepts

The basic circular flow model tells us that if we add up all the spending, it equals all the income, and either measure provides us with GDP. This simplicity is a bit deceiving, because in practice there are several necessary accounting entries that complicate matters. We keep it simple enough for the AP exam and leave the accounting to those who wear the pocket protectors.

Aggregate Income

Calculating GDP from the income half of the circular flow (aka "the income approach") must begin with incomes that are paid to the suppliers of resources. These are the households, and they supply labor, land, capital, and entrepreneurial talents. See Table 7.3. Payments to these resources are usually referred to as wages, rents, interest, and profits. With some accounting adjustments, the sum of all income sources is approximately equal to the sum of all spending sources, or GDP.

Table 7.3

RESOURCE SUPPLIED	INCOME RECEIVED
Labor	Wages
Land	Rent
Capital	Interest
Entrepreneurial Talent	Profits

A third approach to calculating GDP considers all stages of production of a final good and the value that was added to the final good along the way. This **value-added approach** can again be demonstrated with the bottle of ketchup example described earlier. The stages of production are summarized in Table 7.4.

Table 7.4

STAGE OF PRODUCTION	COST OF INPUTS (CI)	PRICE OF OUTPUT (P)	VALUE ADDED = P – CI
Growing 1 pound of tomatoes	\$0	\$0.50	\$0.50
Processing tomatoes into ketchup	\$0.50	\$1.50	\$1.00
Sale of ketchup to customer	\$1.50	\$3.00	\$1.50

At each stage of production, there is a firm that is creating an item that has more market value than it had at the previous stage. The farmer adds $0.50 of value in growing the tomatoes, the food-processing firm adds another $1.00, and the retail grocer adds a final $1.50. When we add up all of these incremental values added, we get the same $3 of GDP.

K.I.S.S.: Keep It Simple, Silly

National income accounting makes my head spin, and studying it usually sends students off to their guidance counselors to investigate majoring in Scandinavian poetry. If we focus on the simplicities of the circular flow model, we can use the relationships between income and spending with some powerful results.

$$\textbf{GDP} = C + I + G + (X - M) = \textbf{Aggregate spending}$$
$$= \textbf{Aggregate income } (Y) = \textbf{Sum of all Value Added}$$

- The most recent AP Macroeconomics curriculum focuses on GDP, or total spending, as the nation's measure of economic output. Your study should therefore focus on the components of GDP and understand how there are three approaches to estimating GDP.

Real and Nominal GDP

Remember that calculation of GDP requires that we take production of goods and services and apply the value of those items. But we know that prices change, so when we compare GDP from one year to the next, we have to account for changing prices. Reporting that GDP has risen without acknowledging that this is simply because prices have risen doesn't tell a very accurate story. We need a way to compare GDP over time by accounting for different prices over time.

Example:

In 2014, our small coffee shop sold 1,000 café lattes at a price of $2 each. The total value of this production was $2,000. In 2015, firms and residents in town experienced a higher cost of living, and our coffee shop increased the price of a latte to $3 and still sold 1,000. The total value of the production has shown an increase of $1,000, but production didn't increase at all.

Nominal GDP. The value of current production at the current prices. Valuing 2021 production with 2021 prices creates nominal GDP in 2021. This is also known as current-dollar GDP or "money" GDP.

Real GDP. The value of current production, but using prices from a fixed point in time. Valuing 2021 production at 2020 prices creates real GDP in 2021 and allows us to compare it to 2020. This is also known as constant-dollar or real GDP.

Keepin' It Real: An Espresso Example

Suppose GDP is made up of just one product, cups of latte. Table 7.5 shows how many lattes have been made in a four-year period, the prices, and a price index. We need a **price index** in order to calculate real GDP. This index is a measure of the price of a good in a given year, when compared to the price of that good in a **reference** (or **base**) **year.** Using 2012 as the base year, I'll create a latte index and use it to adjust nominal GDP to real GDP for this one good. First the latte price index, or LPI:

LPI in year t = 100 × (Price of a latte in year t)/(Price of a latte in base year)

Table 7.5

YEAR	# OF LATTES	PRICE PER CUP	NOMINAL GDP	PRICE INDEX	REAL GDP
2012	1,000	\$2	\$2,000	= 100 × \$2/\$2 = 100	= \$2,000
2013	1,200	\$3	\$3,600	150	\$2,400
2014	1,800	\$4	\$7,200	200	\$3,600
2015	1,600	\$5	\$8,000	250	\$3,200

Notice that a price index always equals 100 in the base year. Even if you didn't know the actual price of a latte in 2012, by looking at the LPI, you can see that the price doubled by 2014, since the LPI is 200 compared to the base value of 100.

Deflating Nominal GDP

To deflate a nominal value, or adjust for inflation, you do a simple division:

Real GDP = 100 × (Nominal GDP)/(Price index) or you can think of it as

Real GDP = (Nominal GDP)/(Price index; in hundreds)

Making this adjustment provides the final column of Table 7.5. While nominal GDP appears to be rapidly rising from 2012 to 2015, you can see that, in real terms, the value of latte production has risen more modestly from 2012 to 2014 but actually fell in 2015.

Using Percentages

Another way to look at the relationship among a price index, real GDP, and nominal GDP is to look at them in terms of percentage change.

TIP

$$\%\Delta \text{ real GDP} = \%\Delta \text{ nominal GDP} - \%\Delta \text{ price index}$$

Example:

If nominal GDP increased by 5 percent and the price index increased by 1 percent, we could say that real GDP increased by approximately 4 percent.

The GDP Deflator

GDP is constructed by aggregating the consumption and production of thousands of goods and services. The prices of these many goods that compose GDP are used to construct a price index informally called the **GDP price deflator.** Nominal GDP is deflated, with this price index, to create real GDP. Economists watch real GDP to look for signs of economic growth and recession. We see these changes in real GDP by looking at the business cycle.

Business Cycles

The **business cycle** is the periodic rise and fall in economic activity, and can be measured by changes in real GDP. Figure 7.2 is a simplification of a complete business cycle. In general, there are four phases of the cycle.

- **Expansion.** A period where real GDP is growing.
- **Peak.** The top of the cycle where an expansion has run its course and is about to turn down.

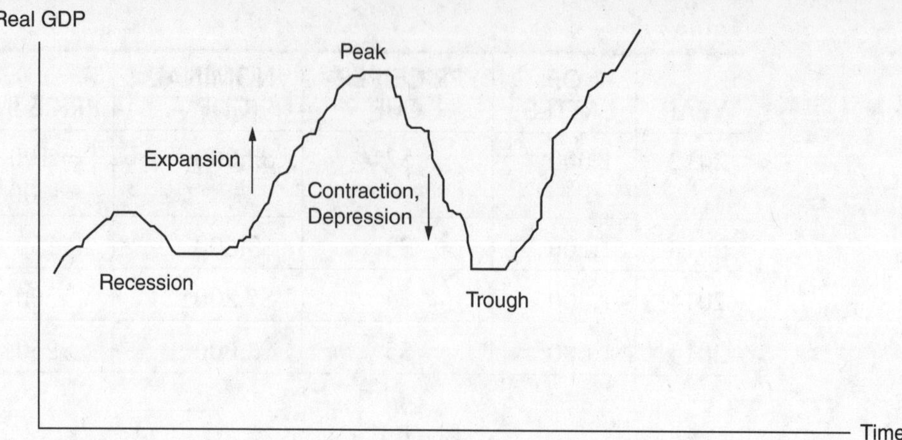

Figure 7.2

- **Contraction.** A period where real GDP is falling. There is no specific criteria for defining one, but a **recession** is unofficially described as two consecutive quarters of falling real GDP. If the contraction is prolonged or deep enough, it is called a **depression.**
- **Trough.** The bottom of the cycle where a contraction has stopped and is about to turn up.

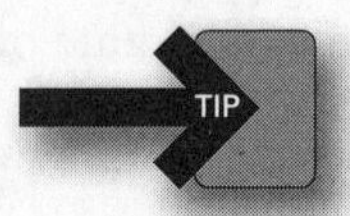

- *Though it is an imperfect measure, GDP is used as a measure of economic prosperity and growth.*
- *You must focus on real GDP, not nominal GDP.*
- *Nominal GDP is deflated to real GDP by dividing by the price index known as the GDP deflator.*

This chapter has stressed that we need to know how economic activity is measured so that we can understand how and why policies can be used to strengthen the economy. Real GDP is one of these important economic indicators and is probably the most all-encompassing of macroeconomic measures of performance, but it is not the only one. The economic indicators of inflation and unemployment are also targets of economic policy and are widely covered by the media. Before getting to macroeconomic models and policy, the next two sections spend some time learning more about what these statistics do, and do not, tell us.

7.3 Inflation and the Consumer Price Index

Main Topics: *Consumer Price Index, Inflation, Is Inflation Bad?, Measurement Issues*

My "Latte Price Index" illustrates that a price index can be constructed to measure changes in the price of anything. Another price index, the GDP price deflator, measures the increase in the price level of items that compose GDP. But not all goods that fall into GDP are goods that the everyday household shops for. If United Airlines buys a 767 from Boeing, it adds to GDP, but the price of a new 767 doesn't exactly fall within what we might call consumer spending. We need a statistic that focuses on consumer prices.

The Consumer Price Index (CPI)

To measure the average price level of items that consumers actually buy, use the **consumer price index (CPI).** The Bureau of Labor Statistics (BLS) selects a base year, and a **market basket** is compiled of hundreds of consumer goods and services bought in that year. A monthly survey is conducted in 50 urban areas around the country, and based on

Table 7.6

	2021 (BASE PERIOD)			2022 (CURRENT PERIOD)	
Items in the Basket	*Quantity Purchased*	Price	*2021 Spending Using 2021 Prices and Quantities*	Price	*2022 Spending Using 2022 Prices and 2021 Quantities*
Chocolate Bars	12	$1.50	$18	$1.75	$21
Concert Tickets	4	$45	$180	$60	$240
Large Pizzas	18	$16	$288	$15	$270
Total Spending			= $486		= $531

the results of this survey, the average prices of the items in the base year market basket is factored into the CPI. Confused yet? Let's do a simple example of a price index for a typical consumer (see Table 7.6).

Price index current year = 100 × (Spending current year)/(Spending base year)

2022 price index = 100 × (531)/(486) = 109.26

Inflation

In the above example, the price index increased from 100 in the base year to 109.26 in 2022. In other words, the average price level increased by 9.26 percent.

On a much larger scale, the official CPI is constructed and used to measure the increase in the average price level of consumer goods. The annual rate of **inflation** on goods consumed by the typical consumer is the percentage change in the CPI from one year to the next.

"Know these things for multiple-choice especially."
—Lucas, AP Student

Example:

Let's use some actual Bureau of Labor Statistics CPI data to calculate the rate of inflation. In January 2000, the CPI was 169.30, and one year later in January 2001 it had risen to 175.60. Remember this value alone isn't the rate of inflation, we need to calculate the percentage change in the CPI to calculate inflation.

Inflation = (175.60 − 169.30)/169.30 = .037 or 3.7%

This tells us that in that particular year the average cost of the market basket of typical consumer goods and services increased by 3.7%.

For the most part, average prices do tend to rise from month to month and year to year but not always.

Example:

In January 2008 the CPI was 212.174 and in January 2009 it was 211.933. Again, let's calculate the percentage change.

Inflation = (211.933 − 212.174)/212.174 = −0.0011 or −0.11%

There was actually deflation, not inflation, in this twelve-month period. Why were average prices slightly falling at this time? In hindsight, this was the beginning of a very difficult time in the economy, a time that came to be known as the Great Recession. As we will see in future chapters, recessions, especially bad ones, are typically linked to falling average price levels.

- *Consumer inflation rate = 100 × (CPI new – CPI old)/CPI old*

Nominal and Real Income

As a consumer, I am also a worker and an income earner. Rising consumer prices hurt my ability to purchase the items that make me happy. In other words, rising prices can cause a decrease in my purchasing power. Ideally, I would like to see my income rise at a faster rate than the price of consumer goods. One way to see if this is happening is to deflate nominal income by the CPI to calculate my real income. Real income is calculated in the same way that real GDP is calculated.

- **Real income this year = (Nominal income this year)/CPI this year (in hundredths)**

Example:

In 2014 Kelsey's nominal income was $40,000, and it increases to $41,000 in 2015. Curious about her purchasing power, she looks up the CPI in 2014 and finds that at the end of that year it was 234.8; at the end of 2015 it was 236.5. This is compared to the base year value of 100 in 1984.

Real income 2015 = $40,000/2.348 = $17,036

Real income 2016 = $41,000/2.365 = $17,336

What we have done here is converted Kelsey's nominal incomes in 2014 and 2015, which were each a function of prices on those two years, into constant 1984 dollars. In other words, we have adjusted (or deflated) incomes measured in two different years so they are measured with the prices that existed in one year. After accounting for inflation, Kelsey's real income increased by $300. Her nominal income increased at a rate slightly faster than the rate of inflation, and so her purchasing power has slightly increased.

Example:

What if Kelsey's wages were frozen and she did not receive that raise in 2015?

Real income 2015 = $40,000/2.365 = $16,913,

or a $123 decrease in purchasing power

Is Inflation Bad?

The previous example illustrates that inflation erodes the purchasing power of consumers if nominal wages do not keep up with prices. In general, inflation impacts different groups in different ways. It can actually help some individuals! The main thing to keep in mind with inflation is that it is the unexpected or sudden inflation that creates winners and losers. If the inflation is predictable and expected, most groups can plan for it and adjust behavior and prices accordingly.

"Make sure you understand the difference between expected and unexpected inflation." —AP Teacher

Expected Inflation

If my employer and I agree that the general price level is going to increase by 3 percent next year, then my salary can be adjusted by at least 3 percent so that my purchasing power does not fall. This **cost of living adjustment** doesn't hurt my employer so long as the prices of the firm's output and any other inputs also increase by 3 percent. Many unions and government employees have cost of living raises written into employment contracts to recognize predictable inflation over time.

Banks and other lenders acknowledge inflation by factoring expected inflation into interest rates. If they do not, savers and lenders can be hurt by rising prices. For this reason, the bank adds an inflation factor on the **real rate** of interest to create a **nominal rate** of interest that savers receive and borrowers pay.

Nominal interest rate = Real interest rate + Expected inflation

Savings Example 1:

When I see the bank offering an interest rate of 1 percent for a savings account and I put $100 in the bank, I expect to have $101 worth of purchasing power a year from now. But if prices increase by 2 percent, my original deposit is only worth $98. So even when I receive my $1 of interest, I have lost purchasing power.

If you have a savings account, the real rate is the rate the bank pays you to borrow your money for a year. You must be compensated for this because you do not have $100 to spend at the mall if you put it into the bank. Look at my savings example again with an inflation expectation of 2 percent and a real interest rate of 1 percent.

Savings Example 2:

- January 1: The purchasing power of my $100 is $100, and the bank offers me a 3 percent nominal interest rate on a savings account.
- Throughout the year, inflation is indeed 2 percent.
- December 31: My bank balance says $103, but $2 of purchasing power on my original deposit has been lost to inflation, leaving me with $1 as payment from the bank for having my money for one year.

Borrowing Example:

If you are looking for a loan of $100, the real interest is the rate the bank will charge you for borrowing the bank's money for a year. After all, if the bank lends the money to you, it will not have those funds for some other profitable opportunity. Again, let's assume that the expected inflation is 2 percent but the real rate of interest is 3 percent.

- January 1: The purchasing power of the bank's $100 is $100, and the bank lends it to me with a 5 percent nominal interest rate.
- Throughout the year, inflation is indeed 2 percent.
- December 31: I pay the bank back $105, but $2 of the bank's purchasing power on the original $100 has been lost to inflation, leaving it with $3 as payment from me for having its money for one year.

- So long as the actual inflation is identical to the expected inflation, workers, employers, savers, lenders, and borrowers are not harmed by the inflation.

Unexpected Inflation

When price levels are unpredictable or increase by a much larger or much smaller amount than predicted, some sectors of the economy gain and others lose. Though not a comprehensive list, some of the groups that win and lose from unexpected inflation include the following:

- *Employees and employers.* If the real income of workers is falling because of rapid inflation, it is possible that firms are benefiting at the expense of the workers. In a simple case, you work at a grocery store and the price of groceries unexpectedly rises by 10 percent a year, but your nominal wages rise by 8 percent. Your employer is clearly benefiting by selling goods at higher and higher prices but paying you wages that are rising more slowly.
- *Fixed-income recipients.* A retiree receiving a fixed pension can expect to see it slowly eroded by rising prices. Likewise, a landlord who is locked into a long-term lease receives payments that slowly decline in purchasing power. If the minimum wage is not frequently adjusted for inflation, then minimum-wage workers see a decline in their purchasing power.
- *Savers and borrowers.* If I put my money in the bank and leave it for a year when inflation is higher than expected, and then withdraw it, the purchasing power is greatly diminished. On the other hand, if I borrow from the bank at the beginning of that year and pay it back after higher-than-expected inflation, I am giving back dollars that are not worth as much as they used to be. This benefits me and hurts the bank.

- Rapid unexpected inflation usually hurts employees if real wages are falling, as well as fixed-income recipients, savers, and lenders.
- Rapid unexpected inflation usually helps firms if real wages are falling, as well as borrowers. It might also increase the value of some assets like real estate or other properties.

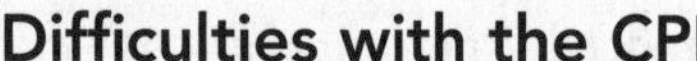

Difficulties with the CPI

Like all statistical measures, we should be careful not to read too much into them and acknowledge that they all have some problematic issues.

- *Consumers substitute.* The market basket uses consumption patterns from the base year, which could be several years ago. As the price of goods begins to rise, we know that consumers seek substitutes. This substitution might make the base year market basket a poor representation of the current consumption pattern.
- *Goods evolve.* Imagine if the CPI market basket were using 1912 as a base year. The basket would include the price of buggy whips and stovepipe hats in the inflation rate. The emergence of new products (smartphones) and extinction of others (manual typewriters) is understood by firms and consumers, but the market basket must reflect this or it risks becoming irrelevant.
- *Quality differences.* Some price increases are the result of improvements in quality. As automakers improve safety features, luxury options, and mechanical sophistication, we should expect the price to rise. Prices that increase because the product is fundamentally better are not an indication of overall inflation. Because the BLS has a difficult time telling the difference between quality improvements and actual inflation, the CPI can be overstated for this reason.

If the market basket is not altered to account for the previously mentioned effects, the CPI is not very accurate. The BLS reviews the market basket from time to time and updates it if necessary. Comparisons over long periods are not very useful, but from month to month and year to year, the CPI is a fairly useful measure of how the average price level of consumer items is changing.

7.4 Unemployment

Main Topics: *Measuring the Unemployment Rate, Types of Unemployment*

Whenever an economy has idle, or unemployed, resources, it is operating inside the production possibility frontier. Though unemployment can describe any idle resource, it is almost always applied to labor.

Measuring the Unemployment Rate

Is an infant unemployed? What about an 85-year-old retiree? A parent staying home with young children? Before we can calculate an unemployment rate, we must first define who is a candidate for employment. Once again, a monthly survey is conducted by the BLS, and through a series of questions, it classifies all persons in a surveyed household above the age of 16 into one of three groups: "Employed" for pay at least one hour per week, "Unemployed" but looking for work, or "Out of the Labor Force." If a person is out of the labor force, they have chosen to not seek employment. Our retiree and stay-at-home parent of young children would fall into this category. Many students, at least those who choose not to work while pursuing their studies, also fall into this latter category.

The non-institutionalized civilian **labor force** (LF) is the sum of all individuals 16 years and older, not in the military or in prison, who are either currently employed (E) or unemployed (U). To be counted as one of the unemployed, you must be actively searching for work.

$$LF = E + U$$

The **labor force participation rate (LFPR)** is also a statistic that is carefully followed by economists. Once the size of the labor force, the sum of the unemployed and employed, has been estimated, the LFPR is the ratio of the labor force to the entire population (Pop) 16 years and older.

$$LFPR = (LF/Pop) * 100$$

The LFPR is essentially a measure of labor market engagement. If a greater percentage of the population is working, or attempting to find work, this is a sign of a healthy job market and a robust economy. On the other hand, if the economy begins to weaken, people get frustrated being unable to find a job and drop out of the labor force, and the LFPR will fall.

The **unemployment rate** is the ratio of unemployed to the total labor force:

$$UR = (U/LF) \times 100$$

Example:

Table 7.7 summarizes the 2022 and 2023 labor market in Smallville.

Table 7.7

	POPULATION	OUT OF THE LABOR FORCE	EMPLOYED	UNEMPLOYED	LABOR FORCE = E + U	LFPR = (LF/POP)∗100	UNEMPLOYMENT RATE = (U/LF) × 100
2022	1,800	800	900	100	1,000	= 55.6%	= 10%
2023	1,800	820	900	80	980	= 54.4%	= 8.2%

In 2022, 100 citizens are unemployed but are seeking work and the reported unemployment rate is 10 percent. After a year of searching, 20 of these unemployed citizens become tired of looking for work and move back home to live in the basement of their parents' home. These **discouraged workers** are not counted in the ranks of the unemployed, and this results in an unemployment rate that falls to 8.2 percent. On the surface, the economy looks to be improving, but these 20 individuals have *not* found employment. The statistic hides their presence. However, the LFPR shows a slight decline, which is a better indicator of the weakening labor market and the presence of discouraged workers.

To give you an idea of the statistical impact that discouraged workers have on the official unemployment rate, we can look at labor force data from January 2016. The BLS estimated a U.S. labor force of 158,335,000 people and of those, 7,791,000 were counted as unemployed. The January 2016 official unemployment rate was 4.9 percent. However, there were an estimated 623,000 people who were not in the labor force because they were discouraged over their job prospects. If you add these people to the ranks of the unemployed and also to the labor force, the adjusted unemployment rate increases to 5.3 percent.

- The presence of discouraged workers understates the true unemployment rate.

Types of Unemployment

"Be sure to give examples of each type."
—AP Teacher

People are unemployed for different reasons. Some of these reasons are predictable and relatively harmless, and others can even be beneficial to the individual and the economy. Other reasons for lost jobs are quite damaging, however, and policies need to target these types of job loss.

Frictional Unemployment. This type of unemployment occurs when someone new enters the labor market or switches jobs. Frictional unemployment can happen voluntarily if a person is seeking a better match for their skills, or has just finished schooling, and is usually short-lived. Employers who fire employees for poor work habits or subpar performance also contribute to the level of frictional unemployment. The provision of unemployment insurance for six months allows for a cushion to these events and assists the person in finding a job compatible with their skills. Because frictional unemployment is typically a short-term phenomenon, it is considered the least troublesome for the economy as a whole. If it results in a better match between workers and employers, it can be an improvement in overall productivity.

Seasonal Unemployment. This type of unemployment emerges as the periodic and predictable job loss that follows the calendar. Agricultural jobs are gained and lost as crops are grown and harvested. Teens are employed during the summers and over the holidays, but most are not employed during the school year. Summer swimming pools close in the winter, and winter ski lodges close in the spring. Workers and employers alike anticipate these changes in employment and plan accordingly, thus the damage is minimal. The BLS accounts for the seasonality of some employment, so such factors are not going to affect the published unemployment rate.

Structural Unemployment. This type of unemployment is caused by fundamental, underlying changes in the economy that can create job loss for skills that are no longer in demand. A worker who manually tightened bolts on the assembly line can be structurally replaced by robotics. In cases of technological unemployment like this, the job skills of the worker need to change to suit the new workplace. In some cases of structural employment, jobs are lost because the product is no longer in demand, probably because a better product has replaced it. This market evolution is inevitable, so the more flexible the skills of the workers, the less painful this kind of structural change. Government-provided job training and subsidized public universities help the structurally unemployed help themselves.

Cyclical Unemployment. Jobs are gained and lost as the business cycle improves and worsens. The unemployment rate rises when the economy is contracting, and the unemployment rate falls as the economy is expanding. This form of unemployment is usually felt throughout the economy rather than on certain subgroups, and therefore, policies are going to focus on stimulating job growth throughout the economy. Structural unemployment might be forever, but cyclical unemployment only lasts as long as it takes to get through the recession.

Full Employment

Economists acknowledge that frictional and structural unemployment are always present. In fact, in a rapidly evolving economy, these are often beneficial in the long run. Because of these forms of unemployment, the unemployment rate can never be zero. Economists define **full employment** as the situation when there is no cyclical unemployment in the economy. The unemployment rate associated with full employment is called the **natural rate of unemployment**, and in the United States, this rate has traditionally been 4 to 6 percent.

› Review Questions

1. Which of the following transactions would be counted in GDP if we were using the spending approach?

(A) The cash you receive from babysitting your neighbor's kids
(B) The sale of illegal drugs
(C) The sale of cucumbers to a pickle manufacturer
(D) The sale of a pound of tomatoes at a supermarket
(E) The eBay resale of a sweater you received from your great aunt at Christmas

2. GDP is $10 million, consumer spending is $6 million, government spending is $3 million, exports are $2 million, and imports are $3 million. How much is spent for investments?

(A) $0 million
(B) $1 million
(C) $2 million
(D) $3 million
(E) $4 million

3. If Real GDP = $200 billion and the price index = 200, Nominal GDP is

(A) $4 billion.
(B) $400 billion.
(C) $200 billion.
(D) $2 billion.
(E) impossible to determine since the base year is not given.

For Questions 4 to 5 use the following information for a small town:

Total population:	2,000
Total employed adults:	950
Total unemployed adults:	50

4. What is the size of the labor force, and what is the labor force participation rate?

(A) 2,000; 100 percent
(B) 950; 47.5 percent
(C) 900; 45 percent
(D) 1,000; 50 percent
(E) 1,000; 5 percent

5. What is the official unemployment rate?

(A) 5 percent
(B) 2.5 percent
(C) 5.5 percent
(D) 7 percent
(E) Unknown, as we do not know the number of discouraged workers

6. You are working at a supermarket bagging groceries, but you are unhappy about your wage, so you quit and begin looking for a new job at a competing grocery store. What type of unemployment is this?

(A) Cyclical
(B) Structural
(C) Seasonal
(D) Frictional
(E) Discouraged

› Answers and Explanations

1. **D**—The supermarket tomatoes are the only final good sale and are counted. Babysitting is a nonmarket, cash "under the table" service. The sale of illegal drugs is a part of an underground economy. The sale of the cucumbers is an intermediate good. The resale of the sweater, even though it was never worn, is a secondhand sale. When your great aunt originally purchased it at the mall, it was counted in GDP.

2. **C**—GDP = $C + I + G + (X - M)$. This would mean that $10 = 6 + I + 3 + (2 - 3)$; therefore, I = \$2 million.

3. **B**—Nominal GDP/price index (in hundredths) = Real GDP. Use this relationship to solve for Nominal GDP. \$200 = (Nominal GDP)/2. Nominal GDP = \$400 billion.

4. **D**—Labor force is the employed + the unemployed. LF = 950 + 50 = 1,000. The remaining citizens are out of the labor force. The LFPR is the ratio of the labor force to the population. LFPR = (1000/2000)∗100 = 50%.

5. **A**—The unemployment rate is the ratio of unemployed to the total labor force. UR = U/LF = 50/1,000 = 5%.

6. **D**—Frictional unemployment occurs when a person is between jobs. This person has not been laid off due to a structural change in the demand for skills, or because of a cyclical economic downturn, or because of a new season. A low wage might be discouraging; a discouraged worker is a worker who has been unemployed for so long that they have ceased the search for work.

› Rapid Review

Circular flow of economic activity: A model that shows how households and firms circulate resources, goods, and incomes through the economy. This basic model is expanded to include the government and the foreign sector.

Closed economy: A model that assumes there is no foreign sector (imports and exports).

Aggregation: The process of summing the microeconomic activity of households and firms into a more macroeconomic measure of economic activity.

Gross domestic product (GDP): The market value of the final goods and services produced within a nation in a given period of time.

Final goods: Goods that are ready for their final use by consumers and firms, for example, a new Harley-Davidson motorcycle.

Intermediate goods: Goods that require further modification before they are ready for final use, e.g., steel used to produce the new Harley.

Double counting: The mistake of including the value of intermediate stages of production in GDP on top of the value of the final good.

Secondhand sales: Final goods and services that are resold. Even if they are resold many times, final goods and services are only counted once—in the year in which they were produced.

Nonmarket transactions: Household work or do-it-yourself jobs are missed by GDP accounting. The same is true of government transfer payments and purely financial transactions like the purchase of a share of Amazon stock.

Underground economy: These include unreported illegal activity, bartering, or informal exchange of cash.

Aggregate spending (GDP): The sum of all spending from four sectors of the economy. GDP $= C + I + G + (X - M)$.

Aggregate income (AI): The sum of all income—Wages + Rents + Interest + Profit—earned by suppliers of resources in the economy. With some accounting adjustments, aggregate spending equals aggregate income and also equals the sum of the value added.

Value-added approach: A third approach to calculating GDP that considers all stages of production of a final good and the value that was added to the final good along the way.

Nominal GDP: The value of current production at the current prices. Valuing 2015 production with 2015 prices creates nominal GDP in 2015.

Real GDP: The value of current production, but using prices from a fixed point in time. Valuing 2015 production at 2014 prices creates real GDP in 2015 and allows us to compare it back to 2014.

Base year: The year that serves as a reference point for constructing a price index and comparing real values over time.

Price index: A measure of the average level of prices in a market basket for a given year, when compared to the prices in a reference (or base) year. You can interpret the price index as the current price level as a percentage of the level in the base year.

Market basket: A collection of goods and services used to represent what is consumed in the economy.

GDP price deflator: The price index that measures the average price level of the goods and services that make up GDP.

Real rate of interest: The percentage increase in purchasing power that a borrower pays a lender.

Expected (anticipated) inflation: The inflation expected in a future period. This expected inflation is added to the real interest rate to compensate for lost purchasing power.

Nominal rate of interest: The percentage increase in money that the borrower pays the lender and is equal to the real rate plus the expected inflation.

Business cycle: The periodic rise and fall (in four phases) of economic activity.

Expansion: A period where real GDP is growing.

Peak: The top of a business cycle where an expansion has ended.

Contraction: A period where real GDP is falling.

Recession: Unofficially defined as two consecutive quarters of falling real GDP.

Trough: The bottom of the cycle where a contraction has stopped.

Depression: A prolonged, deep contraction in the business cycle.

Consumer price index (CPI): The price index that measures the average price level of the items in the base year market basket. This is the main measure of consumer inflation.

Inflation: The percentage change in the CPI from one period to the next.

Nominal income: Today's income measured in today's dollars. These are dollars unadjusted by inflation.

Real income: Today's income measured in base year dollars. These inflation-adjusted dollars can be compared from year to year to determine whether purchasing power has increased or decreased.

Employed: A person is employed if they have worked for pay at least one hour per week.

Unemployed: A person is unemployed if they are not currently working but are actively seeking work.

Labor force: The sum of all individuals 16 years and older who are either currently employed (E) or unemployed (U). LF = E + U.

Out of the labor force: A person is classified as out of the labor force if they have chosen to not seek employment.

Labor force participation: The ratio of the size of the labor force to the size of the population 16 years and older. LFPR = (LF/Pop)∗100

Unemployment rate: The percentage of the labor force that falls into the unemployed category. Sometimes called the *jobless rate.* UR = 100 × U/LF.

Discouraged workers: Citizens who have been without work for so long that they become tired of looking for work and drop out of the labor force. Because these citizens are not counted in the ranks of the unemployed, the reported unemployment rate is understated.

Frictional unemployment: A type of unemployment that occurs when someone new enters the labor market or switches jobs. This is a relatively harmless form of unemployment and not expected to last long.

Seasonal unemployment: A type of unemployment that is periodic, is predictable, and follows the calendar. Workers and employers alike anticipate these changes in employment and plan accordingly, thus the damage is minimal.

Structural unemployment: A type of unemployment that is the result of fundamental, underlying changes in the economy such that some job skills are no longer in demand.

Cyclical unemployment: A type of unemployment that rises and falls with the business cycle. This form of unemployment is felt economy-wide, which makes it the focus of macroeconomic policy.

Full employment: Exists when the economy is experiencing no cyclical unemployment.

Natural rate of unemployment: The unemployment rate associated with full employment, somewhere between 4 to 6 percent in the United States.

Consumption, Saving, Investment, and the Multiplier

IN THIS CHAPTER

Summary: Having described GDP as the macroeconomic measure of a nation's output, we begin to build a model that helps to explain how and why GDP fluctuates. As the largest component of GDP, we spend some time on consumption. Investment is also a component of GDP, and because investment plays an important role in monetary policy, we investigate it as well. The market for loanable funds combines savings and investment, and is a prelude to the interaction of interest rates and the role of financial institutions. This chapter begins to show how changes in spending affect output and employment through the multiplier process. Discussion of the spending multiplier previews how policy affects the macroeconomy and leads to the aggregate demand and supply model in the next chapter.

Key Ideas

- Consumption and Saving Functions
- Investment
- Market for Loanable Funds
- The Spending Multiplier, Tax Multiplier, and Balanced-Budget Multiplier

8.1 Consumption and Saving

Main Topics: *Consumption and Saving Functions, Marginal Propensity to Consume and Save, Changes in Consumption and Saving*

The circular flow model illustrates the importance of consumption in the production of goods and the employment of resources. A better understanding of consumption allows us to build a model of the macroeconomy and see the role of policy in affecting macroeconomic indicators like GDP, employment, and inflation.

Consumption and Saving Functions

Though not the only factor, the most important element affecting consumption (and savings) is disposable income. **Disposable income (DI)** is what consumers have left over to spend or save once they have paid out their net taxes:

$$\textbf{DI} = \textbf{Gross income} - \textbf{Net taxes}$$

where Net taxes = (Taxes paid − Transfers received).

With no government transfers or taxation, DI $= C + S$. Though not all consumers save part of their income, typical consumers spend the majority of their disposable income and save whatever is left over. To see the relationship between disposable income and consumption, we create a **consumption function.**

Consumption and Saving Schedules

The consumption and saving schedules are the direct relationships between disposable income and consumption and savings. As DI increases for a typical household, C and S both increase. Table 8.1 provides an example.

Table 8.1

DISPOSABLE INCOME (DI)	CONSUMPTION (*C*)	SAVINGS (*S*)
0	40	−40
100	120	−20
200	200	0
300	280	20
400	360	40
500	440	60

Consumption

Even with zero disposable income, households still consume as they liquidate wealth (sell assets), spend some savings, or borrow (dissavings). For every additional $100 of disposable income, consumers increase their spending by $80 and increase saving by $20. We can convert the above consumption schedule to a linear equation or **consumption function:**

$$C = 40 + .80(\text{DI})$$

The constant $40 is referred to as **autonomous consumption** because it does not change as DI changes. The slope of the consumption function is .80. This function is plotted in Figure 8.1.

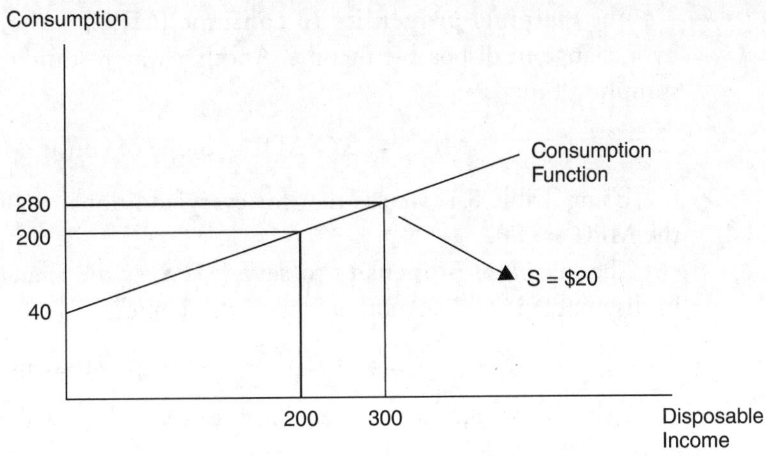

Figure 8.1

At every level of DI, the consumption function tells us how much is consumed. Both Table 8.1 and Figure 8.1 tell us that at incomes below $200, the consumer is consuming more than his income. As a result, saving is negative, and this is referred to as **dissaving.** But at incomes above $200, the consumer is spending less than his income, and so saving is positive.

Saving

The saving schedule above can also be converted into a linear equation, or **saving function**:

$$S = -40 + .20(\text{DI})$$

The constant $–40 is referred to as **autonomous saving** because it does not change as DI changes. With zero disposable income, the household would need to borrow $40 to consume $40 worth of goods. The slope of the saving function is .20. This function is plotted in Figure 8.2.

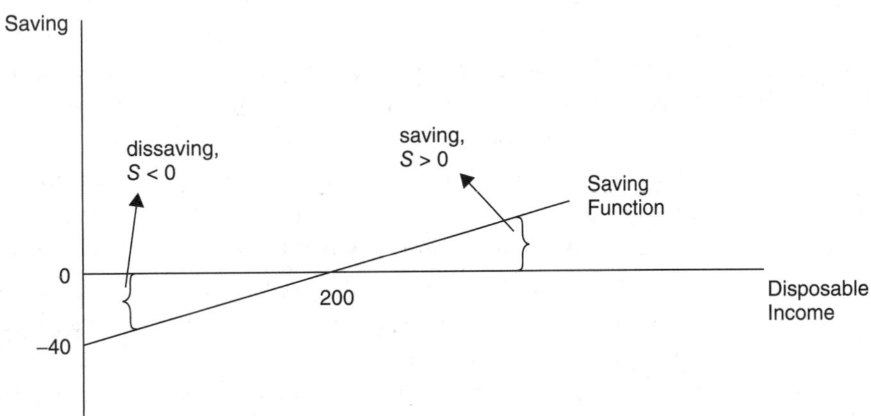

Figure 8.2

KEY IDEA

Marginal Propensity to Consume and Save

An important lesson from the study of microeconomics is the marginal concept. You can think of it in two equivalent ways. *Marginal* always means an incremental change caused by an external force, or it is always the slope of a "total" function. The same is true here.

The **marginal propensity to consume (MPC)** is the change in consumption caused by a change in disposable income. Another way to think about it is the slope of the consumption function:

$$\text{MPC} = \Delta C/\Delta \text{DI} = \text{Slope of consumption function}$$

Using Table 8.1, we see that for every additional \$100 of DI, *C* increases by \$80, so the MPC = .80.

The **marginal propensity to save (MPS)** is the change in saving caused by a change in disposable income. Another way to think about it is the slope of the saving function:

$$\text{MPS} = \Delta S/\Delta \text{DI} = \text{Slope of saving function}$$

Using Table 8.1, we can see that for every additional \$100 of DI, *S* increases by \$20, so the MPS = .20.

There is a nice relationship between the MPC and the MPS. For every additional dollar not consumed, it is saved. So if the consumer gains \$100 in disposable income, they increase their consumption by \$80 and increase saving by \$20. In other words, MPC + MPS = 1. If you know one, you can find the other.

- MPC = $\Delta C/\Delta$DI = Constant slope of consumption function
- MPS = $\Delta S/\Delta$DI = Constant slope of saving function
- MPC + MPS = 1

Changes in Consumption and Saving

A change in disposable income causes a movement along the consumption and savings functions. Economists typically recognize four external determinants of household consumption and saving that shift the functions upward or downward.

Determinants of Consumption and Saving

- *Wealth.* When the value of accumulated wealth increases, consumption functions shift upward, and the saving function shifts downward, because households can sell stock or other assets to consume more goods at their current level of disposable income.
- *Expectations.* Uncertainty or a low expectation about future income usually prompts a household to decrease consumption and increase saving. An expectation of a higher future price level spurs higher consumption right now and less saving.
- *Household debt.* Households can increase consumption with borrowing, or debt. However, as households accumulate more and more debt, they need to use more and more disposable income to pay off the debt and thus decrease consumption.
- *Taxes and transfers.* A change in taxes impacts both consumption and saving in the same direction. If the government increases taxes, households see both consumption and saving decrease because more of their gross income is sent to the government. On the other hand, an increase in government transfer payments increases both consumption and saving functions. In the case of taxes and transfers, consumption and saving functions shift in the same way.

An upward shift in consumption tells us that at all levels of disposable income, consumption is greater (C_{High}). If consumption is greater at all levels of disposable income, saving must be lower (S_{Low}), and vice versa. The only exception is the case of taxes and transfers described earlier. Figures 8.3 and 8.4 illustrate these simultaneous shifts in the opposite directions.

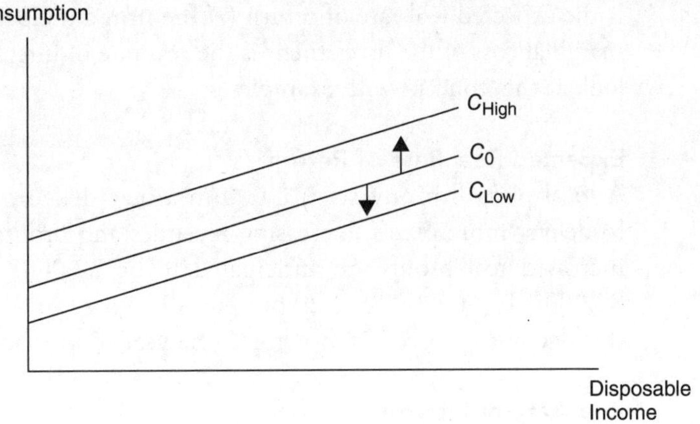

Figure 8.3

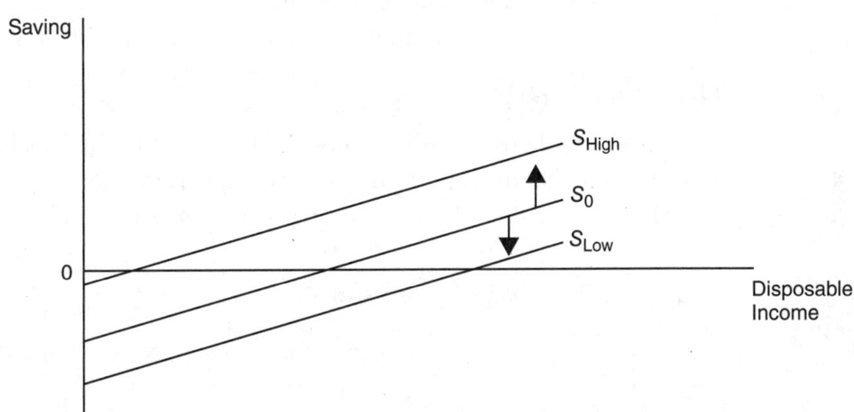

Figure 8.4

- With the exception of taxes and transfers, when the consumption function shifts upward, the saving function shifts downward.
- With the exception of taxes and transfers, when the consumption function shifts downward, the saving function shifts upward.
- When taxes increase (or transfers decrease), both consumption and saving functions shift downward.
- When taxes decrease (or transfers increase), both consumption and saving functions shift upward.

8.2 Investment

Main Topics: *Decision to Invest, Investment Demand, Investment and GDP, Market for Loanable Funds*

Investment is the other source of private domestic spending. We spend a little time examining why firms increase or decrease investment, build the investment demand curve, and then introduce the market for loanable funds.

Decision to Invest

The decision of a firm to spend money on new machinery or construction is simply a decision based on marginal benefits and marginal costs. The marginal benefit of an investment is the expected real rate of return (r) the firm anticipates receiving on the expenditure. The marginal cost of the investment is the real rate of interest (i), or the cost of borrowing. Let's look at this concept with examples.

Expected Real Rate of Return

A local pizza firm invests $10,000 in a new delivery car. The owner expects this to help to deliver more pizzas, increasing revenues and profits. The car lasts exactly one year, and increased real profits are anticipated to be $2,000. This expected real rate of return is $2,000/$10,000 = .20 or 20 percent. Of course an actual car lasts more than one year, but this decision to invest is shown for one year to keep it simple, while still making the point.

Real Rate of Interest

The owner goes to the bank and asks for a one-year loan to purchase the new delivery car. The bank offers a nominal rate of interest of 15 percent; this includes 5 percent for expected inflation and 10 percent as the real rate of borrowing the money for a year. At the end of the year, the owner spends $1,000 as real interest on the $10,000 loan.

The Decision

Since the new delivery car provides $2,000 in additional real profits ($r = 20\%$), and the loan costs $1,000 in real interest ($i = 10\%$), this investment should be made. Another way to make this decision is with a comparison of interest rates.

- If $r\% \geq i\%$, make the investment.
- If $r\% < i\%$, do not make the investment.

Investment Demand

Like any demand curve, the quantity demanded increases as the price falls. The same is true for investment demand. The rational firm invests in all projects up to the point where the real rate of interest equals the expected real rate of return ($i = r$). Very few investment projects are available at extremely high rates of return, and so those opportunities are taken first. As the real rate of return (r) falls, those very profitable opportunities are gone, but many less profitable investments remain. So as the expected real rate falls, the cumulative amount of investment dollars rises. Likewise, as the real cost of borrowing (i) falls, more and more projects become worthwhile, so dollars of investment rises. Either way, as interest rates fall, the total amount of investment rises. Figure 8.5 illustrates the **investment demand curve**, which shows the inverse relationship between the interest rate and the cumulative dollars invested. At an interest rate of 5 percent, $20 billion might be invested.

Investment and GDP

In the simple model of private investment outlined in Figure 8.5, there is no mention of GDP or disposable income. With no government or foreign sector, GDP = DI. To keep the model simple, we assume that investment spending (I) is determined from the investment demand curve and is constant at all levels of GDP.

Example:

In Figure 8.5 if the interest rate was 5%, firms would invest $20 billion this year, regardless of the level of disposable income or GDP. This **autonomous investment** is illustrated in Figure 8.6 as a horizontal line with GDP on the x-axis. If something happened to interest rates, or to investment demand, autonomous

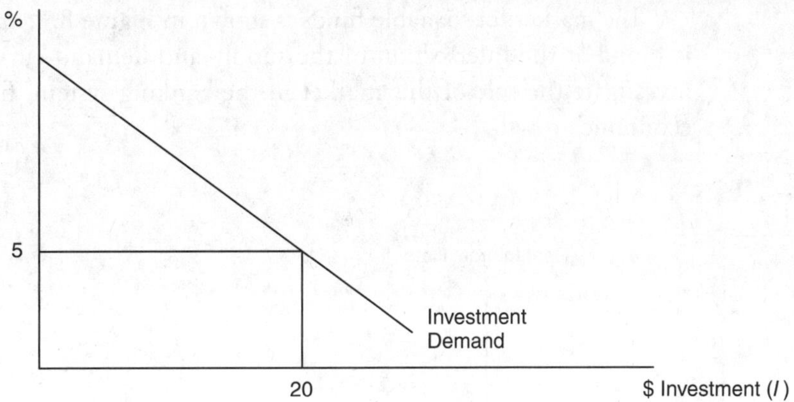

Figure 8.5

Figure 8.6

investment could increase or decrease but, at that new level, would once again be constant at any value of GDP.

Market for Loanable Funds

It is useful to see the relationship between saving and investment by looking at the **market for loanable funds.** When savers place their money in banks or buy bonds, those funds are available to be borrowed by firms for private investment.

Demand for Loanable Funds

The inverse relationship between investment and the real interest rate is fairly straightforward. As the real interest rate falls, borrowing becomes less costly, and large investment projects become more attractive to firms. This investment demand curve can also be thought of as a **demand for loanable funds,** and this demand is the result of the borrowing by private firms and the government.

Supply of Loanable Funds

The **supply of loanable funds** comes from saving on the part of households, both domestic and foreign. If disposable income is greater than consumption, this **private saving** exists and is positively related to the real interest rate.

The market for loanable funds is shown in Figure 8.7, and the equilibrium interest rate is found at the intersection of the supply and demand curves. In upcoming chapters, we investigate the role of this market in the banking system, fiscal and monetary policy, and economic growth.

"Make the connections between concepts learned in a previous chapter to what you are learning now, because everything is cumulative."
—Caroline, AP Student

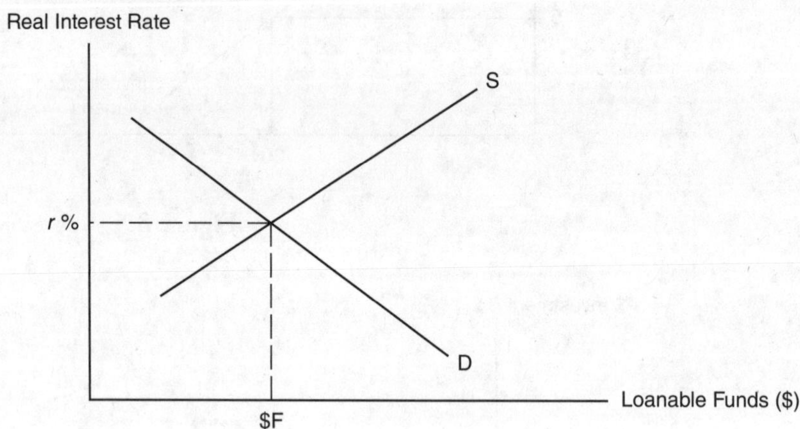

Figure 8.7

- The supply of loanable funds comes from saving and lending.
- The demand for loanable funds comes from investment and borrowing.
- Equilibrium is at the real interest rate where dollars saved equals dollars invested.

8.3 The Multiplier Effect

Main Topics: *Multiplier Effect and Spending Multiplier, Public and Foreign Sectors, Tax Multiplier, Balanced-Budget Multiplier*

The most simple circular flow consists solely of consumers and firms; in other words, GDP $= C + I$. But the public sector (G) and the foreign sector ($X - M$) are also important sources of domestic spending and income. The inclusion of these two sectors provides very little in the way of complications; they introduce the concept of the spending multiplier, the tax multiplier, and the balanced budget multiplier. This also paves the way for fiscal policy aimed at macroeconomic stability.

Multiplier Effect and Spending Multiplier

When you buy an ear of corn at the farmers' market, those dollars serve as income to several people. The farmers use those dollars to pay employees, to run their farm equipment, and to buy their own food. Farm employees use those wages to buy bacon, pay the rent, and many other goods and services. The circular flow explains how the injection of a few dollars of spending creates many more dollars of spending. Follow the dollars for a few rounds to see how it works. With the marginal propensity to consume (MPC) of .80, if households receive $1 of new income they spend $0.80 and save $0.20.

Round 1: Firms *increase* **investment spending by $10**, which acts as an injection of new money into the economy.

Round 2: The **$10** acts as income to resource suppliers (households) and with an MPC = .80, **households spend $8** and save $2.

Round 3: The **$8** of new consumption spending (*C*) is income for other households, and they spend 80 percent, or **$6.40**, and save $1.60.

Round 4: The **$6.40** of new *C* is income for other households, and they spend 80 percent, or **$5.12**, and save $1.28.

This process repeats. Each time the dollars circulate through the economy, 80 percent is spent and 20 percent is saved. After four rounds, there has been $10 + $8 + $6.40 + $5.12 = **$29.52 of new GDP**. The process continues until households are trying to consume 80 percent of virtually nothing and the increase in new GDP comes to an eventual stop.

This is called the **multiplier effect**. A change in any component of autonomous spending creates a larger change in GDP. The discussion of the "rounds" of spending earlier implies that the marginal propensities to consume and save play a critical role in determining the magnitude of the multiplier. There are two equivalent ways to calculate the multiplier if you know the MPC or MPS. The magnitude of the **spending multiplier** is found by taking a ratio:

$$\text{Multiplier} = 1/(1 - \text{MPC}) = 1/(1 - .80) = 5$$
$$\text{Since MPC} + \text{MPS} = 1,$$
$$\text{Multiplier} = 1/\text{MPS} = 1/.20 = 5.$$

The spending multiplier can be found by using one of the following equations:

- Multiplier = 1/MPS
- Multiplier = 1/(1 − MPC)
- Multiplier = (Δ GDP)/(Δ Spending)

Some common spending multipliers are as follows:

- MPC = .90, Multiplier = 1/.10 = 10
- MPC = .80, Multiplier = 1/.20 = 5
- MPC = .75, Multiplier = 1/.25 = 4
- MPC = .50, Multiplier = 1/.50 = 2

Public and Foreign Sectors

The inclusion of government spending (*G*) and net exports (*X* − *M*) act in the very same way as the change in investment illustrated in the preceding example.

Government Spending (*G*)

With the MPC = .80, we have found the spending multiplier equal to 5. If autonomous government spending is incorporated into the circular flow model, the multiplier effect is again felt throughout the economy. If *G* = $20, we could expect those $20 to multiply to $100 in new GDP.

Net Exports (*X* − *M*)

The final sector of the macroeconomy is the foreign sector. The addition or subtraction (if imports exceed exports) of autonomous net exports is an increase (or decrease) of dollars in the circular flow. Using a spending multiplier of 5, if $(X - M) = \$10$, GDP would increase by $50.

Tax Multiplier

The preceding discussion of the public sector shows that when the government injects money into the economy (G), it multiplies by a factor of the spending multiplier. But the government can also have an impact on aggregate expenditures and real GDP by changing taxes and/or transfers.

The Multiplier Effect

Recipients of a decrease in taxes treat it as an increase in disposable income. The typical household increases consumption by a factor of the MPC and increases saving by a factor of the MPS. It is important to keep in mind that less than 100 percent of this increase in disposable income circulates through the economy because most households save a proportion of it.

Example:

The MPC is equal to .90, and the government transfers back tax revenue to consumers by sending each taxpayer a $200 check. With an MPC = .90, $180 is consumed and $20 is saved. The multiplier process kicks in, but not on the entire $200, only on the consumed portion of $180. The multiplier being 1/.10 = 10, GDP increases by $1,800.

In other words, a $200 change in tax policy (a tax rebate in this case) caused an $1,800 change in real GDP. This tax multiplier (Tm) of 9 measures the magnitude of the multiplier process when there is a change in taxes.

"Remember that taxes will have a smaller multiplier than government spending!"
—Richard, AP Student

The Difference in Multipliers

With an MPC = .90, the spending multiplier is 10, but the tax multiplier is smaller, Tm = 9. Why? The spending multiplier begins to work as soon as there is a change in autonomous spending (C, I, G, net exports), but the tax multiplier must first go through a person's consumption function as disposable income. In that first "round" of spending, some of those injected dollars are leakages in the form of savings. In the earlier example, 10 percent of those injected dollars fail to be recirculated, and therefore, the final multiplier effect is smaller. The relationship between the spending multiplier and the tax multiplier (Tm) is as follows:

$$\text{Tm} = \text{MPC} \times (\text{Spending multiplier}) = .90 \times (1/.10) = 9 \text{ in our example}$$

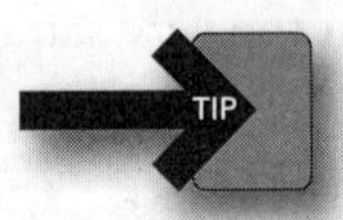

Be prepared to respond to a free-response question that asks you to explain why the tax multiplier is smaller than the spending multiplier.

Example:

The MPC = .80 and the government decides to impose a $50 increase in taxes. What happens to GDP?

$$\text{Tm} = .80 \times \text{Multiplier} = .80 \times (1/.20) = 4$$

Because the tax multiplier is equal to 4, we determine that GDP falls by $200. How do we know? Because taxes were *increased*, disposable income falls, and consumption falls, causing GDP to fall, in this case by a factor of 4.

The tax multiplier is found as follows:

- Tm = (Δ GDP)/(Δ taxes)
- Tm = MPC × M = MPC/MPS

Balanced-Budget Multiplier

The government both collects and spends tax revenue. In a simplified model, if the dollars spent equal the dollars collected, the budget is balanced. We have already discussed how the spending multiplier and tax multiplier are different. A quick example of a balanced budget policy illustrates what is called the **balanced-budget multiplier.**

Example:

The government wants to spend $100 on a federal program and pay for it by collecting $100 in additional taxes. The MPC = .90 in this example.

Spending Effect

The spending multiplier = 10 implies that the $100 of new spending ($G$) creates a $1,000 *increase* in real GDP.

Taxation Effect

The tax multiplier Tm = 9 implies that a $100 increase in taxes *decreases* real GDP by $900.

Balanced Budget Effect

Change in real GDP = +$1,000 − $900 = +$100

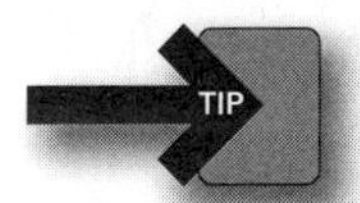

So a $100 increase in spending, financed by a $100 increase in taxes, created only $100 in new GDP. *The balanced-budget multiplier is always equal to 1, regardless of the MPC.*

- Balanced-budget multiplier = 1

❯ Review Questions

1. When disposable income increases by $X,

   (A) consumption increases by more than $X.
   (B) saving increases by less than $X.
   (C) saving increases by exactly $X.
   (D) saving remains constant.
   (E) saving decreases by more than $X.

2. Which of the following is true about the consumption function?

   (A) The slope is equal to the MPC.
   (B) The slope is equal to the MPS.
   (C) The slope is equal to MPC + MPS.
   (D) It shifts upward when consumers are more pessimistic about the future.
   (E) It shifts downward when consumer wealth increases in value.

3. Which of the following events most likely increases real GDP?

   (A) An increase in the real rate of interest
   (B) An increase in taxes
   (C) A decrease in net exports
   (D) An increase in government spending
   (E) A lower value of consumer wealth

4. Which of the following choices is most likely to create the greatest decrease in real GDP?
   (A) The government decreases spending, matched with a decrease in taxes.
   (B) The government increases spending with no increase in taxes.
   (C) The government decreases spending with no change in taxes.
   (D) The government holds spending constant while increasing taxes.
   (E) The government increases spending, matched with an increase in taxes.

5. The tax multiplier increases in magnitude when
   (A) the MPS increases.
   (B) the spending multiplier falls.
   (C) the MPC increases.
   (D) government spending increases.
   (E) taxes increase.

6. Which of the following is the source of the supply of loanable funds?
   (A) The stock market
   (B) Investors
   (C) Net exports
   (D) Banks and mutual funds
   (E) Savers

› Answers and Explanations

1. **B**—A \$1 increase in DI increases consumption by a factor of the MPC and increases saving by a factor of the MPS. Because both MPC and MPS represent the fraction of new income that is consumed and saved, consumption and saving increase by less than the increase in DI.
2. **A**—The slope of the consumption function is the MPC. The slope of the saving function is the MPS.
3. **D**—An increase in GDP is the result of an increase in *C*, *I*, *G*, or (*X* – *M*). All other choices represent less spending in some economic sector.
4. **C**—Look for choices that decrease GDP by the largest magnitude. Choices B and E actually improve the economy (and GDP), so they are eliminated. A decrease in spending lowers GDP by a magnitude equal to the spending multiplier, which is larger than the tax multiplier, which in turn is larger than the balanced budget multiplier. This question is a prelude to fiscal policy.
5. **C**—Knowing the relationship between the tax and spending multipliers allows you to make the right choice. Tm = MPC × Multiplier = MPC/MPS.
6. **E**—Banks help facilitate lending to investors, but the real supply of those loanable funds are the savers who choose to place some of their disposable income dollars in those banks as saving.

› Rapid Review

Disposable income (DI): The income a consumer has left over to spend or save once they have paid out net taxes. DI = *Y* – *T*.

Consumption function: A linear relationship showing how increases in disposable income cause increases in consumption.

Consumption and saving schedules: Tables that show the direct relationships between disposable income and consumption and saving. As DI increases for a typical household, *C* and *S* both increase.

Autonomous consumption: The amount of consumption that occurs no matter the level of disposable income. In a linear consumption function, this shows up as a constant and graphically it appears as the *y*-intercept.

Dissaving: Another way of saying that saving is less than zero. This can occur at low levels of disposable income when the consumer must liquidate assets or borrow to maintain consumption.

Saving function: A linear relationship showing how increases in disposable income cause increases in saving.

Autonomous saving: The amount of saving that occurs no matter the level of disposable income. In a linear saving function, this shows up as a constant, and graphically it appears as the *y*-intercept.

Marginal propensity to consume (MPC): The change in consumption caused by a change in disposable income, or the slope of the consumption function: MPC = $\Delta C/\Delta$DI.

Marginal propensity to save (MPS): The change in saving caused by a change in disposable income, or the slope of the saving function: MPS = $\Delta S/\Delta$DI.

Determinants of consumption and saving: Factors that shift the consumption and saving functions in the opposite direction are wealth, expectations, and household debt. The factors that change consumption and saving functions in the same direction are taxes and transfers.

Expected real rate of return (*r*): The rate of real profit the firm anticipates receiving on investment expenditures. This is the marginal benefit of an investment project.

Real rate of interest (*i*): The cost of borrowing to fund an investment. This can be thought of as the marginal cost of an investment project.

Decision to invest: A firm invests in projects as long as $r \geq i$.

Investment demand: The inverse relationship between the real interest rate and the cumulative dollars invested. Like any demand curve, this is drawn with a negative slope.

Autonomous investment: The level of investment determined by investment demand. It is autonomous because it is assumed to be constant at all levels of GDP.

Market for loanable funds: The market for dollars that are available to be borrowed for investment projects. Equilibrium in this market is determined at the real interest rate where the dollars saved (supply) is equal to the dollars borrowed (demand).

Demand for loanable funds: The negative relationship between the real interest rate and the dollars invested and borrowed by firms and by the government.

Supply of loanable funds: The positive relationship between the dollars saved and the real interest rate.

Private saving: Saving conducted by households and equal to the difference between disposable income and consumption.

Multiplier effect: Describes how a change in any component of aggregate expenditures creates a larger change in GDP.

Spending multiplier: The magnitude of the spending multiplier effect is calculated as Multiplier = (Δ GDP)/(Δ spending) = 1/MPS = 1/(1 − MPC).

Tax multiplier: The magnitude of the effect that a change in taxes has on real GDP. Tm = (Δ GDP)/(Δ taxes) = MPC × Multiplier = MPC/MPS.

Balanced-budget multiplier: When a change in government spending is offset by a change in lump-sum taxes, real GDP changes by the amount of the change in *G*; the balanced-budget multiplier is thus equal to 1.

Aggregate Demand and Aggregate Supply

"This is the bulk of the Macro exam—very important!"
—AP Teacher

IN THIS CHAPTER

Summary: Chapter 7 addressed three widely used measures of macroeconomic performance: real GDP, inflation, and unemployment. Economists have built upon the model of supply and demand for microeconomic markets to model an aggregate picture of the macroeconomy. The model of Aggregate Demand (AD) and Aggregate Supply (AS) have been extremely useful to predict how real GDP, employment, and the aggregate price level are affected by external factors and government policy. Before discussing macroeconomic policy, we first need to describe the AD/AS model.

Key Ideas

- Aggregate Demand (AD)
- Aggregate Supply (AS)
- Short-Run and Long-Run AS
- Macroeconomic Equilibrium
- The Inflation and Unemployment Trade-Off

9.1 Aggregate Demand (AD)

Main Topics: *What Is Aggregate Demand?, Components of AD, The Shape of AD, Changes in AD*

When we discussed microeconomic markets, we described the shape of any microeconomic demand curve with the Law of Demand, income, and substitution effects. Both effects work to change quantity demanded in the opposite direction of any price change.

What tends to be the case for the demand of a microeconomic good is also the case for AD but for different theoretical reasons.

What Is Aggregate Demand?

A microeconomic demand curve for peaches illustrates the relationship between the quantity of peaches demanded and the price of peaches. When economists aggregate all microeconomic markets to build AD, we include peaches and all other items that are domestically produced. **Aggregate demand** is the inverse relationship between all spending on domestic output and the aggregate price level of that output.

Components of AD

Demand in the macroeconomy comes from four general sources, and we have already seen these components when we described how total production is measured in the economy. In the previous chapter we defined real GDP as $= C + I + G + (X - M)$.

So AD measures, for any price level, the sum of consumption spending by households, investment spending by firms, government purchases of goods and services, and the net exports bought by foreign consumers.

The Shape of AD

When the price of peaches rises, consumers find another microeconomic good (with a lower relative price) to substitute for peaches, and this helps explain why the demand for peaches is downward sloping. But if the overall price level is rising, the prices of peaches, pears, and apples might all be rising. Remember that this aggregate price level is not the same as the price of one good relative to another. Where are the substitutes when the "good" we are discussing is a unit of real GDP? Macroeconomists describe three general groups of substitutes for national output:

- Goods and services produced in other nations (foreign sector substitution effect)
- Goods and services in the future (interest rate effect)
- Money and financial assets (wealth effect)

Foreign Sector Substitution Effect. When the price of U.S. output (as measured by the CPI or some other price index) increases, consumers naturally begin to look for similar items produced elsewhere. A Japanese computer, a German car, and a Mexican textile all begin to look more attractive when inflation heats up in the United States. The resulting increase in imports pushes real GDP down at a higher price level.

Interest Rate Effect. Remember that consumers have two general choices with their disposable income: they can consume it or they can save it for future consumption. If the aggregate price level rises, consumers might need to borrow more money for big-ticket items like autos or college tuition. When more and more households seek loans, the real interest rate begins to rise, and this increases the cost of borrowing. Firms postpone their investment in plant and equipment, and households postpone their consumption of more expensive items for a future when their spending might go further and borrowing might be more affordable. This wait-and-see mentality reduces current consumption of domestic production as the price level rises and real GDP falls.

Wealth Effect. Wealth is the value of accumulated assets like stocks, bonds, savings, and especially cash on hand. As the aggregate price level rises, the purchasing power of wealth and savings begins to fall. Higher prices therefore tend to reduce the quantity of domestic output purchased.

The combination of the foreign sector substitution, interest rate, and wealth effects predict a downward-sloping AD curve. For all three reasons, as the aggregate price level rises, consumption of domestic output (real GDP) falls along the AD curve. This is seen as a movement from points *a* to *b* in Figure 9.1. It should be noted that some textbooks label the horizontal axis as "Aggregate output." Basically, this is the same thing as real GDP, so don't sweat it.

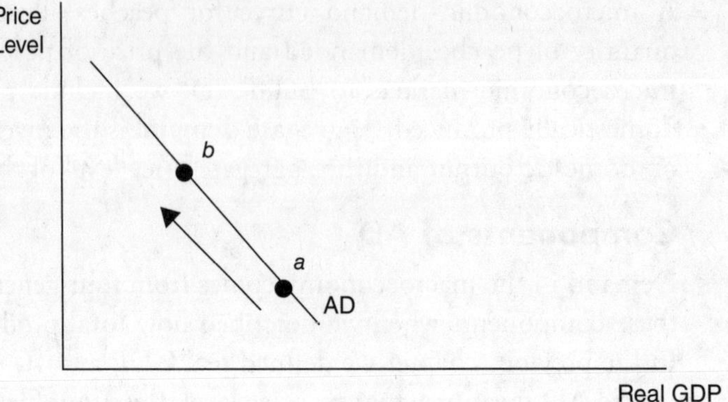

Figure 9.1

- Aggregate demand is not the vertical or horizontal summation of the demand curves for all microeconomic goods and services.
- AD is a model of how domestic purchasing changes when the aggregate price level changes.

Changes in AD

Since AD is the sum of the four components of domestic spending [*C, I, G,* (*X* – *M*)], if any of these components increases, holding the price level constant, AD increases, which increases real GDP. This is seen as a shift to the right of AD. If any of these components decreases, holding the price level constant, AD decreases, which decreases real GDP. This is seen as a shift to the left of AD. Figure 9.2 illustrates these shifts in AD.

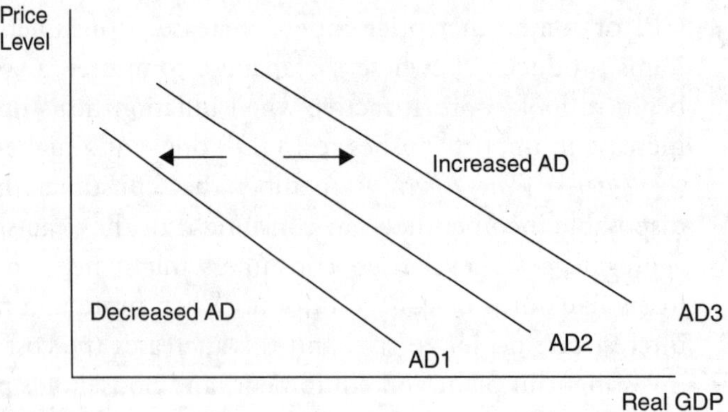

Figure 9.2

This is a preview for policy to manipulate the macroeconomy. If you want to stimulate real GDP and lower unemployment, you need to boost any or all of the components of AD. If you feel AD must slow down, you need to rein in the components of AD. Policies are tackled in more depth in the next chapter, but for now we'll take a quick look at some variables that can increase C, *I, G,* or (*X* – *M*).

Consumer Spending (C). If you put more money in the pockets of households, expect them to consume a great deal of it and save the rest. Consumers also increase their consumption if they are more optimistic about the future.

Investment Spending (I). Firms increase investment if they believe the investment will be profitable. This expected return on the investment is increased if investors are optimistic about the future profitability or if the necessary borrowing can be done at a low rate of interest.

Government Spending (G). The government injects money into the economy by spending more on goods and services, by reducing taxes, or by increasing transfer payments.

1. *Government spending* on goods and services acts as a direct increase in AD.
2. *Taxes and transfers.* Lowering taxes and increasing transfer payments increase AD through C by increasing DI.

Net Exports ($X - M$). When we sell more goods to foreign consumers and buy fewer goods from foreign producers, this component of AD increases.

1. *Foreign incomes.* Exports (X) increase with a strong Canadian, Mexican, or Brazilian economy. When foreign consumers have more disposable income, this increases the AD in the United States because those consumers spend some of that income on U.S.-made goods.
2. *Consumer tastes.* Consumer tastes and preferences, both foreign and domestic, are constantly changing. If American blue jeans become more popular in France, American AD increases. If French wines become more preferred by American consumers, AD in France increases.
3. *Exchange rates.* Imports (M) decrease when the exchange rate between the U.S. dollar and foreign currency falls. The model of foreign currency exchange is covered in a later chapter, but the idea is that foreign goods become relatively more expensive and so domestic consumers buy fewer foreign-produced items.

9.2 Aggregate Supply (AS)

Main Topics: *What Is Aggregate Supply?, Short-Run and Long-Run Shape of AS, Changes in AS*

Again, there are parallels between our coverage of supply in micro markets and aggregate supply. The law of supply describes the positive relationship between the micro price of a product and the quantity of that product that firms supply and is explained in part by increasing marginal cost as output rises. What tends to be the case for the supply of a micro good is also the case for AS but for different theoretical reasons.

What Is Aggregate Supply?

A microeconomic supply curve for salt illustrates the relationship between the price of salt and the quantity of salt supplied. When economists aggregate all microeconomic markets to build AS, we include salt and all other items that are domestically supplied. **Aggregate supply** is the relationship between the aggregate price level of all domestic output and the level of domestic output produced.

Short-Run and Long-Run Shape of AS

The model of AS and the resulting shape of the AS curve depend on whether the economy has fully adjusted to market forces and price changes.

Macroeconomic Short Run

In the **macroeconomic short run** period of time, the prices of goods and services are changing in their respective markets, but input prices have not yet adjusted to those product market changes. This lag between the increase in the output price and the increase in input prices gives us a shape of the short-run AS curve that is sometimes described in three stages. Figure 9.3 illustrates the stages of short-run AS.

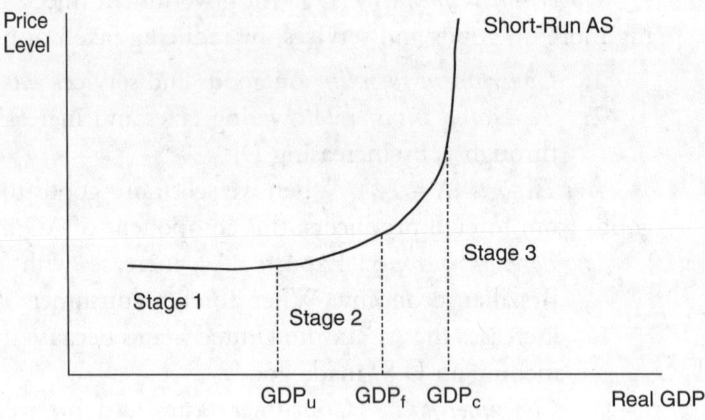

Figure 9.3

If the economy is in a recession with low production (GDP_u), there are many unemployed resources. Increasing output from this low level puts little pressure on input costs and subsequent minimal increase in the aggregate price level. The first stage of AS is drawn as almost horizontal. The Keynesian school of economics believes that when aggregate spending is extremely weak, the economy can be modeled in this way.

As real GDP increases in the second stage of AS and approaches full employment (GDP_f), available resources become more difficult to find, and so input costs begin to rise. If the price level for output rises at a faster rate than the rising costs, producers have a profit incentive to increase output. Most of the time the economy is operating in this upward-sloping range of AS, and so you see short-run AS (SRAS) commonly drawn with a positive slope.

If the economy grows and approaches the nation's productive capacity (GDP_c), firms cannot find unemployed inputs. Input costs and the price level rise much more sharply, and so in this third stage of AS, the curve is almost vertical.

Macroeconomic Long Run

The period known as the **macroeconomic long run** is long enough for input prices to have fully adjusted to market forces. Now all product and input markets are in equilibrium, and the economy is at full employment. In this long-run equilibrium, the AS curve is vertical at GDP_f. The classical school of economics asserts that the economy always gravitates toward full employment, so a cornerstone of classical macroeconomics is a vertical AS curve. Figure 9.4 illustrates the long-run AS (LRAS) curve.

- When drawing the AD/AS graph for a free-response question, it is *not* acceptable to label the vertical axis "P" or "$" and the horizontal axis "Q." You want to be *very* careful to use terms like "Aggregate price level" or "PL" on the vertical axis and "Real output" or "Real GDP" on the horizontal axis to earn these graphing points.

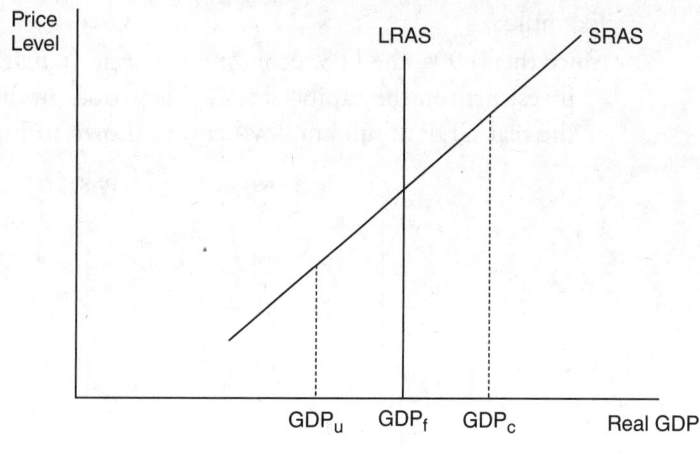

Figure 9.4

Changes in AS

In the short run, AS may fluctuate without changing the level of full employment. There are some factors, however, that can cause a fundamental shift in the long-run AS curve because they can change the level of output at full employment.

Short-Run Shifts

The most common factor that affects short-run AS is an economy-wide change in input (or factor) prices. Taxes, government policy, and short-term political or natural events can change the short-term ability of a nation to supply goods and services.

- *Input prices.* If input prices fall economy-wide, the short-run AS curve increases (shifting to the right) without changing the level of full employment.
- *Tax policy.* Some taxes are aimed at producers rather than consumers. If these "supply-side taxes" are lowered, short-run AS shifts to the right.
- *Deregulation.* In some cases, the regulation of industries can restrict their ability to produce (for good reasons in many cases). If these regulations are lessened, the short-run AS likely increases.
- *Political or environmental phenomena.* For a nation as large as the United States, wars and natural disasters can decrease the short-run AS without permanently decreasing the level of full employment. For a smaller nation or a large nation hit by an epic disaster, this could be a permanent decrease in the ability to produce.

Long-Run Shifts

There are a few main factors that affect both long-run and short-run AS and fundamentally affect the level of full employment in a nation's macroeconomy:

- *Availability of resources.* A larger labor force, larger stock of capital, or more widely available natural resources can increase the level of full employment.
- *Technology and productivity.* Better technology raises the productivity of both capital and labor. A more highly trained or educated populace increases the productivity of the labor force. These factors increase long-run AS over time.
- *Policy incentives.* Different national policies like unemployment insurance provide incentives for a nation's labor force to work. If policy provides large incentives to quickly find a job, full-employment real GDP rises. If government gives tax incentives to invest in capital or technology, GDP_f rises.

Example:

Since the 1990s, the U.S. economy has seen dramatic increases in technology and investment in the capital stock. This period produced a significant increase in the real GDP at full employment, as shown in Figure 9.5.

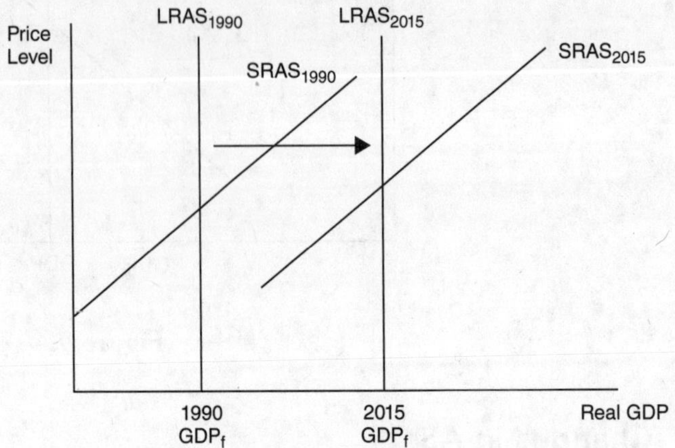

Figure 9.5

- When the LRAS curve shifts to the right, this indicates economic growth, just as an outward shift in the production possibility curve does.

9.3 Macroeconomic Equilibrium

Main Topics: *Equilibrium Real GDP and Price Level, Recessionary and Inflationary Gaps, Shifting AD, The Multiplier Again, Shifting SRAS, Classical Adjustment from Short-Run to Long-Run Equilibrium*

We use supply and demand models to predict changes in the prices and quantities of microeconomic goods and services. Now that we have built a model of aggregate demand and aggregate supply, we use similar analysis to predict changes in real GDP and the aggregate price level.

Equilibrium Real GDP and Price Level

When the quantity of real output demanded is equal to the quantity of real output supplied, the macroeconomy is said to be in equilibrium. Figure 9.6 illustrates **macroeconomic**

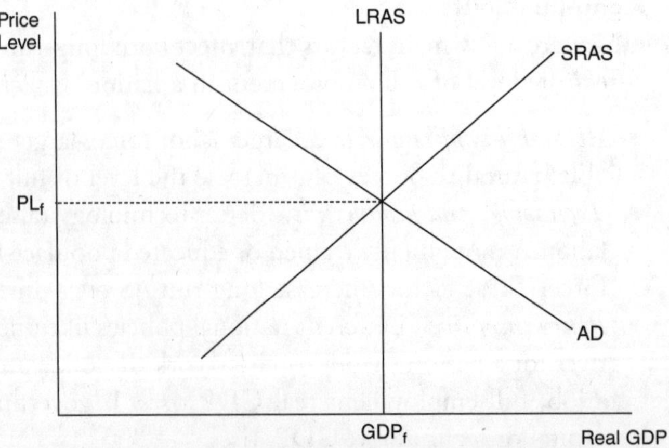

Figure 9.6

equilibrium at full employment GDP_f and price level PL_f at the intersection of AD, SRAS, and LRAS.

Recessionary and Inflationary Gaps

When the economy is in equilibrium, but not at the level of GDP that corresponds to full employment (GDP_f), the economy is experiencing either a recessionary or an inflationary gap. As the name implies, a **recessionary gap** exists when the economy is operating below GDP_f and the economy is likely experiencing a high unemployment rate. In Figure 9.7, the recessionary gap is the difference between GDP_f and GDP_r, or the amount that current real GDP must rise to reach GDP_f.

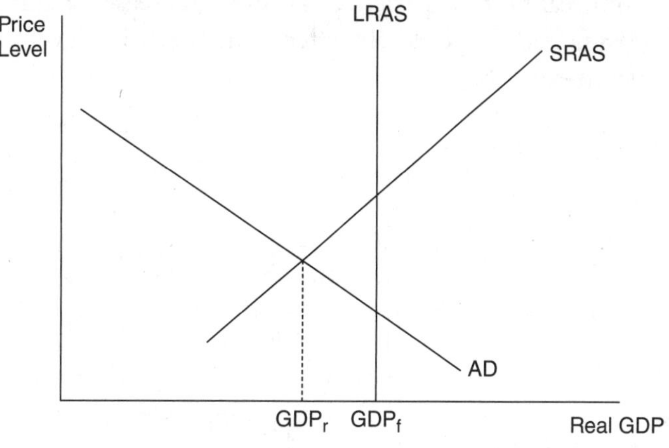

Figure 9.7

"Be able to locate these on a graph."
—AP teacher

An **inflationary gap** exists when the economy is operating above GDP_f. Because production is higher than GDP_f, a rising price level is the greatest danger to the economy. In Figure 9.8, the inflationary gap is the difference between GDP_i and GDP_f, or the amount that real GDP must fall to reach GDP_f.

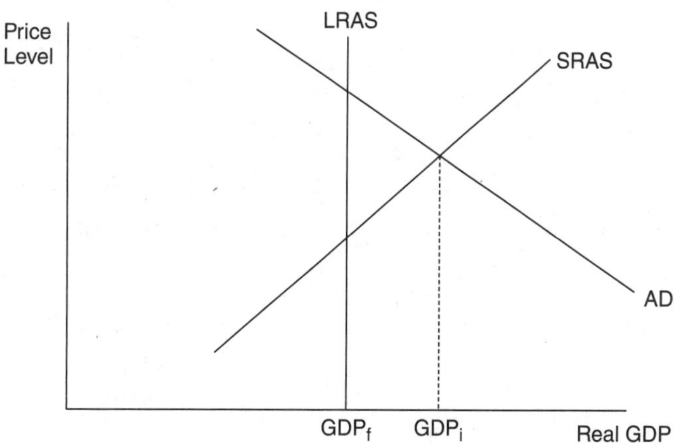

Figure 9.8

Shifting AD

Since you have mastered the microeconomic tools of supply and demand, you should have little trouble predicting how macroeconomic factors affect real GDP and the price level.

Shifts in AD

Let's assume again that the SRAS curve has three stages, nearly horizontal, upward sloping, and nearly vertical. The economy is currently in equilibrium but at a very low recessionary level of real GDP. If AD increases from AD_0 to AD_1 in the nearly horizontal range of SRAS, the price level may only slightly increase, while real GDP significantly increases and the unemployment rate falls.

If AD continues to increase to AD_2 in the upward-sloping range of SRAS, the price level begins to rise and inflation is felt in the economy. This **demand-pull inflation** is the result of rising consumption from all sectors of AD.

If AD increases much beyond full employment to AD_3, inflation is quite significant and real GDP experiences minimal increases. Figures 9.9, 9.10, and 9.11 illustrate how rising AD has different effects on the price level and real GDP in the three stages of short-run AS.

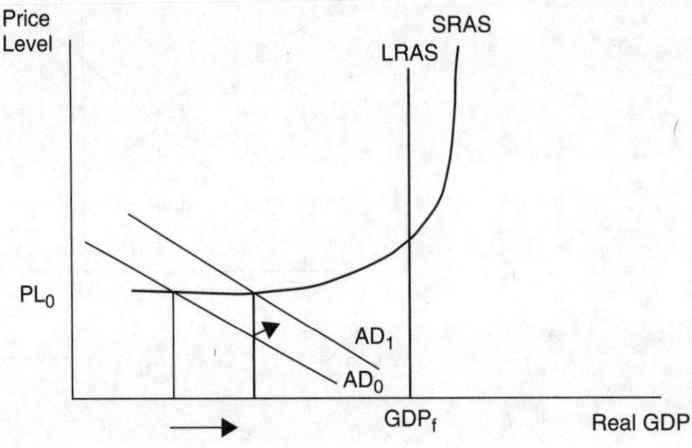

Figure 9.9

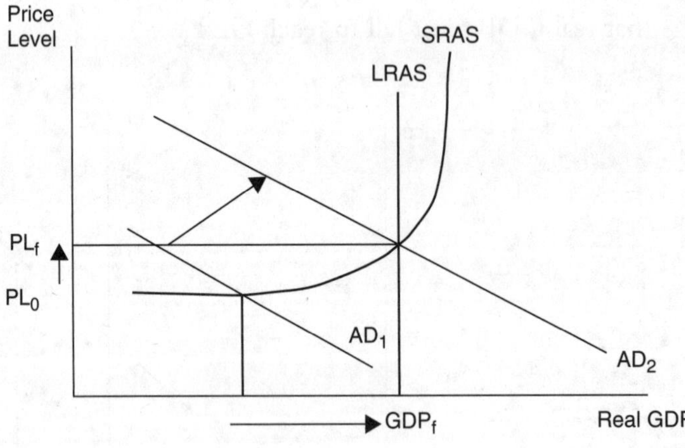

Figure 9.10

If aggregate demand weakens, we can expect the opposite effects on price level and real GDP. In fact, one of the most common causes of a recession is falling AD as it lowers real GDP and increases the unemployment rate. Inflation is not typically a problem with this kind of recession, as we expect the price level to fall, or **deflation**, with a severe decrease in AD. This is seen in Figure 9.12.

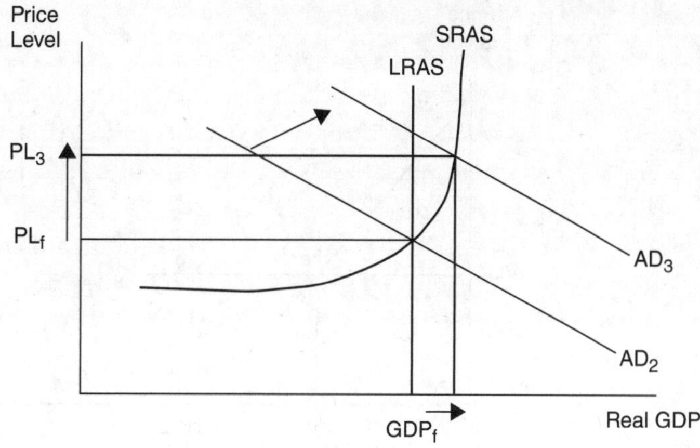

Figure 9.11

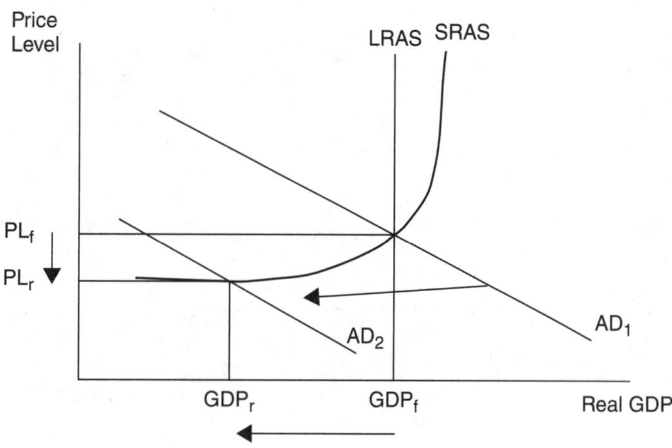

Figure 9.12

The Multiplier Again

One of the important topics of the previous chapter is the spending multiplier. When a component of autonomous spending increases by $1, real GDP increases by a magnitude of the multiplier. The full multiplier effect is only observed if the price level does not increase, and this only occurs if the economy is operating on the horizontal range of the SRAS curve. Figure 9.13 shows the full multiplier effect. (Note that the SRAS curve is likely a much smoother curve, but the multiplier effect can be illustrated more clearly with more linear segments.)

But what if the economy is operating in the upward-sloping range of SRAS? Figure 9.14 shows an identical rightward shift in AD. If there were no increase in the price level, the new equilibrium GDP would be at GDP_1, but with a rising price level, it is somewhat smaller at GDP_2. This means that the full multiplier effect is not felt because the rising price level weakens the impact of increased spending in the macroeconomy.

- The multiplier effect of an increase in AD is greater if there is no increase in the price level.
- The multiplier effect of an increase in AD is smaller if there is a larger increase in the price level.

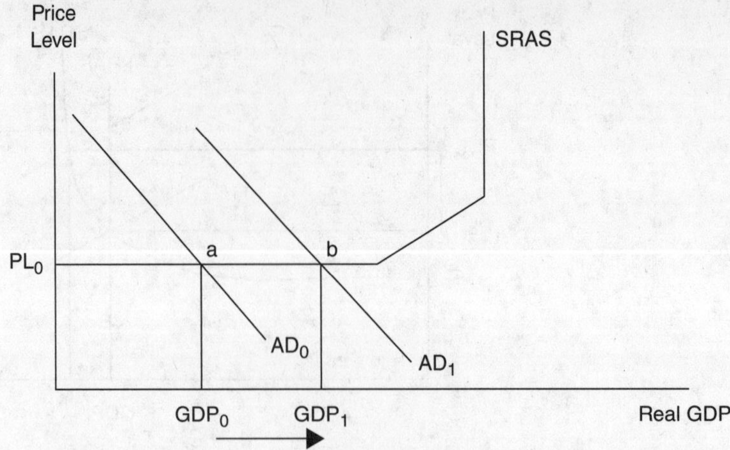

Figure 9.13

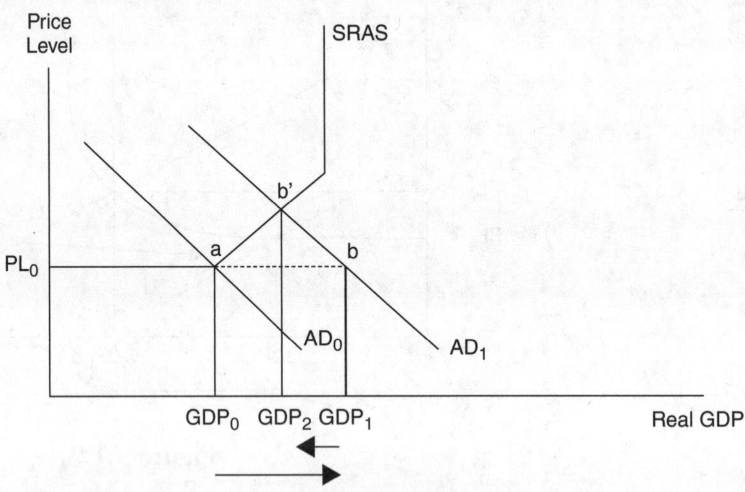

Figure 9.14

Shifting SRAS

The macroeconomy is currently in equilibrium at full employment. In Figure 9.15, we simplify the short-run aggregate supply curve by drawing only the upward-sloping segment (and this is the usual treatment of SRAS in the AP curriculum). If nominal input prices were to fall, the SRAS curve shifts to the right. Assuming that the AD curve stays constant, the price level falls, real GDP increases, and the unemployment rate falls. This kind of **supply-side boom** would seemingly be the best of all situations, though it is likely to only be temporary. When the economy is producing beyond GDP_f, eventually the high demand for production inputs will increase the prices of those inputs, shifting the SRAS curve back to the left and returning the economy to full employment.

If an increase in SRAS is the best of possible macroeconomic situations, a decrease in SRAS is one of the worst. Figure 9.16 shows that a decrease, or leftward shift, in SRAS creates inflation, lowers real GDP, and increases the unemployment rate. This **cost-push inflation**, or **stagflation**, creates very unpleasant economic conditions in the short run.

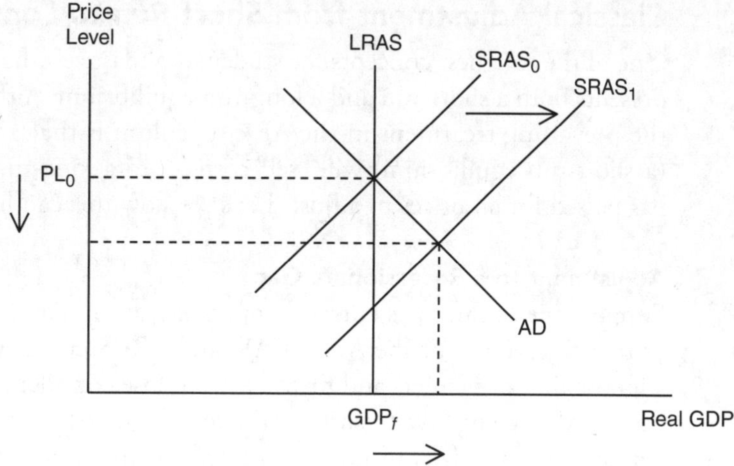

Figure 9.15

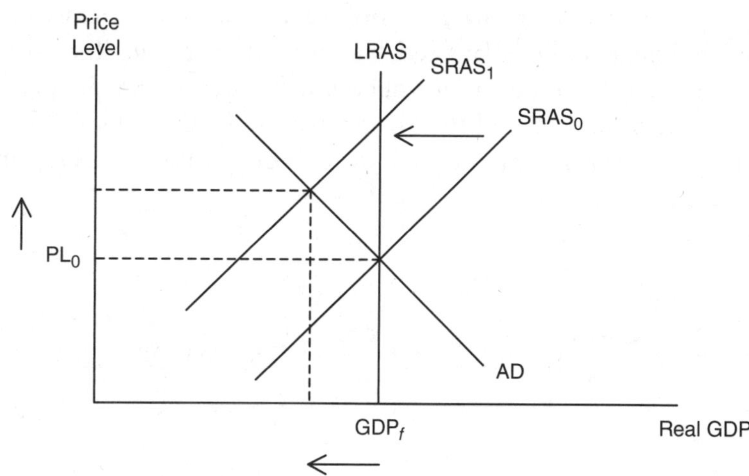

Figure 9.16

In the long run, however, the high unemployment should eventually relieve pressure on nominal input prices. When the input prices begin to fall, the SRAS shifts back to the right, returning the economy to full employment.

> "Make it easier for the graders and use flow charts to answer free-response questions instead of long essays." —Justine, AP Student

Supply Shocks

These shifts in SRAS are caused by events that are called **supply shocks**. A supply shock is an economy-wide phenomenon that affects the costs of firms, positively or negatively. Positive supply shocks might be the result of higher productivity or lower energy prices. Negative supply shocks usually occur when economy-wide input prices suddenly increase, like the OPEC oil embargoes of the 1970s or the Gulf War of 1990 to 1991 or the supply chain disruptions in the aftermath of the Covid-19 pandemic.

- ↑ AD causes ↑ real GDP, ↓ unemployment and ↑ price level.
- ↓ AD causes ↓ real GDP, ↑ unemployment and ↓ price level.
- ↑ SRAS causes ↑ real GDP, ↓ unemployment and ↓ price level.
- ↓ SRAS causes ↓ real GDP, ↑ unemployment and ↑ price level.

Classical Adjustment from Short-Run to Long-Run Equilibrium

One of the toughest concepts for students to master is the way in which the AD/AS model presents both a short-run and a long-run equilibrium. Although some economists disagree, the prevailing treatment in the AP curriculum is that a recessionary or inflationary gap (a short-run equilibrium) will "self-correct" to a long-run equilibrium once enough time has passed for all prices to adjust. Let's see how this can happen.

Adjustment to a Recessionary Gap

Suppose the economy is currently operating at full employment, as shown in Figure 9.17 at the intersection of the AD, SRAS, and LRAS curves with a real GDP of GDP_f. Now suppose that consumers and firms begin to lose confidence in the labor market and overall economy, causing AD to shift to the left. In the short run, this will cause a recessionary gap as real GDP falls to GDP_r (unemployment rises), and the aggregate price level falls from PL_1 to PL_2. Ignoring any kind of fiscal or monetary policy intervention (which we will discuss in the next two chapters), this short-run recessionary gap can self-correct. How does this happen?

One of the hallmarks of a recession is a decreased demand for many factors of production, like labor, steel, oil, and other commodities. This decreased demand for critical factors of production will eventually decrease the prices of those factors, causing a gradual rightward shift of the SRAS curve to $SRAS_2$. The SRAS curve shifts to the right until the recessionary gap is closed, the economy is back at GDP_f, and an even lower aggregate price level exists at PL_3.

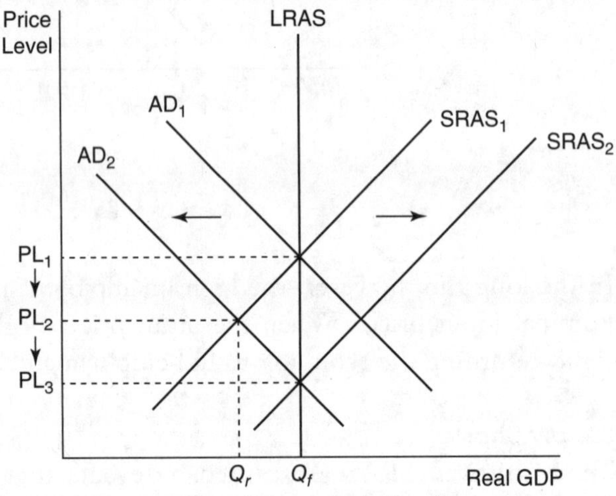

Figure 9.17

Adjustment to an Inflationary Gap

Let's begin again with long-run equilibrium at a real GDP of GDP_f. When we incorporate an increase in the AD curve, we create an inflationary gap. Figure 9.18 shows that this increase to AD_2 causes an increase in real GDP to GDP_i (a lower unemployment rate) and an increase in the aggregate price level to PL_2. How would this self-correct?

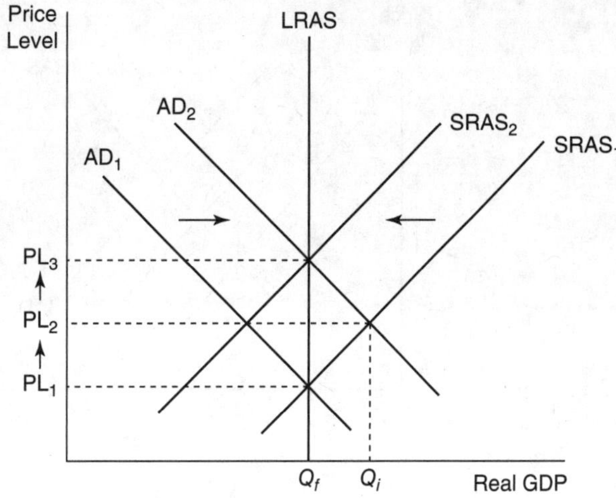

Figure 9.18

When the economy is really booming, there is stronger demand for labor and all of those other factors of production, and this causes factor prices to rise. As the factor prices rise, the SRAS curve begins to shift to the left to $SRAS_2$. Eventually, the inflationary gap is eliminated, and the economy is back in long-run equilibrium at GDP_f, though at an even higher aggregate price level of PL_3.

- Using the AD/AS model to show the long-run adjustment to equilibrium after a short-run shift in AD is a very common FRQ on the AP Macroeconomics exam.

9.4 The Trade-Off Between Inflation and Unemployment

Main Topics: *Short-Run Changes in AD, The Phillips Curve, The Long-Run Phillips Curve, Expectations*

Changes in AD and AS create changes in our main macroeconomic indicators of inflation and unemployment. Many economists have studied the relationship between inflation and unemployment, and this section provides a very brief overview of one prominent theory, the Phillips curve. We also take another look at the effects of supply shocks and expectations.

Short-Run Changes in AD

In the upward-sloping range of the SRAS curve, there is a positive relationship between the price level and output. If AD is rising, the price level and real GDP are both rising. Since rising real GDP creates jobs and lowers unemployment, we connect these points of equilibrium and show an inverse relationship between inflation and the unemployment rate. See Figure 9.19.

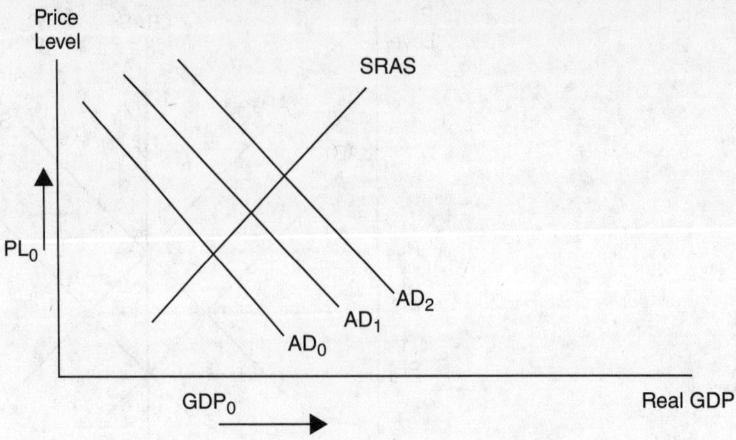

Figure 9.19

The Phillips Curve

The inverse relationship between inflation and the unemployment rate has come to be known as the Phillips curve and in the short-run is downward sloping. The short-run Phillips curve is drawn in Figure 9.20. Though Figure 9.20 does not show it, the possibility of deflation at extremely high unemployment rates means that the Phillips curve may actually continue falling below the *x*-axis.

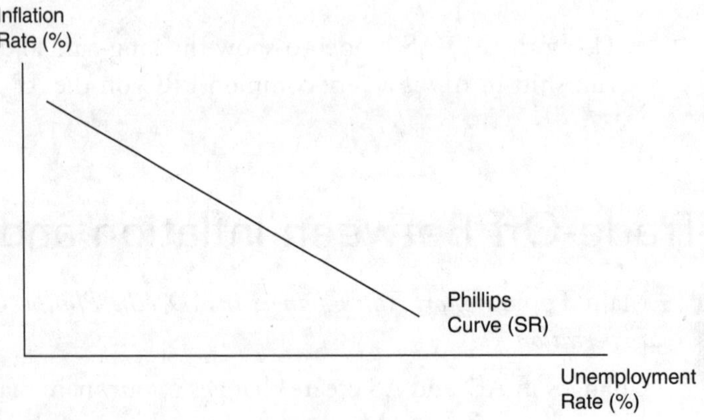

Figure 9.20

Supply Shocks and the Phillips Curve

We saw that when SRAS shifts to the right, holding AD constant, both the price level and unemployment rate fall. On the other hand, when SRAS shifts to the left, we get stagflation because inflation and unemployment rates are both rising. Figure 9.21 shows how supply shocks shift the Phillips curve inward when SRAS shifts to the right and outward when SRAS shifts to the left.

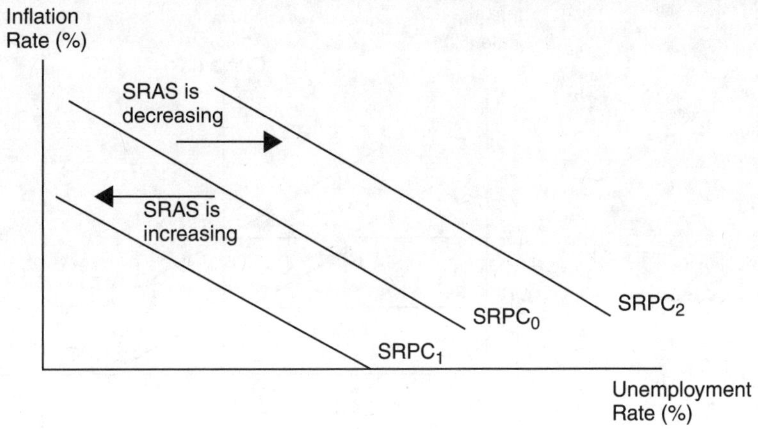

Inflation Rate (%)

SRAS is decreasing

SRAS is increasing

$SRPC_2$

$SRPC_0$

$SRPC_1$

Unemployment Rate (%)

Figure 9.21

The Long-Run Phillips Curve

The AD and AS model presumes that the long-run AS curve is vertical and located at full employment. As a result, the Phillips curve in the long run is also vertical at the natural rate of employment. You might recall that the natural rate of employment is the unemployment rate where cyclical unemployment is zero. Suppose this occurs at a measured unemployment rate of 4 percent. Figure 9.22 illustrates the long-run Phillips curve.

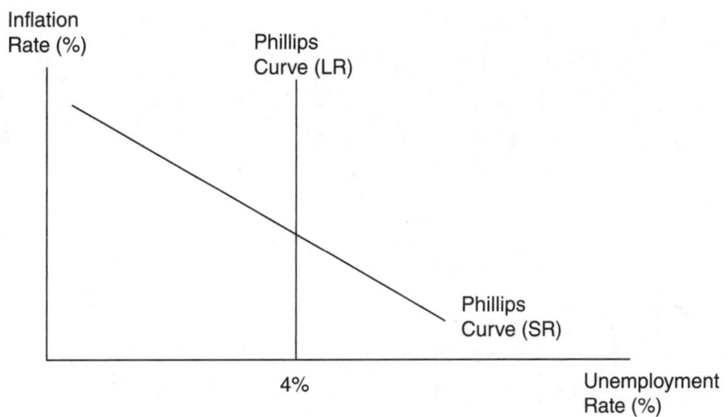

Figure 9.22

Expectations

The idea that there is, in the short term, an inverse relationship between inflation and unemployment and, in the long term, unemployment is always at the natural rate can be confusing. The reason is that sometimes a gap exists between the actual rate of inflation and the expected rate of inflation. Inflationary expectations play a role here in the derivation of the long-run Phillips curve. Figure 9.23 illustrates this concept with an example.

The expected inflation rate is 2 percent at a 4 percent natural rate of unemployment (point *a*). If AD unexpectedly rises, this drives up the rate of inflation to 5 percent, and as a result, firms are earning higher profits. Firms respond with more hiring, and this temporarily drops the unemployment rate to 2 percent (point *b*). This is seen as a movement along the short-run PC above from *a* to *b*.

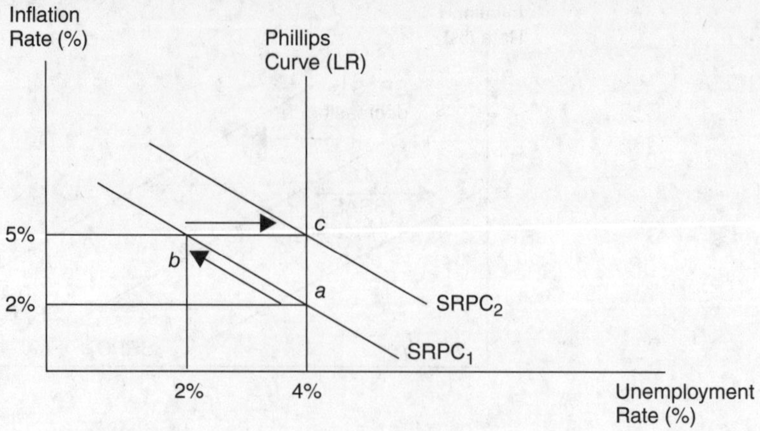

Figure 9.23

The point at 5 percent inflation and 2 percent unemployment will not last. Workers realize that their real wages are falling and insist on a raise! As wages rise, the profits of firms begin to fall, and so too does employment back to the natural rate of 4 percent (point *c*). At this point both actual and expected inflation is 5 percent. Another short-run Phillips curve runs through this point. Points *a* and *c* must lie on one long-run Phillips curve, and that curve must be vertical. The process can repeat itself if AD continues to increase, or it can reverse itself if AD falls. You might notice that this adjustment from a point on the SRPC back to the LRPC follows the adjustment from a short-run equilibrium to the long-run equilibrium in the AD/AS model.

What happens if citizens and firms expect a higher rate of inflation than the actual rate? Expecting higher prices in the future, consumers and firms increase purchasing now and AD increases, which serves to increase the price level. The expectation in this case is really a self-fulfilling prophecy.

› Review Questions

1. Using the model of AD and AS, what happens in the short run to real GDP, the price level, and unemployment with more consumption spending (*C*)?

	REAL GDP	PRICE LEVEL	UNEMPLOYMENT
(A)	Increases	Decreases	Decreases
(B)	Decreases	Increases	Increases
(C)	Increases	Increases	Decreases
(D)	Decreases	Decreases	Decreases
(E)	Decreases	Decreases	Increases

2. Which is the best way to describe the AS curve in the long run?

(A) Always vertical in the long run.
(B) Always upward sloping because it follows the Law of Supply.
(C) Always horizontal.
(D) Always downward sloping.
(E) Upward sloping at low levels of aggregate output and downward sloping at higher levels of aggregate output.

3. Stagflation most likely results from

(A) increasing AD with constant SRAS.
(B) decreasing SRAS with constant AD.
(C) decreasing AD with constant SRAS.
(D) a decrease in both AD and SRAS.
(E) an increase in both AD and SRAS.

4. Equilibrium real GDP is far below full employment, and the government lowers household taxes. Which is the likely result?
   (A) Unemployment falls with little inflation.
   (B) Unemployment rises with little inflation.
   (C) Unemployment falls with rampant inflation.
   (D) Unemployment rises with rampant inflation.
   (E) No change occurs in unemployment or inflation.

5. What is the difference between the short-run Phillips curve (SRPC) and the long-run Phillips curve (LRPC)?
   (A) The SRPC is downward sloping and the LRPC is horizontal.
   (B) The SRPC is upward sloping and the LRPC is downward sloping.
   (C) The SRPC is vertical and the LRPC is horizontal.
   (D) The SRPC is downward sloping and the LRPC is vertical.
   (E) The SRPC is downward sloping and the LRPC is upward sloping.

6. The effect of the spending multiplier is lessened if
   (A) the price level is constant with an increase in aggregate demand.
   (B) the price level falls with an increase in aggregate supply.
   (C) the price level is constant with an increase in long-run aggregate supply.
   (D) the price level falls with an increase in both aggregate demand and aggregate supply.
   (E) the price level rises with an increase in aggregate demand.

› Answers and Explanations

1. **C**—An increase in consumption spending increases the AD curve, or shifts it to the right. Along the SRAS curve, we see increasing real GDP, a rising aggregate price level, and a lower unemployment rate.

2. **A**—All resources are employed at full employment in the long run, so firms cannot respond to an increase in the price level by increasing production. Thus, any increase in prices cannot increase production in the long run, and so AS is assumed to be vertical. Any short-run discrepancy in GDP, above or below, full employment adjusts back to GDP_f in the long run.

3. **B**—Stagflation is an increase in the price level and an increase in unemployment. This is most often the result of falling SRAS and a constant AD. Choice D is incorrect because a simultaneous decrease in AD puts downward pressure on the price level, which offsets the upward pressure from falling SRAS.

4. **A**—A deep recession describes macroeconomic equilibrium in the horizontal section of SRAS. Here, rising AD increases real GDP, and lowers unemployment, with little inflation.

5. **D**—The short-run Phillips curve shows an inverse relationship between inflation rates and unemployment rates but the long-run Phillips curve is vertical at the natural rate of unemployment.

6. **E**—The full spending multiplier effect of an increase in AD is felt only if there is no rise in the price.

› Rapid Review

Aggregate demand (AD): The inverse relationship between all spending on domestic output and the aggregate price level of that output. AD measures the sum of consumption spending by households, investment spending by firms, government purchases of goods and services, and net exports (exports minus imports).

Foreign sector substitution effect: When the aggregate price of U.S. output increases, consumers naturally begin to look for similar items produced elsewhere.

Interest rate effect: If the aggregate price level rises, consumers and firms might need to borrow more money for spending and capital investment, which increases the interest rate and delays current consumption. This postponement reduces current consumption of domestic production as the price level rises.

Wealth effect: As the aggregate price level rises, the purchasing power of wealth and savings begins to fall. Higher prices therefore tend to reduce the quantity of domestic output purchased.

Determinants of AD: AD is a function of the four components of domestic spending: *C*, *I*, *G*, and ($X - M$). If any of these components increases (decreases), holding the others constant, AD increases (decreases), or shifts to the right (left).

Short-run aggregate supply (SRAS): The positive relationship between the level of domestic output produced and the aggregate price level of that output.

Macroeconomic short run: A period of time during which the prices of goods and services are changing in their respective markets, but the input prices have not yet adjusted to those changes in the product markets. In the short run, the SRAS curve is typically drawn as upward sloping.

Macroeconomic long run: A period of time long enough for input prices to have fully adjusted to market forces. In this period, all product and input markets are in a state of equilibrium and the economy is operating at full employment (GDP_f). Once all markets in the economy have adjusted and there exists this long-run equilibrium, the LRAS curve is vertical at GDP_f.

Determinants of AS: AS is a function of many factors that impact the production capacity of the nation. If these factors make it easier, or less costly, for a nation to produce, AS shifts to the right. If these factors make it more difficult, or more costly, for a nation to produce, AS shifts to the left.

Macroeconomic equilibrium: Occurs when the quantity of real output demanded is equal to the quantity of real output supplied. Graphically this is at the intersection of AD and SRAS. Equilibrium can exist at, above, or below full employment.

Recessionary gap: The amount by which full-employment GDP exceeds equilibrium GDP.

Inflationary gap: The amount by which equilibrium GDP exceeds full-employment GDP.

Demand-pull inflation: This inflation is the result of stronger consumption from all sectors of AD as it continues to increase in the upward-sloping range of SRAS. The price level begins to rise, and inflation is felt in the economy.

Recession: In the AD and AS model, a recession is typically described as falling AD with a constant SRAS curve. Real GDP falls far below full employment levels and the unemployment rate rises.

Deflation: A sustained falling price level, usually due to severely weakened aggregate demand and a constant SRAS.

Supply-side boom: When the SRAS curve shifts outward and the AD curve stays constant, the price level falls, real GDP increases and the unemployment rate falls.

Stagflation: A situation in the macroeconomy when inflation and the unemployment rate are both increasing. This is most likely the cause of falling SRAS while AD stays constant.

Supply shocks: A supply shock is an economy-wide phenomenon that affects the costs of firms and the position of the SRAS curve, either positively or negatively.

Phillips curve: A graphical device that shows the relationship between inflation and the unemployment rate. In the short run it is downward sloping, and in the long run it is vertical at the natural rate of unemployment.

Fiscal Policy, Economic Growth, and Productivity

IN THIS CHAPTER

Summary: The model of AD and AS is a useful mechanism for looking at how the macroeconomy can be deliberately expanded, or contracted, by the government. **Fiscal policy** measures include government spending and tax collection to affect economic output, unemployment, and the price level. We use graphical analysis to show how fiscal policy attempts to move the economy to full employment and also discuss some of the ways in which fiscal policy is less effective than predicted by theory. This chapter concludes with a discussion of economic growth and productivity and how policy might affect growth.

Key Ideas

- Fiscal Policy
- Budget Deficits and Crowding Out
- Economic Growth
- Productivity and Supply-Side Policy

10.1 Expansionary and Contractionary Fiscal Policy

Main Topics: *Expansionary Fiscal Policy, Contractionary Fiscal Policy, Deficits and Surpluses, Automatic Stabilizers*

This section of the chapter uses AD and AS to illustrate how fiscal policy can work in theory. Fiscal policy stresses the importance of a hands-on role for government in manipulating AD to "fix" the economy. Difficulties in fiscal policy and the supply-side perspective are addressed in the following section.

Expansionary Fiscal Policy

When the economy is suffering a recession, real GDP is low and unemployment is high. In the AD and AS model, a recessionary equilibrium is located below full employment, as shown in Figure 10.1. If the government increases its spending or lowers net taxes, the AD curve increases. *Net taxes*, if you recall, are tax revenues minus transfer payments. Of course, if the government is using tax cuts, rather than government spending, to expand the economy, the multiplier is smaller, so to get the same increase in real GDP, the size of the tax cut must be larger than an increase in government spending.

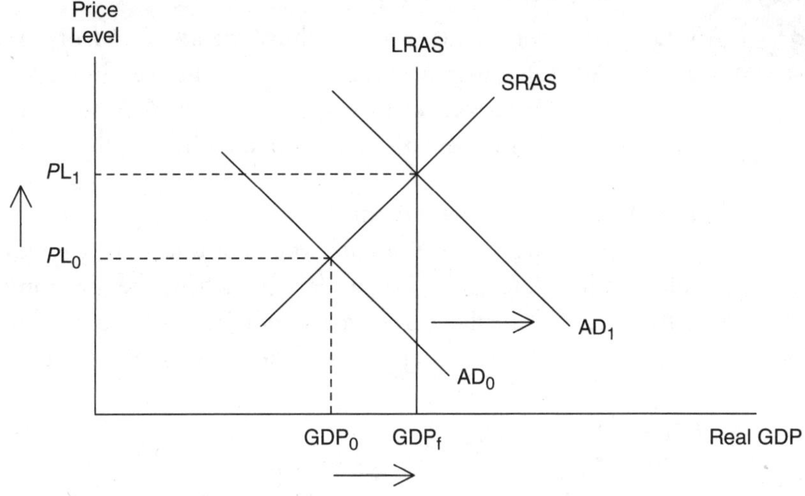

Figure 10.1

Contractionary Fiscal Policy

If the economy is operating beyond full employment and inflation is becoming a problem, the government might need to contract the economy. This inflationary equilibrium is seen beyond full employment, as shown in Figure 10.2. This can be done by decreasing government spending or by increasing net taxes, both of which cause a leftward shift in AD. The economy should see a little decrease in real GDP but ideally a substantial decrease in the rate of inflation.

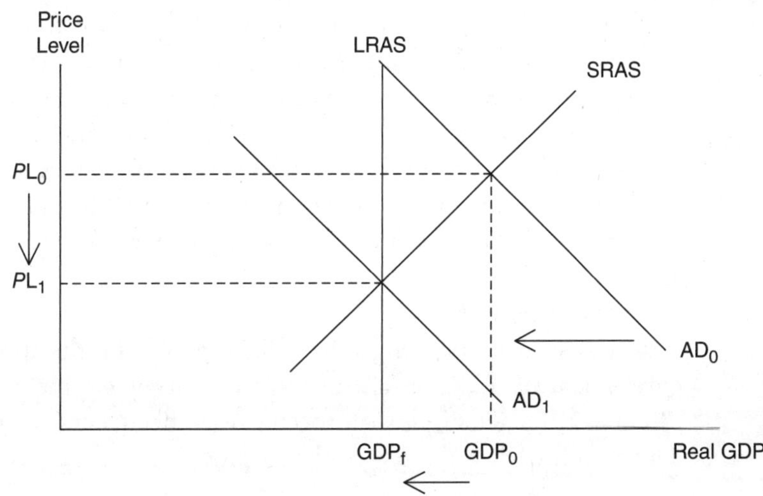

Figure 10.2

Are Prices Sticky?

Do prices fall, as Figure 10.2 seems to indicate? One of the points of contention is whether the price level can fall. Many economists (Keynesians) predict that prices are fairly inflexible, or "sticky" in the downward direction, so efforts to fight inflation are really efforts to slow inflation, not to actually lower the price level. Conversely, Classical school economists believe that the long-run economy naturally adjusts to full employment, and so they see the AS curve as vertical. This argument implies that prices are flexible and can rise and fall, as seen in Figure 10.2.

Deficits and Surpluses

When the government starts to adjust spending and/or taxation, there is an effect on the budget. A **budget deficit** exists if government spending exceeds the revenue collected from taxes in a given period of time, usually a year. A **budget surplus** exists if the revenue collected from taxes exceeds government spending.

The Difference Between Deficit and Debt

An annual budget deficit occurs when, in one year, the government spends more than is collected in tax revenue. To pay for the deficit, the government must borrow funds. When deficits are an annual occurrence, a nation begins to accumulate a **national debt**. The national debt is therefore an accumulation of the borrowing needed to cover past annual deficits.

Expansionary Policy

If the economy is in a recession, the appropriate fiscal policy is to increase government spending or lower taxes. When the government spends more, or collects less tax revenue, budget deficits are likely. There are two ways to finance the deficit, and each has the potential to weaken the expansionary policy:

- *Borrowing*. If a household wants to spend beyond its means, it enters the market for loanable funds as a borrower. The borrowed funds provide a short-term ability to purchase goods and services, but they must be paid back, with interest, when the loan is due. The same is true when the government borrows, but when an entity as large as the federal government is borrowing from the banking system, the public, or foreign lenders, in the form of Treasury bonds, it increases the demand for loanable funds. This, in turn, increases the real rate of interest and reduces the quantity of funds available for private investment opportunities. So what? Well, if the goal is to expand the macroeconomy, then borrowing to finance the deficit slows down the expansion by increasing interest rates. This **crowding-out effect** is examined in the next section of this chapter.
- *Creating money*. The creation of new money to fund a deficit can avoid the higher interest rates caused by borrowing. The primary disadvantage of creating more money is the risk of inflation, which can also lessen the effectiveness of expansionary fiscal policy. The effect that inflation has on the multiplier was illustrated in the previous chapter, and more detailed effects of expanding the money supply are looked at in the next chapter.

Contractionary Policy

If the economy is operating above full employment, the appropriate fiscal policy is to lower government spending or raise taxes. When the government spends less, or collects more tax revenue, a budget surplus can occur. The effectiveness of the contractionary fiscal policy depends on what is done with the surplus.

- *Pay down debt*. If the government pays down debt and retires bonds ahead of schedule, the demand for loanable funds decreases, decreasing interest rates. Lower interest rates stimulate investment and consumption, which counters the contractionary fiscal policy and lessens the downward effects on the price level.

- *Do nothing*. By making regularly scheduled payments on Treasury bonds and retiring them on schedule, idle surplus funds are removed from the economy. By not allowing these funds to be recirculated through the economy, the anti-inflationary fiscal policy can be more effective.

Automatic Stabilizers

An **automatic stabilizer** is anything that increases a deficit during a recessionary period and increases a budget surplus during an inflationary period, without any discretionary change on the part of the government. There are some mechanisms built into the tax system that automatically regulate, or stabilize, the macroeconomy as it moves through the business cycle by changing net taxes collected by the government.

Progressive Taxes and Transfers

When the economy is booming and GDP is increasing, more and more households and firms begin to fall into higher and higher tax brackets. This means that a larger percentage of income is taken as income tax, which slows down the consumption of both households and firms. In addition, a strong economy reduces the need for such transfer payments as unemployment insurance and welfare. Thus, net taxes increase with GDP. Our progressive tax system is therefore contractionary when the economy is very strong. By automatically putting the brakes on spending, this reduces the threat of inflation and contributes to a budget surplus.

When the economy is suffering a recession and GDP is falling, households and firms find themselves in lower tax brackets. With a smaller percentage of income being taken as income tax, this provides a way for more consumption than would have been possible at the higher tax rate. Simultaneously, a weak economy increases the need for transfer payments like welfare payments. Thus, net taxes decrease with GDP. When the economy is sluggish, the progressive tax system is expansionary in nature. The lower tax brackets soften the effect of a recession and contribute to a deficit.

Figure 10.3 shows how, for a given level of government spending, net taxes rise and fall with GDP. These automatically reduce the threat of inflation when the economy is strong (GDP_i) and reduce the negative effects of a recession when the economy is weak (GDP_r). Ideally, at full employment (GDP_f), the budget should be balanced.

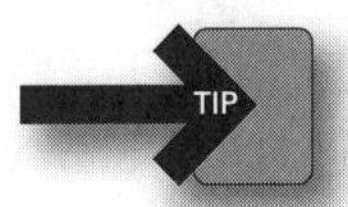

- Automatic stabilizers lessen, but do not eliminate, the business cycle swings.
- Automatic stabilizers lead to deficits during recession and surpluses during economic growth.

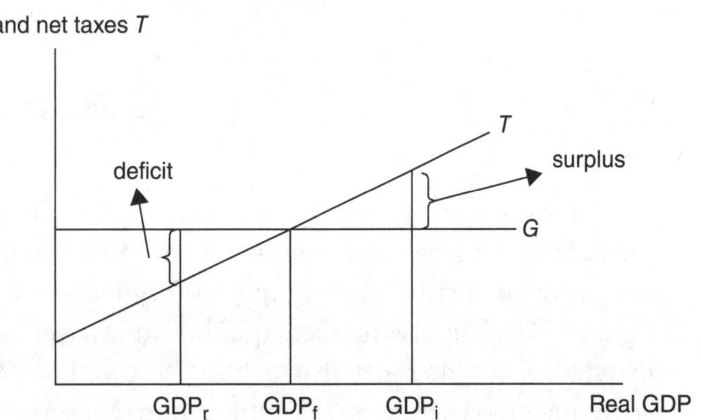

Figure 10.3

10.2 Difficulties of Fiscal Policy

Main Topics: *Crowding Out, Net Export Effect, State and Local Policies*

In theory, aggregate demand can be expanded or contracted, with government spending and/or taxes, to move the economy closer to full employment. In practice, there are some factors that lessen the effectiveness of fiscal policy. There are also some economists who disagree on fiscal policy targets.

Crowding Out

If the government must borrow funds to pay for expansionary fiscal policy, the government has an effect on the market for loanable funds. The market for loanable funds was introduced earlier in this text, and you might recall that public borrowing (in the form of a budget deficit) affects the demand for loanable funds. A government deficit increases the total demand for loanable funds but, by raising the real interest rate, reduces the quantity of loanable funds available to the private borrowers and investors. Less investment spending on capital goods is likely to reduce a nation's growth rate, a topic we'll explore at the end of this chapter.

"Crowding out is an important concept that may get asked more than once."
—AP Teacher

Figure 10.4 shows how a government budget deficit affects the demand for loanable funds and how we see crowding out. At the initial equilibrium, the real interest rate is 5%, the government has a balanced budget, and \$100 billion is being saved by households and invested by firms.

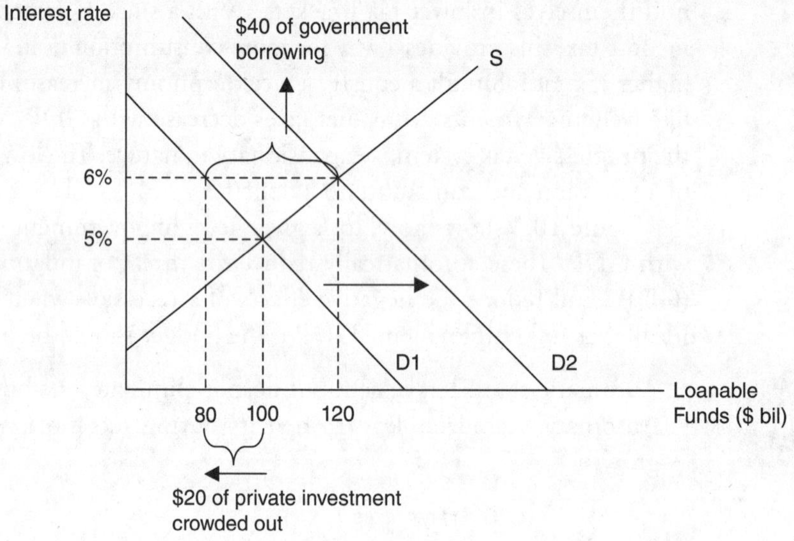

Figure 10.4

Now suppose that government fiscal policy creates a \$40 billion budget deficit. To cover the deficit, the government must borrow \$40 billion in the market for loanable funds. The new demand curve (D2) is simply the original demand curve, only it lays \$40 billion to the right of D1. The new market equilibrium interest rate is 6%, and \$120 billion is saved and invested. But remember that of this \$120 billion, \$40 billion is due to borrowing by the government. That leaves \$80 billion in **private** borrowing and investment. So the government budget deficit caused private borrowing and investment to fall from \$100 billion to \$80 billion, and that is where we see the crowding out of \$20 billion in private investment.

To see the full impact of crowding out, let's go back to a horizontal SRAS curve that depicts a severe recession. Ideally, expansionary fiscal policy would increase output from GDP_0 to GDP_1. When the interest rate increases, households and firms are **crowded out** of the market for loanable funds. This decrease in *C* and *I* dampens the effect of expansionary fiscal policy. The crowding out is seen in Figure 10.5 as a movement from AD_1 to AD_2.

As we saw in Chapter 9, if increases in AD continue into the upward-sloping range of AS, some of the multiplier effect of the fiscal policy is consumed by inflation, and thus, it is less effective.

When the government is fighting inflation with contractionary policy, we are likely to see the opposite of the crowding-out problem. If a budget surplus is the result of the contractionary policy, and government debt is retired, the demand for loanable funds decreases, interest rates fall and private investment increases ("crowding in," perhaps), thus lessening the impact of contractionary fiscal policy.

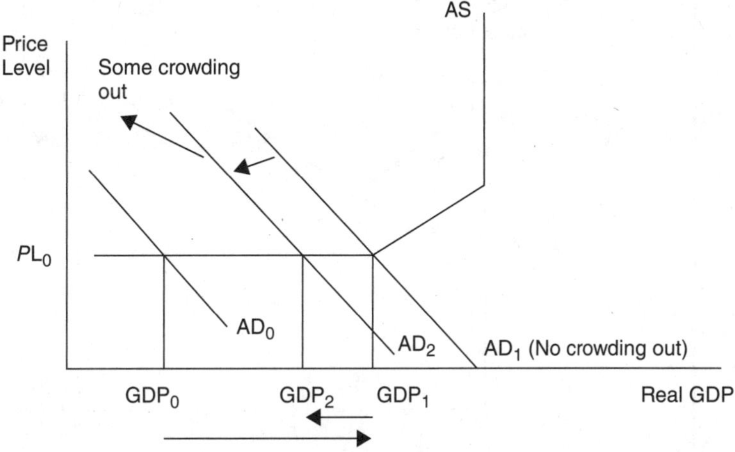

Figure 10.5

Another Way of Looking at Crowding Out

There are two different ways to show how a government budget deficit affects the market for loanable funds and crowds out private investment. I know that can be frustrating, but, hey, that's macro for you! Luckily, the outcomes are the same, and each approach is considered correct on the AP Macroeconomics exam.

The fundamental difference in these approaches is where the loanable funds model places the government. In the model presented, government borrowing (or saving, if there is a budget surplus) resides in the demand curve. Most textbooks use this approach. The demand curve represents the total of all of the private investing and borrowing (from firms) and public borrowing (from government). When the government has a budget deficit, the demand for loanable funds shifts to the right and the real interest rate rises. Private investment, the other source of the demand for loanable funds, decreases and is thus "crowded out."

Other popular macroeconomics textbooks, including the one that your teacher probably chose to use, place the government in the supply curve. The supply curve represents the sum of both private saving (from households) and public saving from the government. If the government has a budget deficit, public saving is negative and the supply of loanable funds shifts leftward. If the government has a budget surplus, public saving is positive and the supply of loanable funds shifts rightward.

Suppose the government is running a budget deficit and public saving is negative. Figure 10.6 shows that a leftward shift of the supply curve increases the interest rate in the market for loanable funds and decreases the quantity of loanable funds both invested and saved.

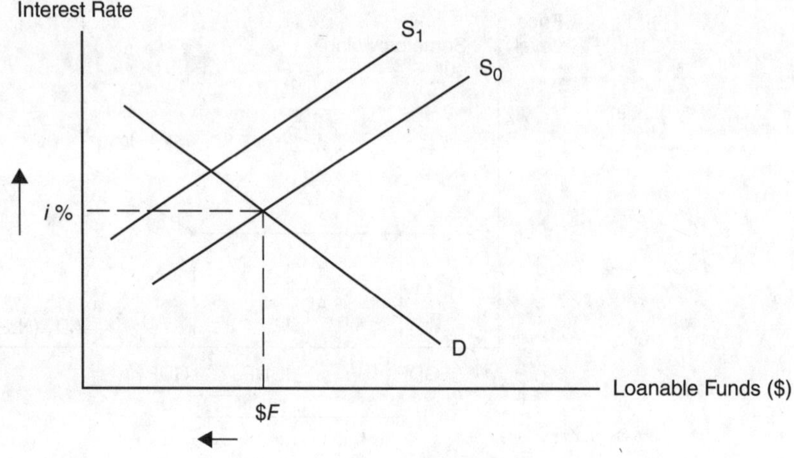

Figure 10.6

So it doesn't matter if your textbook (or teacher) treats crowding out as a leftward shift in supply of, or as a rightward shift in demand for, loanable funds. As long as you can see (or show) the impact of government budget deficits as a higher interest rate and lower private investment, you will score highly on those exam questions.

Net Export Effect

If the government is borrowing to conduct fiscal policy, the resulting increase in interest rates has a similar crowding-out effect on net exports through foreign exchange rates. Again, this is a topic that is addressed in a later chapter, but the basics can be described here. If you are a German, a Malaysian, or a Brazilian and you see interest rates rising in the United States, this higher interest rate makes the United States an attractive place to invest your money and earn higher interest payments. However, you need dollars to purchase a U.S. security (e.g., a U.S. Treasury bond). The increased demand for dollars drives up the "price" of a dollar, which is measured in how many euros, ringgits, or reals it takes to buy a dollar on the currency market. The market for U.S. dollars is illustrated in Figure 10.7, where the price is measured in the number of euros it takes to acquire one dollar.

"Don't try to figure it out in your head. Draw the graphs and read your answers from them."
—Nate, AP Student

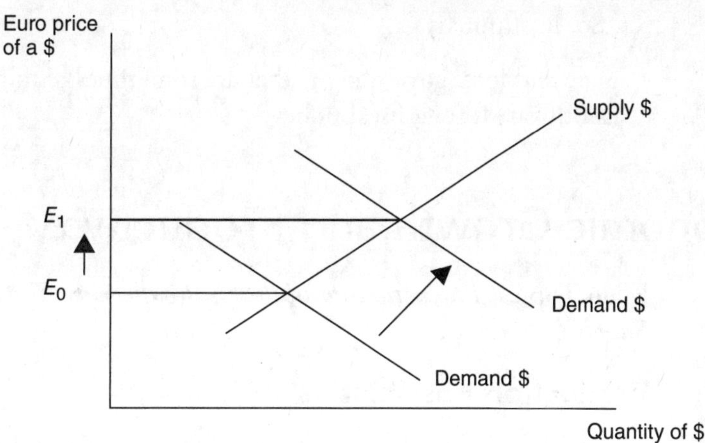

Figure 10.7

When the price of a dollar rises from E_0 to E_1, it now becomes more expensive for European citizens to buy goods made in the United States. All else equal, net exports in the United States fall when the dollar appreciates in value. Falling net exports decreases AD, which lessens the impact of the expansionary fiscal policy. This would be seen in much the same way as in Figure 10.5.

If the government is using contractionary fiscal policy to fight inflation, and interest rates begin to fall, the demand for dollars falls, depreciating the dollar and increasing net exports. This increase in net exports lessens the effectiveness of the contractionary fiscal policy.

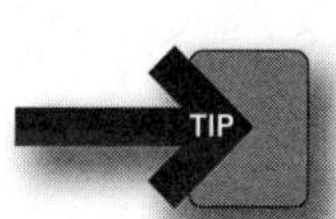

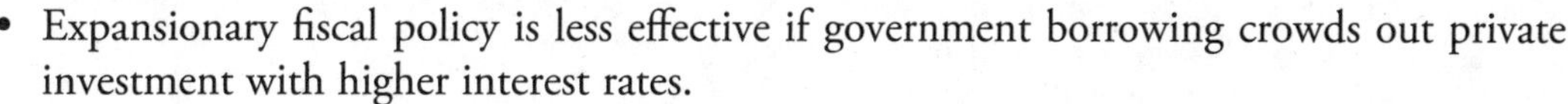
- Expansionary fiscal policy is less effective if government borrowing crowds out private investment with higher interest rates.

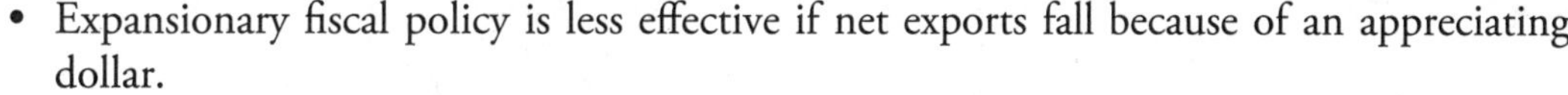
- Expansionary fiscal policy is less effective if net exports fall because of an appreciating dollar.

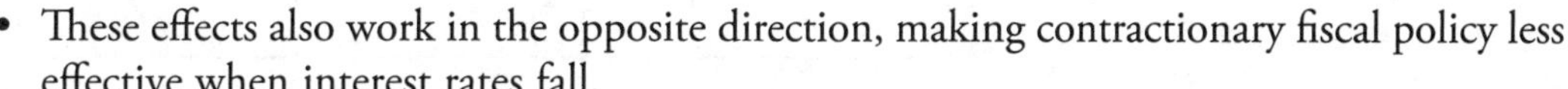
- These effects also work in the opposite direction, making contractionary fiscal policy less effective when interest rates fall.

State and Local Policies

The U.S. Constitution does not require that the federal government balance the budget, and most economists would agree that this is a good thing. After all, when the economy is in a recession, tax revenues are going to be low and deficits are likely to occur. Balancing the budget requires a combination of higher taxes and lower spending, which only exacerbates the recession! Likewise, during a period of economic expansion, tax revenues are high and surpluses occur. Balancing the budget requires lower taxes or higher levels of spending to eliminate the surplus, which continues the expansion and risks higher inflation rates.

On the other hand, many state and local governments are required by law to balance their budgets. During recessions, tax revenue collected by these levels of government fall and elected officials are required to increase taxes and make difficult decisions on which state and local programs need to be cut.

So while the federal government is cutting taxes to increase your disposable income and spur economic growth, your state and local governments are increasing your taxes to make up for the budgetary shortfalls caused by the very recession the federal government is trying to fix. Argh!

So, in summary:

- State and local governments that are sometimes required by law to balance their budgets can thwart federal fiscal policy.

10.3 Economic Growth and Productivity

Main Topics: *Production Possibilities, Productivity, Determinants of Productivity, Supply-Side Policies*

Production Possibilities

Way back in Chapter 5, the topic of the PPC (or PPF) was introduced, and that chapter illustrated how the curve, or frontier, can move outward over time. This simple graphical technique can be extremely useful and adaptable to seeing how growth can be impacted by government policy. Before we move on to policy, here is a quick refresher course in economic growth and productivity.

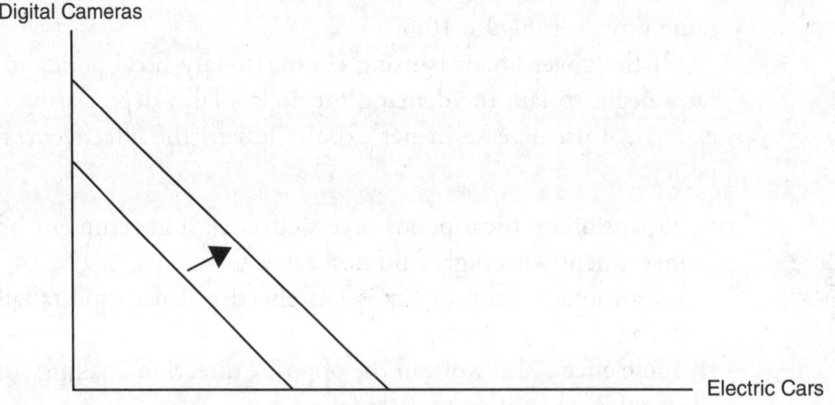

Figure 10.8

Figure 10.8 shows that this nation's production possibilities in electric cars and digital cameras can grow over time if

1. the quantity of economic resources increases,
2. the quality of those resources improves, and/or
3. the nation's technology improves.

Productivity

The factors that shift a PPC outward over time make a lot of sense, but what they all have in common is that each has the potential to represent increased **productivity**. Productivity is typically described as measuring the quantity of output that can be produced per worker in a given amount of time. If a nation's labor force can produce more output per worker from one year to the next, we say that productivity has increased and the nation's PPC has shifted outward.

Determinants of Productivity

The determinants of productivity help to explain why some nations have grown at faster rates than other nations. This short list of determinants provides policy makers with a list of targets that can help focus policy on factors that increase a nation's growth rate.

Stock of Physical Capital

Workers are more productive when they have tools at their disposal. Try painting a house without a brush, digging a hole without a shovel, or writing a term paper without a computer, and you'll find out how important tools can be to your productivity. The nice thing about increasing the quantity of physical capital in an economy is that, in many cases, the capital helps increase the quantity of more capital. There should be policies that provide incentives to invest in physical capital. The supply-side policies described later in the chapter are examples of policies that can increase investment in physical capital.

Human Capital

Labor is a much more productive resource when it has more **human capital**. Human capital is the amount of knowledge and skills that labor can apply to the work that they do. An accountant who takes extra courses so that she can earn her stockbroker's license has increased her human capital. A nurse who studies to become a physician's assistant is increasing her human capital and becoming more productive. Human capital also includes the general health of the nation's labor force. A labor force that has been vaccinated against debilitating disease can bring more productivity to the nation's workplace than the labor force of a nation that has not received these vaccinations. There should be national policies that provide incentives to invest in human capital. How about subsidies to public education to decrease the price to households? Or low-interest federal student loans to help fund college? Or government agencies to research and promote the general physical and psychological health of the population?

Natural Resources

Productive resources provided by nature are called natural resources. A nation's stocks of minerals, fertile soil, timber, clean air and water, or navigable waterways contribute to productivity. **Nonrenewable** resources, such as oil and coal, have a finite supply and cannot replenish themselves. **Renewable** resources, such as timber and salmon, have the ability to repopulate themselves. Environmental protection laws are designed to maintain the quality and quantity of natural resources, so the productivity does not rapidly depreciate.

Technology

Technology is thought of as a nation's knowledge of how to produce goods in the best possible way. Imagine the technological leap that was made when humankind created fire, or the wheel, or the radio, or the assembly line, or the pizza crust with cheese in the middle. Amazing stuff! There should be policies that provide incentives to increase the rate of technological progress. The government's provision of research grants to university professors and laboratories helps to further our state of technology.

What Do All of These Productivity Determinants Have in Common?

They all require an investment, and funds for investment come from **saving**. Firms invest in physical capital and individuals invest in human capital. Nations invest in the conservation of their natural resources, and entrepreneurs invest in technological research.

"Productivity-friendly" policies should make it easier to invest, easier to save, or both. Some economists believe that supply-side policies have the potential to increase productivity and therefore economic growth.

Supply-Side Policies

So far the discussion of fiscal policy is centered on changing government spending and/or taxing to expand or contract AD as a way to move the economy closer to full employment. Other economists believe that the government's fiscal policy should not be so proactive in manipulation of AD. These economists advocate a government that is more hands-off when it comes to fiscal policy. These economists believe that the economy generally moves to full employment without government intervention, but if the government does get involved, fiscal policy should focus on, or at least strongly consider, the AS half of the equation by providing incentives to increase saving and investment. The main idea behind **supply-side fiscal policy** is that tax reductions targeted to AS increase AS so that real GDP increases with very little inflation. This was our "best of all possible macroeconomic situations" from the previous chapter.

Saving and Investment

Supply-side proponents would suggest policies that lower, or remove, taxes on income earned from savings. This would encourage saving and increase the supply of loanable funds, decrease the real interest rate, and increase the amount of money that firms invest. Figure 10.9 shows an increase in the supply of loanable funds. These economists would also propose an **investment tax credit**, which reduces a firm's taxes if it invests in physical capital.

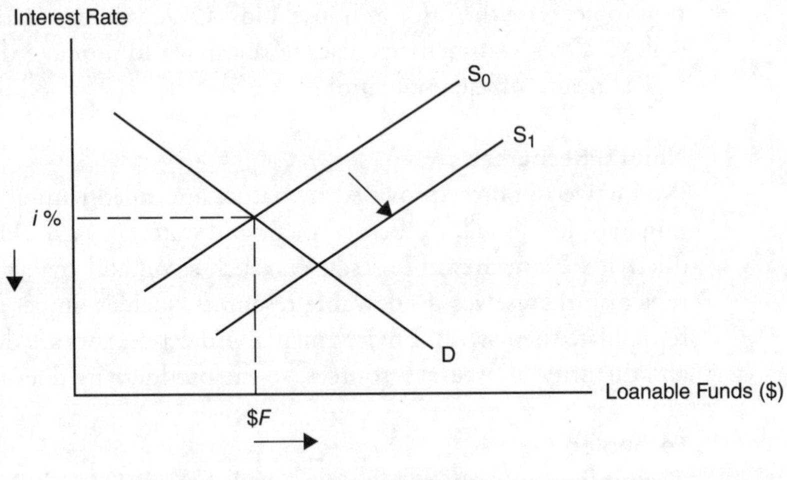

Figure 10.9

Lower income taxes increase disposable income for households, increase both consumption and savings from households, and increase the profitability of investment for firms. This increase in saving and investment allows for an increase in the productive capacity of a nation because more capital stock is accumulated. Ideally, this increase in investment increases the long-run AS curve. The increase in long-run AS is illustrated in Figure 10.10. Tax incentives to increase saving and investment on the supply side are likely to also increase AD. (Note: The price level is shown to remain constant, but this does not have to be, depending on the magnitudes of the two curves' shifts.)

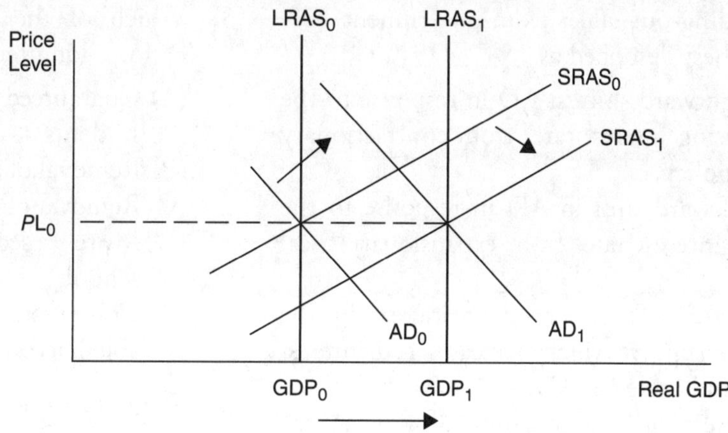

Figure 10.10

Though not all economists agree with their effectiveness, supply-side economists typically advocate other explanations for how lower taxes can increase AS as well as AD:

- *Productivity incentives.* Lower taxes mean workers take more of their pay home, which might prompt wage earners to work harder, take less time off, and be more productive. How hard would you work if 90 percent of your pay were lost to taxes? People not currently in the workforce seek employment at lower tax rates. If the government has a large role in social programs, citizens learn to rely on the government and do less on their own.
- *Risk-taking.* Entrepreneurs take big risks to start businesses and invest in new capital. Lowering the tax rate on profits increases the expected rate of return and encourages more investment.

❯ Review Questions

1. Which of the following would *not* be an example of contractionary fiscal policy?

(A) Decreasing money spent on social programs
(B) Increasing income taxes
(C) Canceling the annual cost of living adjustments to the salaries of government employees
(D) Increasing money spent to pay for government projects
(E) Doing nothing with a temporary budget surplus

2. In a long period of economic expansion the tax revenue collected ____ and the amount spent on welfare programs ____ , creating a budget ____ .

(A) increases, decreases, surplus
(B) increases, decreases, deficit
(C) decreases, decreases, surplus
(D) decreases, increases, deficit
(E) increases, increases, surplus

3. The crowding-out effect from government borrowing is best described as
   (A) the rightward shift in AD in response to the decreasing interest rates from contractionary fiscal policy.
   (B) the leftward shift in AD in response to the rising interest rates from expansionary fiscal policy.
   (C) the effect of the president increasing the money supply, which decreases real interest rates and increases AD.
   (D) the effect on the economy of hearing the chairperson of the central bank say that they believe that the economy is in a recession.
   (E) the lower exports due to an appreciating dollar versus other currencies.

4. Which of the following fiscal policies is likely to be most effective when the economy is experiencing an inflationary gap?
   (A) The government decreases taxes and keeps spending unchanged.
   (B) The government increases spending and keeps taxes unchanged.
   (C) The government increases spending matched with an increase in taxes.
   (D) The government decreases spending and keeps taxes unchanged.
   (E) The government increases taxes and decreases spending.

5. Which of the following would likely slow a nation's long-term economic growth?
   (A) Guaranteed low-interest loans for college students
   (B) Removal of a tax on income earned on saving
   (C) Removal of the investment tax credit
   (D) More research grants given to medical schools
   (E) Conservation policies to manage the renewable harvest of timber

6. The U.S. economy currently suffers a recessionary gap, and a budget deficit exists. If the government wishes to fix the recession, which of the following choices best describes the appropriate fiscal policy, the impact on the market for loanable funds, the interest rate, and the market for the U.S. dollar?

	FISCAL POLICY	LOANABLE FUNDS	INTEREST RATE	MARKET FOR $
(A)	Tax increase	Demand rises	Falling	Demand falls
(B)	Tax cut	Supply rises	Rising	Demand rises
(C)	Tax cut	Demand rises	Rising	Demand rises
(D)	Tax increase	Supply falls	Falling	Demand rises
(E)	Tax cut	Supply falls	Rising	Demand falls

› Answers and Explanations

1. **D**—This is expansionary policy, and the others either contract the economy or do nothing.

2. **A**—In an expansion, households should earn more income, which increases the taxes paid to the government. At the same time, people who needed welfare, or other government assistance, do not need it now because the unemployment level is low and wages are high. In this time of prosperity, the government should run a budget surplus.

3. **B**—If the government borrows to expand the economy, interest rates rise, thus crowding out private investors. This shifts AD leftward, weakening the fiscal policy impact.

4. **E**—Real GDP is at a level above full employment, so AD must be shifted leftward. Choice D shifts AD to the left and lessens the inflationary gap, but choice E couples higher taxes with lower spending and therefore is the most effective remedy. All other choices increase AD and worsen the inflationary gap.

5. C—An investment tax credit rewards firms that invest in physical assets. Removal of this tax credit slows investment, productivity, and growth. All other policies would increase the productivity of resources or increase technological innovation.

6. C— If you understand the nature of a recession, the first step is to eliminate any option indicating higher taxes. When a recessionary gap exists, the appropriate fiscal policy is to cut taxes and run an even larger budget deficit. The borrowing necessary to pay for a budget deficit increases the demand for loanable funds and increases the interest rate. Rising interest rates create a stronger demand for the U.S. dollar because U.S. Treasury bondholders are receiving more interest income.

❯ Rapid Review

Fiscal policy: Deliberate changes in government spending and net tax collection to affect economic output, unemployment, and the price level. Fiscal policy is typically designed to manipulate AD to "fix" the economy.

Expansionary fiscal policy: Increases in government spending or lower net taxes meant to shift AD to the right.

Contractionary fiscal policy: Decreases in government spending or higher net taxes meant to shift AD to the left.

Sticky prices: If price levels do not change, especially downward, with changes in AD, then prices are thought of as sticky or inflexible. Keynesians believe the price level does not usually fall with contractionary policy.

Budget deficit: Exists when government spending exceeds the revenue collected from taxes.

Budget surplus: Exists when the revenue collected from taxes exceeds government spending.

Automatic stabilizers: Mechanisms built into the tax system that automatically regulate, or stabilize, the macroeconomy as it moves through the business cycle by changing net taxes collected by the government. These stabilizers increase a deficit during a recessionary period and increase a budget surplus during an inflationary period, without any discretionary change on the part of the government.

Crowding-out effect: When the government borrows funds to cover a deficit, the interest rate increases and households and firms are crowded out of the market for loanable funds. The resulting decrease in *C* and *I* dampens the effect of expansionary fiscal policy.

Net export effect: A rising interest rate increases foreign demand for U.S. dollars. The dollar then appreciates in value, causing net exports from the United States to fall. Falling net exports decreases AD, which lessens the impact of the expansionary fiscal policy. This is a variation of crowding out.

Productivity: The quantity of output that can be produced per worker in a given amount of time.

Human capital: The amount of knowledge and skills that labor can apply to the work that they do and the general level of health that the labor force enjoys.

Nonrenewable resources: Natural resources that cannot replenish themselves. Coal is a good example.

Renewable resources: Natural resources that can replenish themselves if they are not over-harvested. Lobster is a good example.

Technology: A nation's knowledge of how to produce goods in the best possible way.

Investment tax credit: A reduction in taxes for firms that invest in new capital like a factory or piece of equipment.

Supply-side fiscal policy: Fiscal policy centered on tax reductions targeted to AS so that real GDP increases with very little inflation. The main justification is that lower taxes on individuals and firms increase incentives to work, save, invest, and take risks.

Money, Banking, and Monetary Policy

IN THIS CHAPTER

Summary: People often think that economics is the study of money. While you have already discovered that, strictly speaking, this is not the case, there is no denying the critical role of money in any economic system in the exchange of goods and services, employment of resources, and macroeconomic stability. This chapter first briefly defines money, the functions that it serves, and the market for it. Following a brief overview of the fractional (or limited) reserve banking system, we discuss money creation. We then focus on the tools of monetary policy that the Federal Reserve has traditionally used to influence the macroeconomy in a limited reserve banking system. Following this traditional coverage of monetary policy, we then look at modern tools of monetary policy in the ample reserves banking system. The chapter concludes with a discussion of fiscal and monetary policy coordination and how one school of economic thought sees the role of monetary policy.

Key Ideas

- Money as an Asset
- The Money Market
- The Money Multiplier
- Monetary Policy

11.1 Money and Financial Assets

Main Topics: *Financial Assets, Functions of Money, Supply of Money, Demand for Money, The Money Market, Changes in Money Supply*

The paper and coin currency that we carry around in our pockets is typically used for one thing: to buy stuff. Before we get into a more thorough discussion about money, let's briefly discuss financial assets other than the money in your pocket.

Financial Assets

We have already discussed investment in physical (or capital) assets like machinery or new construction as components of GDP. The firm invests in a physical asset if the expected rate of return is at least as high as the real interest rate. Sometimes firms and households seek other forms of assets as a place to invest their money. Financial investments also yield a rate of return. We spend much more time discussing money as a short-term financial asset but quickly address other financial assets like stocks and bonds.

Stocks

A share of stock represents a claim on the ownership of the firm and is exchanged in a stock market. Firms that wish to raise money for capital investment can issue, and sell, these partial shares of ownership. This form of **equity financing** avoids debt but relinquishes a small degree of control over the management, and profits, of the firm.

Bonds

A bond is a certificate of indebtedness. When a firm wants to raise money by borrowing, it can issue corporate bonds that promise the bondholders the principle amount, plus a specified rate of interest, with repayment on a specific maturity date. This form of **debt financing** commits the corporation to interest payments but does not relinquish shares of ownership. Like stocks, bonds can be bought and sold in a secondary market. We shall see how the central bank can intervene in this market in a way that has profound effects on the economy.

Functions of Money

In general, money is anything that is used to facilitate an exchange of goods between buyers and sellers. Human history has seen many things used as money, from shells and tobacco to gold and spices. These different forms of money have all performed certain functions.

Today's paper and coin money is called **fiat money** because it has no intrinsic value (like gold) and no value as a commodity (like tobacco). It serves as money because the government declares it to be legal tender and, in doing so, the government assures us that it performs three general functions:

- *Medium of exchange.* Your employer exchanges dollars for an hour of your labor. You exchange those dollars for a grocer's pound of apples. The grocer exchanges those dollars for an orchard's apple crop and on and on. If it weren't for money, we would still be engaging in the barter system, an extremely inconvenient way to exchange goods and services. If I were a cheese maker and I wanted apples, I would need to find an orchard that also needed cheese, and this would be a supremely difficult way to do my shopping.
- *Unit of account.* Units of currency (dollars, euro, yen, etc.) measure the relative worth of goods and services just as inches and meters measure relative distance between two points. Again, this is an improvement over the barter system where all goods are measured in terms of many other goods. The value of a pound of cheese in a barter economy is measured in a dozen eggs or a half pound of sausage or three pints of ale. With money, the value of cheese, and all other goods and services, is measured in terms of a monetary unit like dollars.
- *Store of value.* So long as prices are not rapidly increasing, money is a decent way to store value. You can put money under your mattress or in a checking account, and it is still useful, with essentially the same value, a week or a month later. If I were the town cheese maker, I must quickly find merchants with whom to exchange my cheese, because if I wait too long, moldy cheese loses its value.

Supply of Money

At the core of monetary policy is regulation of the supply of money. Because our paper money is not backed by precious metals or crown jewels, we trust the government to keep the value of our money as stable as possible. This value is guaranteed by stabilizing the **money supply**, which is measured by the central bank as ***M*1 and *M*2**, the latter being more broadly defined and less liquid than the former. **Liquidity** refers to how easily an asset can be converted to cash. A five-dollar bill, already being cash, is as liquid as it gets. A Van Gogh painting hidden in your attic is also an asset but not a very liquid one.

"There are a couple of questions on this. Know what is included in each category."
—Kristy, AP Student

We can say that

- *M*1 = Cash + Coins + Checking deposits + Savings deposits. *M*1 is the most liquid of money definitions.
- *M*2 = *M*1 + Small (i.e., under $100,000 certificates of deposit) time deposits + Money market deposits + Money market mutual funds. *M*2 is slightly less liquid because the holders of these assets would likely incur a penalty if they wished to immediately convert the asset to cash.

At any given point in time, the supply of money is assumed to be constant. This implies that the current money supply curve is vertical. Because other measures of money supply are based on the most liquid *M*1, when we discuss the money supply, we focus on *M*1. Insight gained from studying the expansion and contraction of *M*1 can be applied to *M*2.

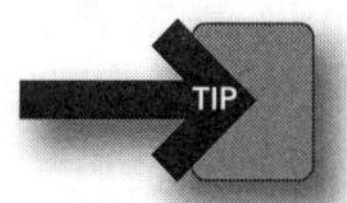

Demand for Money

People demand goods like cheese because cheese helps satisfy wants. People demand money because it facilitates the purchase of cheese and other goods. In addition to this transaction demand for money, people also demand money as an asset, just as a government bond or a share of Intel stock is an asset. We quickly look at demand for money as the sum of money demand for transactions and money demand as an asset.

Transaction Demand. As nominal GDP increases, consumers demand more money to buy goods and services. For a given price level, if output increases, more money is demanded. Or for a given level of output, if the price level rises, more money is demanded. If nominal GDP is $1,000 and each dollar is spent an average of four times each year, money demand for transactions would be $1,000/4 = $250. If nominal GDP increases to $1,200, money demand for transactions increases to $1,200/4 = $300. We assume that the nominal rate of interest does not affect transaction demand for money, so when plotted on a graph with the nominal interest rate on the *y*-axis, it is a constant.

Asset Demand. Money can be held as an asset at very little risk. If you put money under your mattress, there is the advantage of knowing that a crashing stock market or real estate market does not diminish the value of this asset. The main disadvantage of putting this asset under your mattress is that it cannot earn any interest as it would were you to invest that money in bonds, for example. As the interest rate on bonds rises, the opportunity cost of holding money under your mattress begins to rise, and so you are more likely to lessen your asset demand for money. At a lower interest rate on bonds, you are more likely to increase your asset demand for money.

Total Demand. Plotted against the nominal interest rate, the transaction demand for money is a constant MD_t. Adding this constant amount of money needed to make transactions to a downward-sloping asset demand for money (MD_a) provides us with the total money demand curve. This is seen in Figure 11.1.

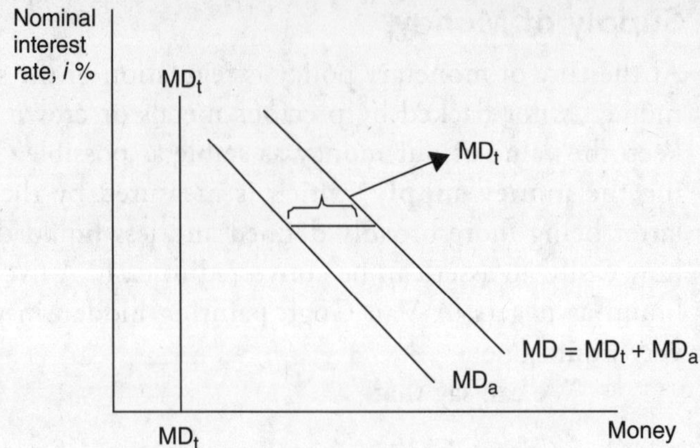

Figure 11.1

The Money Market

The central bank, having established a given level of money supply circulating in the economy, allows us to incorporate a vertical money supply (MS) curve with a downward-sloping money demand curve to complete the money market. John Maynard Keynes developed the *theory of liquidity preference*, which postulates that the equilibrium "price" of money is the interest rate where money supply intersects money demand. Just like any market, if the price is below equilibrium (a shortage), the price must rise, and if the price is above equilibrium (a surplus), the price must fall. Money demand can increase if more transactions are being made, but the real focus of the rest of this chapter is on changes in money supply. Equilibrium is shown in Figure 11.2.

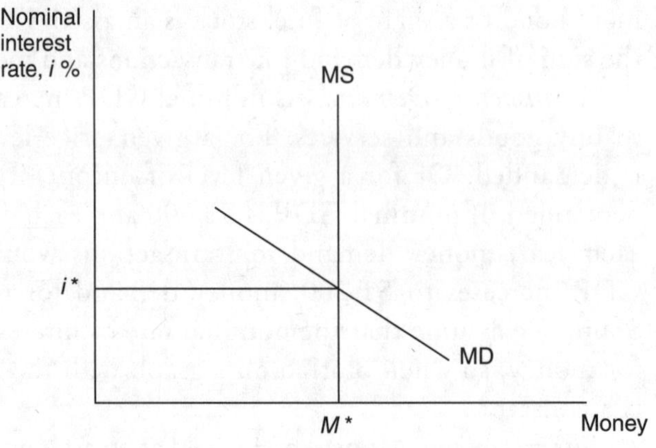

Figure 11.2

How Is the Money Market Different from the Market for Loanable Funds?

"This is an important question. Know the difference." —AP Teacher

Understanding the difference between the money market and the loanable funds market can be tough, so we'll take it in two and a half parts. I'm sure the first is much more helpful, the second much more esoteric, and the half is going to earn you the graphing points.

1. *Breadth of scope.*

The supply of loanable funds, which varies directly with the interest rate, comes from saving. The supply of money is more inclusive than just saving; it includes currency and checking deposits. A $100 bill in your wallet would fall into the money supply curve but not into the supply of loanable funds. The demand for loanable funds comes from investment demand. The demand for money includes the money used not only for investment but also for consumption (transaction demand) and for holding as an asset (asset demand). So basically the money market, both on the supply and the demand side, is broader, and more inclusive, than the market for loanable funds. The price (aka the interest rate) appears to be the same in both markets and is the result of . . .

2. *Different philosophies.*

   We don't want to delve too much into the Keynesian versus Classical philosophical debates because they are quite unlikely to appear on your AP Macroeconomics exam. It can seem a little confusing to show the interest rate as the "price" in both the market for loanable funds and the market for money. The reason that both markets are presented here, and in your textbook, is that they represent fundamental differences in macroeconomic philosophies:

   - Classical economists believe that the price level is flexible and long-run GDP adjusts to the natural rate of employment. For any level of GDP, the interest rate adjusts to balance the supply and demand for loanable funds, and the price level adjusts to keep the money market in equilibrium.
   - Keynesian economists believe that the price level is sticky. For any price level, the interest rate adjusts to balance the supply and demand for money, and this interest rate influences aggregate demand and thus the short-run level of GDP.
   - Bottom line here: The two different ways of looking at the interest rate are the result of two different ways of looking at the overall economy and the difference in the long-run (Classical) and short-run (Keynesian) views of the economy.

   . . . and ½. *Graphing.*

   While it *appears* that the same interest rate is graphed on the vertical axis of both the loanable funds and money market graphs, they are not in fact the same. It is correct to label the vertical axis of the money market with a nominal interest rate and the vertical axis of the loanable funds market with the real interest rate. Changes in the money market can be viewed as short-term changes, and therefore, the role of expected inflation is negligible. For long-term decisions like investment and saving, the price of investment, or return on saving, does depend on expected inflation, and so it makes sense to focus on the real rate of interest when making long-term plans. Here's a way to keep it straight: "Loanable funds are REAL-ly fun."

TIP

   - When asked to draw the money market, the best way to ensure that you receive the graphing point is to label the vertical axis in the money market as the "Nominal interest rate" or "n.i.r."
   - If you simply label the vertical axis in the money market as "%" or "Interest rate" you may not earn all the graphing points.

Changes in Money Supply

When we talk about traditional monetary policy, we are really talking about money supply policy. The traditional tools used to expand or contract the money supply are discussed later in this chapter, but it's useful to see what is happening in the money market when the money supply increases or decreases.

An Increase in the Money Supply

Like the market for any commodity, when the supply increases, there exists a temporary surplus at the original equilibrium price. The money market is no different. At the original interest rate of 10 percent, the supply of money is \$1,000. Now the central bank increases the money supply to \$1,500. In Figure 11.3, you can see that at 10 percent, there is now a surplus of money.

With surplus money on their hands, people (and banks) find other assets, like bonds, as places to put the extra money. As more people increase the demand for bonds, the bond price rises, and this lowers the effective interest rate paid on the bonds.

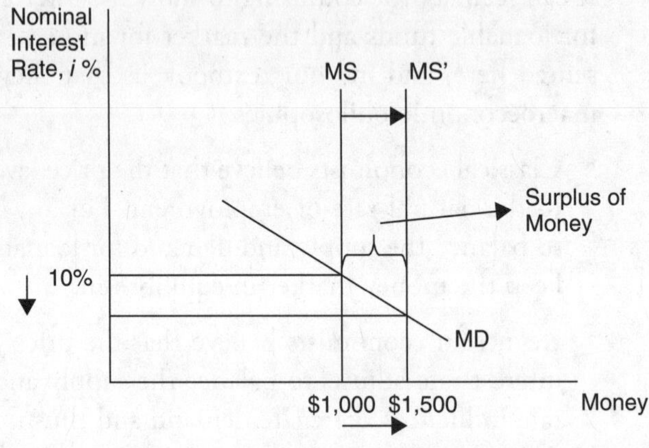

Figure 11.3

How does this work?

A bond is selling at a price of \$100 and promises to pay \$10 in interest. The interest rate = \$10/\$100 = 10 percent. But if the price of the bond is driven up to \$125, the same \$10 of interest actually yields only \$10/\$125 = 8.0 percent. With lower interest rates available in the bond market, the opportunity cost of holding cash falls and the quantity of money demanded increases along the downward-sloping MD curve until MD = \$1,500. An increase in the money supply therefore decreases the interest rate.

A Decrease in the Money Supply

If the central bank decides to decrease the supply of money from \$1,000 to \$500, there is a shortage of money at the 10 percent interest rate. A shortage of money sends some bondholders to sell their bonds so that they have money for transactions. An increase in the supply of bonds in the bond market decreases the price and increases the rate of interest earned on those assets.

How does this work?

If the original price of the bond is \$100, promising to pay \$10 in interest, the interest rate is 10 percent. If the price falls to \$90, the same \$10 of interest now yields \$10/\$90 = 11.1 percent. Higher interest rates on bonds increase the opportunity cost of holding cash, and so the quantity of money demanded falls until the interest rate rises to the point where MD = \$500. This adjustment is seen in Figure 11.4.

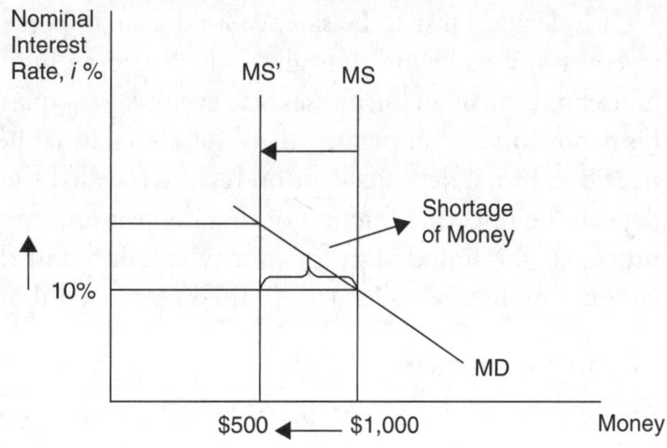

Figure 11.4

- Increasing the money supply lowers interest rates as surplus money moves into the bond market, increasing bond prices.
- Decreasing the money supply increases interest rates as a shortage of money creates a sell-off of bonds, decreasing bond prices.

11.2 Traditional Fractional Reserve Banking and Money Creation

Main Topics: *Fractional Reserve Banking, Money Creation, The Money Multiplier*

If you asked 10 bank tellers in your hometown, "Do you create money here?" I'm guessing that 9 or 10 of them would reply, "No way." They're wrong. The fractional reserve system of banking, plus the bank's profit motive, creates money and opens the door for the central bank to promote or inhibit such money creation.

Fractional Reserve Banking

Fractional reserve banking is a system in which only a fraction of the total money supply is held in reserve as currency. To be consistent with the language used by the Federal Reserve and the updated AP Macro curriculum, we will be referring to this as a "limited reserve framework."

As you will soon learn, the United States and other major economies no longer have a limited reserve banking system. The AP Macro curriculum still includes the limited reserve framework for money creation, so it is important to know how it works. The short story that follows illustrates how fractional reserve banking might have evolved.

Eli's Community Bank (ECB) opens its doors and is now accepting deposits from citizens who want a safe place to put their money. Eli promises to always keep 100 percent of their money on hand so that if a person needs to buy groceries, they can simply withdraw some money and take it to the store.

One day, a citizen comes up to the bank asking to borrow some money to start a lemonade stand, but Eli has to turn her down because if any of his customers comes to withdraw money for groceries and finds that it was not in the vault, they would be extremely irritated. After a month or so, Eli observes that on any given day, there are very few withdrawals and that most of the time the deposited money just sits there in the vault, doing nothing.

Eli decides, just to be safe, to hold a small percentage of his total deposits in the vault to cover any daily withdrawals, and earn some interest income by lending out the rest to households or small businesses. He even realizes that he must offer a small rate of interest to his depositors to compensate them for the fact that he has their money and they do not. The fraction of total deposits kept on reserve is called the **reserve ratio**. Each time he receives a deposit, he puts that fraction of that deposit on reserve in the vault and lends the rest. This process is the foundation for money creation and the central bank's traditional ability to conduct monetary policy in a limited reserve banking system.

Money Creation

A specific example of how the fractional reserve system can multiply one new bank deposit into new created money illustrates the process of money creation.

The reserve ratio is 10 percent. In other words,

$$\text{Reserve ratio } (rr) = \text{Cash reserves/Total deposits} = 0.10$$

One way to see how checking deposits turn into loans and how loans turn into new money is to create a basic T-account, or **balance sheet**. The idea of a balance sheet is to show the assets and liabilities of a bank. In our example, total assets must equal total liabilities.

Asset. Anything owned by the bank or owed to the bank is an asset of the bank. Cash on reserve is an asset, and so are loans made to citizens.

Liability. Anything owned by depositors or lenders to the bank is a liability. Checking deposits of citizens or loans made to the bank are liabilities to the bank.

Let's look at an example:

Step 1. Katie takes $1,000 from under her mattress, deposits it at ECB, and opens a checking account. If the Federal Reserve, the central bank of the United States, tells the ECB that it must hold 10 percent of all deposits in reserve, then the ECB must comply and keep no less than $100 of Katie's deposit as "required" reserves. The remaining $900 of the deposit are excess reserves and can be kept on reserve in the bank or lent to another person.

Balance Sheet ECB (Step 1)

ASSETS		LIABILITIES	
Required Reserves	$100	Checking Deposits	$1,000
Excess Reserves	$900		
Total Assets	$1,000	Total Liabilities	$1,000

It is important to understand that Katie's deposit is not initially creating an increase in the money supply. When she takes $1,000 of cash and puts it into a checking account, the quantity of money in $M1$ remains the same. What happens next will eventually create an increase in the money supply.

Step 2. ECB lends all $900 in excess reserves to Theo, a local farmer.

Balance Sheet ECB (Step 2)

ASSETS		LIABILITIES	
Required Reserves	$100	Checking Deposits	$1,000
Excess Reserves	$0		
Loans	$900		
Total Assets	$1,900	Total Liabilities	$1,000

Step 3. Theo uses his $900 at Tractor Supply, which has a checking account with ECB. Checking deposits have now increased by $900, and this is new money. ECB must keep $90 as required reserves, and excess reserves now total $810.

Balance Sheet ECB (Step 3)

ASSETS		LIABILITIES	
Required Reserves	$190	Checking Deposits	$1,900
Excess Reserves	$810		
Loans	$900		
Total Assets	$1,900	Total Liabilities	$1,900

Step 4. ECB makes an $810 loan to Max, who wants to buy some furniture. Max spends $810 at Furniture Factory, which also banks with ECB, increasing checking deposits by $810. ECB must keep $81 in required reserves, leaving $729 in excess reserves.

Balance Sheet ECB (Step 4)

ASSETS		LIABILITIES	
Required Reserves	$271	Checking Deposits	$2,710
Excess Reserves	$729		
Loans	$1,710		
Total Assets	$2,710	Total Liabilities	$2,710

The Money Multiplier

An initial deposit of $1,000 creates, after only two loans are made and redeposited, $2,710 of checking deposits. This process could continue until there are no more excess reserves to be loaned, ultimately creating $10,000 of deposits. Of this $10,000 of deposits, $1,000 was already in the money supply (cash under Katie's mattress) but $9,000 has been created as new money, seemingly out of thin air. This process is known as the money multiplier, which measures the maximum amount of new checking deposits that can be created by a single dollar of excess reserves. The idea of the money multiplier, not to mention the mathematics, is identical to our coverage of the spending multiplier.

$$M = 1/(\text{Reserve requirement}) = 1/rr\ (= 1/.10 = 10 \text{ in our example})$$

We had $900 in initial excess reserves and this would have multiplied into a maximum of $9,000 if (a) at every stage the banks kept only the required dollars in reserve, (b) at every stage borrowers redeposit funds into the bank and keep none as cash, and (c) borrowers are willing to take out excess reserves as loans.

- The maximum, or simple, money multiplier $M = 1/rr$.
- An initial amount of excess reserves multiplies by, at most, a factor of M.

This process works in reverse if, instead of an initial deposit, Katie makes a $1,000 withdrawal and puts the cash under her mattress. Rather than money creation, this could be called money destruction.

11.3 Monetary Policy with Limited Reserves

Main Topics: *Expansionary Monetary Policy, Contractionary Monetary Policy, Open Market Operations, Changing the Discount Rate, Changing the Required Reserve Ratio, Coordination of Fiscal and Monetary Policy, Quantity Theory of Money*

The previous example of how multiple deposits create a multiplier effect in the money supply only happens if the central bank requires banks to keep a percentage of every deposit in reserve. Such policies create the limited reserve banking system. Central banks like the Federal Reserve have traditionally had three general tools of monetary policy at their disposal. In a system with limited reserves, the central bank could engage in open market operations, change the discount rate, and change the required reserve ratio. Each of these can be used to expand or contract the money supply to stabilize prices and move the economy to full employment. So let us first take a look at the intended effects of expansionary and contractionary monetary policy and then investigate each of the traditional tools in more detail. After presenting the monetary policies that can be used in a limited reserve banking system, we will look at how a system of *ample reserves* changes the way in which monetary policy is currently conducted by many central banks.

Expansionary Monetary Policy

Unlike fiscal policy, which has a relatively direct impact on spending, aggregate demand, real GDP, unemployment, and the price level, monetary policy affects the economy by changing interest rates in the money market. Expansionary monetary policy, conducted in a limited reserve banking system, is designed to fix a recession and increase aggregate demand, lower the unemployment rate, and increase real GDP. By increasing the money supply, the interest rate is lowered. A lower rate of interest increases private consumption and investment, which shifts the aggregate demand curve to the right. This process is illustrated in Figures 11.5 and 11.6.

Contractionary Monetary Policy

As you might imagine, contractionary monetary policy has the opposite effect as expansionary and is designed to avoid inflation by decreasing aggregate demand, which lowers the price level and decreases real GDP back to the full employment level. By decreasing the money supply, the interest rate is increased. A higher rate of interest decreases private consumption and investment, which shifts the aggregate demand to the left. This process is illustrated in Figures 11.7 and 11.8.

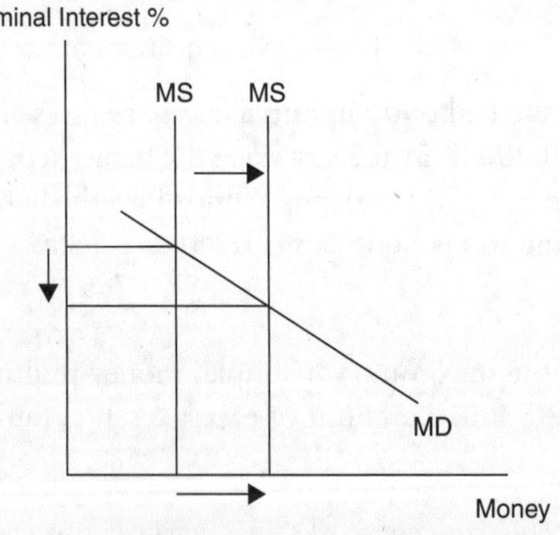

Figure 11.5

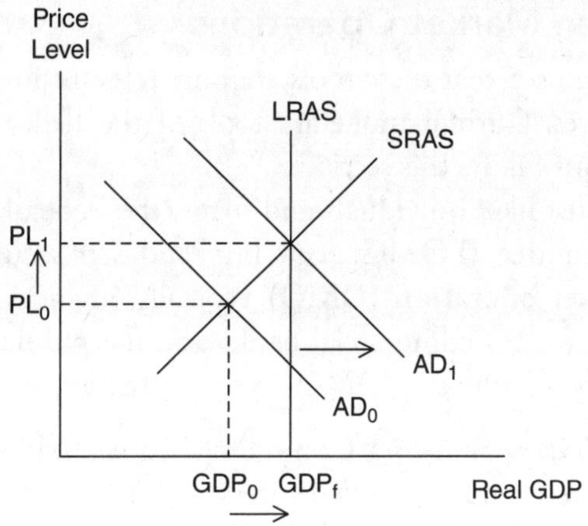

Figure 11.6

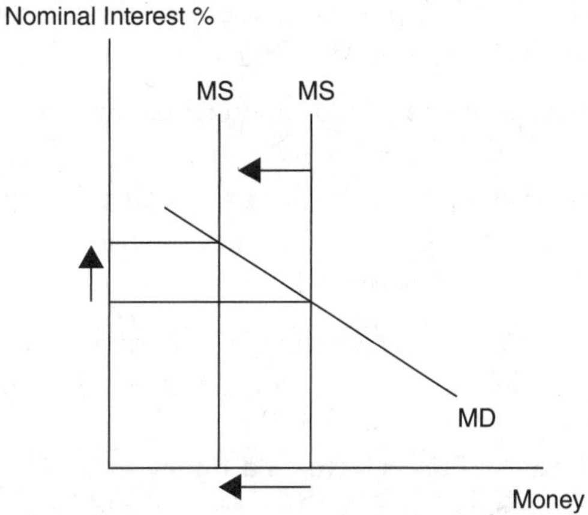

Figure 11.7

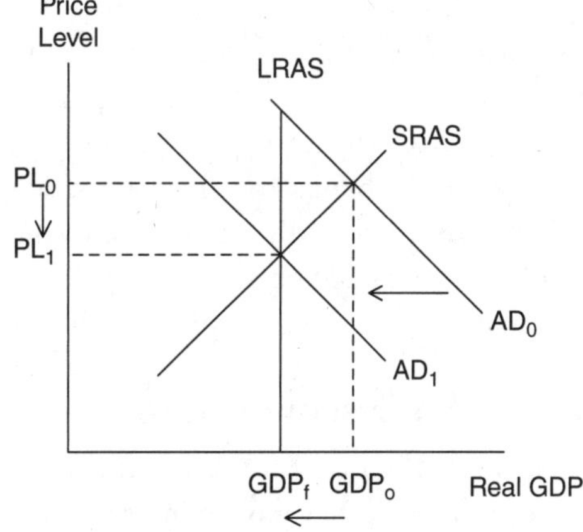

Figure 11.8

The traditional chain of events for expansionary and contractionary monetary policy is as follows.

- *Unemployment is too high* →↑MS, ↓*i*%, ↑*I*, ↑AD, ↑real GDP, ↓unemployment
- *Inflation is too high* →↓MS, ↑*i*%, ↓*I*, ↓AD, ↓real GDP, ↓price level

Open Market Operations

TIP

Remember that these tools are only relevant in a banking system with limited (or fractional) reserves. Current monetary tools of the Federal Reserve and other ample reserve banking systems follow this section.

Just like individuals and firms, the Federal Reserve, through the Federal Open Market Committee (FOMC), can buy and sell securities on the open market. Such an **open market operation (OMO)** typically involves the buying (or selling) of Treasury bonds from (or to) commercial banks and the public. Of the three traditional tools of monetary policy, conducting OMOs is by far the approach most frequently taken by the Fed.

Buying Securities. Commercial banks hold Treasury bonds as an asset rather than excess cash reserves. If the Fed offers to buy some of those securities, the banks would receive excess cash reserves and the Fed would get the bonds. When banks have excess reserves, the money creation process begins. The money supply increases and the interest rate falls.

"This is a great way to remember this!" —AP Teacher

- When the Fed buys securities, the money supply expands. If it helps you remember, use this: "**B**uying **B**onds = **B**igger **B**ucks" (a larger money supply).

Selling Securities. Commercial banks might be in the market to buy Treasury bonds as an asset rather than excess cash reserves. If the Fed offers to sell some of their securities, the banks would get the bonds and their excess cash reserves would fall. When banks have fewer excess reserves, the money destruction process begins. The money supply decreases and the interest rate rises.

- When the Fed sells securities, the money supply contracts. If it helps you remember, use this: "**S**elling **B**onds = **S**maller **B**ucks" (a smaller money supply).

The Federal Funds Rate as a Policy Rate

The discussion of OMOs seems to indicate that the buying and selling of securities is the main policy tool. If the FOMC wants to lower the interest rate, it buys bonds. If the FOMC wants to increase the interest rate, it sells bonds. In reality, many central banks have a target range for interest rates on overnight lending between banks. This "policy rate" in the U.S. is called the *federal funds rate.* Traditional monetary policy would see the Federal Reserve using the federal funds rate as a target interest rate and the FOMC then proceeds to engage in OMOs to hit that target rate. The **federal funds rate** is the interest rate that banks charge other banks for short-term loans. One bank might need to borrow funds from other banks, primarily to cover an unexpected dip in reserves. The important thing to remember is that our analysis of traditional monetary policy is the same whether we talk about changes in the money supply or changes in the target federal funds interest rate.

Changing the Discount Rate

There are times when commercial banks need a short-term loan from the Fed. When they borrow from the Fed, they pay an interest rate called the **discount rate**. When the Fed lowers the discount rate, it makes it more affordable for commercial banks to increase excess reserves by borrowing from the Fed. The entire amount of the loan goes into excess reserves and can be borrowed by customers of the bank, increasing the money supply. As a practical matter, the Fed tends to change the discount rate in lockstep with the federal funds target rate.

To summarize:

- Lowering the discount rate (or federal funds rate) increases excess reserves in commercial banks and expands the money supply.
- Raising the discount rate (or federal funds rate) decreases excess reserves in commercial banks and contracts the money supply.

Changing the Required Reserve Ratio

When there are limited reserves in the banking system, a central bank can change the fraction of deposits that must be kept as required reserves. If the reserve ratio is 0.50, half of all deposits must be kept in the vault, leaving half to be loaned as excess reserves. The money multiplier in this case is two. But if the required reserve ratio were lowered to 0.10, 90 percent of all deposits could be lent as excess reserves. The money multiplier increases to 10.

So:

- Lowering the reserve ratio increases excess reserves in commercial banks and expands the money supply.
- Increasing the reserve ratio decreases excess reserves in commercial banks and contracts the money supply.

Table 11.1 summarizes how the traditional tools of monetary policy in a limited reserve banking system can be used to target high unemployment or high inflation.

Table 11.1

	PROBLEM: HIGH UNEMPLOYMENT	PROBLEM: HIGH INFLATION
Monetary tool could be used to . . .	Buy bonds in an OMO, lowering the fed funds rate.	Sell bonds in an OMO, increasing the fed funds rate.
Or . . .	Lower the discount rate.	Raise the discount rate.
Or . . .	Lower the required reserve ratio.	Raise the required reserve ratio.
The effect would be . . .	↑MS, ↓*i*%, ↑*I*, ↑AD, ↑real GDP, ↓unemployment	↓MS, ↑*i*%, ↓*I*, ↓AD, ↓real GDP, ↓price level

11.4 Modern Monetary Policy with Ample Reserves

As a student of economics, you might be saying to yourself, "OK, I understand the traditional tools of central bank policy, but my teacher keeps talking about *quantitative easing* and *ample reserves regime.* What's going on here? What do I need to know?"

The new revision of the AP Macroeconomics course description include the three traditional tools of monetary policy, which were covered in the previous section of this chapter. There are still banking systems that operate with limited reserves. Until this changes, you must study that material and be ready for questions about those tools. Be prepared to discuss the buying and selling of bonds to influence interest rates!

If a question includes language such as "the central bank in an economy with limited reserves . . ." then you should discuss one of the three traditional tools of monetary policy.

Before we get into monetary policy with ample reserves, some quick backstory: Central banks around the world have adapted monetary policy in response to the global financial crisis that spawned the global financial crisis and subsequent "Great Recession" of 2007–2009. Open market operations are still occasionally used but play a much smaller role than they did prior to the crisis. Below is a short summary of how current monetary policy influences interest rates in pursuit of the twin goals of stable prices and full employment.

As the financial crisis began to rapidly threaten the global banking system, banks were faced with many defaulting home mortgages and other loans from their borrowers, and reserves were dangerously low. Central banks like the Federal Reserve flooded bank reserves to give banks more liquidity (cash). The trillions of dollars in reserves kept banks afloat and prevented reserves from drying up, an outcome that would have devastated the economy.

This massive increase in cash reserves drove the federal funds rate down to approximately zero. At the point of zero interest rates, any further increase in the money supply would have no effect on interest rates. Because of this decision to maintain bank reserves at such high levels, the Fed came to refer to this new strategy as the "ample reserves" framework for conducting monetary policy. The Fed still sets targets for the federal funds rate, but instead of using open market operations to meet that target, the Fed adjusts the federal funds rate by making deliberate changes to two administered interest rates: the interest on reserves (IOR) and the overnight reverse repurchase agreement (ON RRP) rate.

How does this work?

Since October 2008, the interest on reserves (IOR) now serves as the primary tool for monetary policy. It's important to keep in mind that banks can do many things with their excess cash reserves. They can lend reserves to another bank and receive the federal funds rate in return. Another option for banks is to deposit excess reserves with the Federal Reserve and earn the interest on reserves rate. To entice more lending between banks, the Fed would lower the IOR, making deposits with the Fed a less attractive option. To induce banks to deposit more reserves with the Fed, the Fed would increase the IOR. Because the federal funds rate and the IOR are so tightly linked, the federal funds rate would rise and fall along with the IOR, impacting other interest rates in the economy.

What happens if these rates don't move together as the Fed intends? Suppose the federal funds rate was significantly lower than the IOR. A smart banker could borrow money from another bank, paying them the low federal funds rate, and then redeposit that money with the Fed and earn the higher IOR. A tidy profit! This "borrow low and save high" strategy is called arbitrage and, as more banks exploit this arbitrage opportunity, the large gap between the interest rates would begin to shrink down to a very small difference again.

This would be the end of the modern monetary policy story except that there are some financial institutions that borrow and lend, but not with the Federal Reserve. To incorporate these institutions, and influence their borrowing and lending, the Fed created a secondary policy tool called the overnight reverse repurchase agreement (ON RRP) facility.

Financial institutions don't earn income by letting money sit idle. As a short-term, and risk-free, way of investing some cash, a financial institution might choose to buy a Treasury bond from the Fed. The next day, the Fed buys it back from them and pays the ON RRP rate. Since buying a Treasury bond from the Fed involves zero risk of losing money, this interest rate is going to be quite low, and the federal funds rate would not dip below it. If the federal funds rate did fall below the ON RRP, investors would again see arbitrage opportunities that would move the federal funds rate back to where it is slightly greater than the ON RRP. For example, if the federal funds rate fell significantly below the ON RRP, a savvy financial institution could borrow from another bank, deposit with the Fed, and earn profit in the difference between the borrowing and saving rates.

The Market for Reserves

Since the College Board announced in June 2022 that ample reserves monetary policy would be part of the AP Macro curriculum, and fair game for testing in 2023 and beyond, educators have been modifying the ways in which monetary policy is taught.

When you are presented with a question that uses a phrase like "the economy has a banking system with ample reserves," then you are no longer dealing with traditional tools like the buying and selling of government bonds to increase or decrease the money supply. In a system of ample reserves, the central bank has infused the system with so much money as to make increases or decreases in the money supply ineffective in changing the **policy rate.**

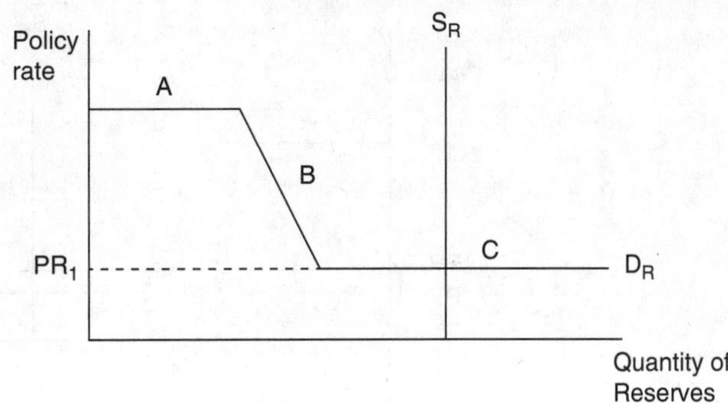

Figure 11.9

So, rather than thinking about a leftward or rightward shift in the money supply curve that causes an indirect change in interest rates, think of a direct increase or decrease in the policy rate.

Figure 11.9 shows the **market for reserves.** This is a graph that is relatively new to the AP Macroeconomics curriculum. The horizontal axis is the quantity of reserves in the banking system. The vertical axis incorporates several different interest rates, but for now let's keep it simple and label it the policy rate. In the U.S., this is the federal funds rate: the overnight interest rate paid by banks when they borrow from other banks.

The supply of reserves (S_R) is vertical because the quantity of reserves is controlled by the central bank. The unique feature of this graph is the three stages of the demand for reserves (D_R) curve. I have labeled them as ranges A, B, and C.

- Range A: If the policy rate is high enough, it will not affect the quantity of reserves being demanded. In the U.S. the discount rate serves as an upper limit that the policy rate *could* take. Recall that the discount rate is the rate that the Fed would charge a bank for overnight borrowing.
- Range B: This is the range that corresponds to a banking system with limited reserves. In this range, changes to the vertical supply of reserves, usually through open market operations, would cause the policy rate to rise or fall. We saw this in Figures 11.5 and 11.7.
- Range C: This is the range that corresponds to a banking system with ample reserves. An increase or decrease in the supply of reserves will have no impact on interest rates. Open market operations are used to maintain ample reserves and to keep S_R in this range. In this case, the policy rate is labeled PR_1.

A policy rate sandwich

Rather than shift the supply curve, the central bank simply changes the administrated interest rates to move the policy rate to a target range. The interest on reserves rate (IOR) and the overnight reverse repurchase agreement rate (ON RRP) are like the two slices of bread on a sandwich. These have been added to Figure 11.10. Tucked inside this sandwich is the policy rate.

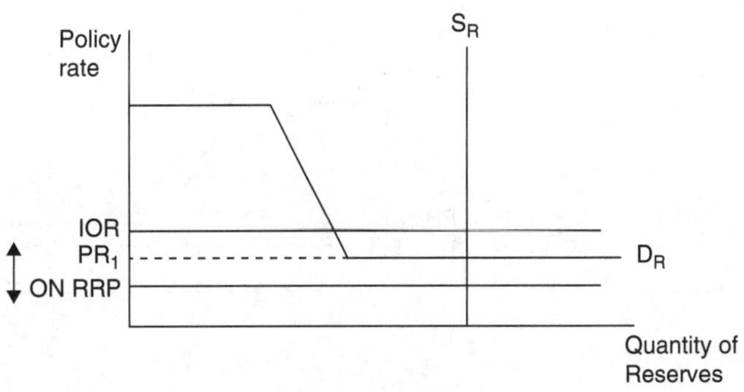

Figure 11.10

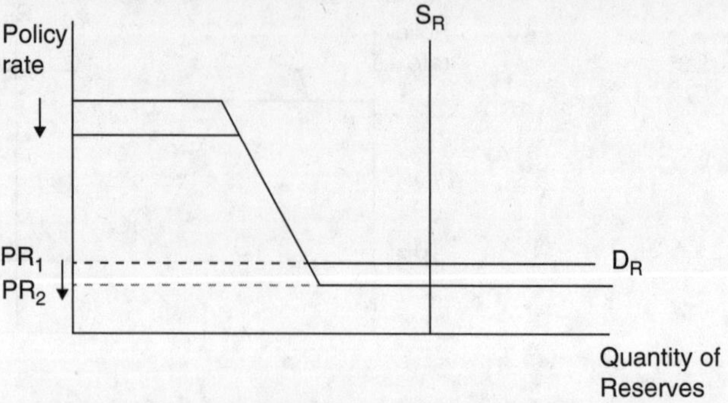

Figure 11.11

Across the broader economy, other interest rates will move with the federal funds rate (PR_1). This will affect the economy in much the same way as we discussed earlier in the chapter with a limited reserve banking system. If the central bank wants to increase the policy rate to counter high inflation, they raise the IOR and ON RRP rates, and the policy rate moves upward within those two bounds. If they want to decrease the policy rate to counter unemployment, they decrease the IOR and ON RRP rates and the policy rate moves downward within those two bounds.

Ample Reserves Monetary Policy with a Recessionary Gap

Suppose the economy is operating below full employment. The central bank would like to boost aggregate demand, so they begin to lower the administered rates to decrease the policy rate. This is shown in Figure 11.11.

As interest rates throughout the economy begin to fall, investment spending and consumer spending begins to increase, shifting aggregate demand to the right and reducing the recessionary gap.

On the other hand, suppose the economy is experiencing high inflation. The central bank would like to slow aggregate demand, so they begin to raise the administered rates to increase the policy rate. This is shown in Figure 11.12.

As interest rates across the economy begin to rise, investment spending and consumer spending begins to fall, shifting aggregate demand to the left and reducing the aggregate price level.

What's the bottom line?

To summarize, today the Fed (and other central banks with ample reserve systems) manipulates interest rates by keeping the federal funds rate within a range that is defined by the gap between the interest on reserves (IOR) and the ON RRP rates. Open market operations

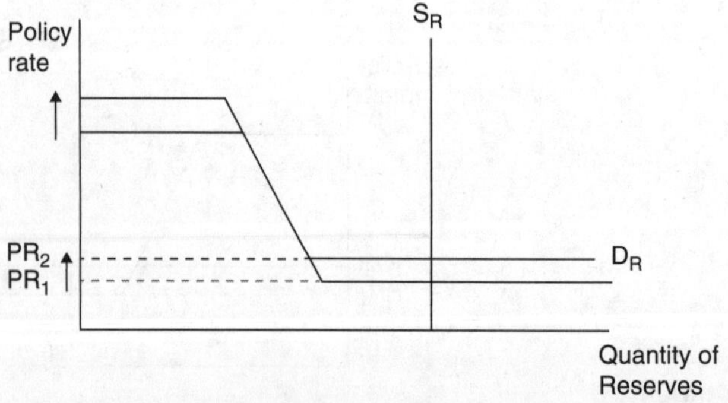

Figure 11.12

are used, but only to ensure that total bank reserves remain "ample." The discount rate, or the rate that a bank would pay to borrow directly from the Fed, serves as an upper limit for the federal funds rate. The reserve requirement is basically obsolete in a system of ample reserves and the Fed eliminated it in 2020.

To reiterate the point made at the top of this section, for the purposes of acing your AP Macro exam, you need to know the three traditional tools of monetary policy (reserve requirement, discount rate, and open market operations). In an economy with limited reserves, you must be able to discuss and draw the money market and AD/AS graphs, to show how buying bonds is used to fight a recessionary gap and selling bonds is used to fight an inflationary gap. You also must be able to describe how a central bank with ample reserves changes the administered rates to influence aggregate demand.

Coordination of Fiscal and Monetary Policy

In the United States, Congress and the president develop fiscal policy through the annual process of approving a spending budget and tax law. Chapter 10 showed how fiscal policy can be used to move the economy closer to full employment but that it has some weakness, especially in the case when private investment is crowded out by government borrowing.

"Monetary policy does not affect government spending."
—Elliot, AP Student

The central bank develops monetary policy and is independent of Congress and the president. This independence of monetary policy is believed to be a critical balance to fiscal policy that can be heavily politicized. After all, the creators of fiscal policy are elected by their constituents and might let an upcoming election taint the policy-making process. The central bank, free of election pressures, can develop monetary policy without this conflict of interest and perhaps work to counterbalance the downsides to fiscal policy. Let's look at three different scenarios where monetary and fiscal policy might be coordinated in Table 11.2.

Table 11.2

THE PROBLEM:	FISCAL POLICY SOLUTION	BUDGET IMPACT	POTENTIAL CONSEQUENCE	MONETARY POLICY COMPLEMENT	KEEP AN EYE ON . . .
Deep recessionary gap and high unemployment	Tax cuts *and* increased spending to rapidly increase AD	Large deficit	Higher interest rates, crowding out private investment, lower net exports, and even weaker AD	Lower interest rates to offset the impact of crowding out. Increases AD to assist fiscal policy	Higher inflation
Mild recessionary gap and moderate unemployment	Tax cuts *or* increased spending to gradually increase AD and real GDP	Moderate deficit	Rising prices, mild crowding out, lower net exports, weakening AD	Consider slight increase to interest rates to keep prices stable. Decreases AD, partially offsetting fiscal policy	Rising interest rates
Inflationary gap	Tax hikes *and/or* decreased spending to rapidly decrease AD and real GDP	Surplus	Lower interest rates "crowding in" private investment, higher net exports, and even stronger AD	Increase interest rates to reduce inflation. Decreases AD to assist fiscal policy	Higher unem-ployment

- In a deep recessionary gap, expansionary monetary policy could be used to assist expansionary fiscal policy to quickly move to full employment. The risk then becomes a burst of inflation.
- In a mild recessionary gap, contractionary monetary policy could be used to partially offset expansionary fiscal policy to gradually move to full employment. The risk then becomes rising interest rates.
- In an inflationary gap, contractionary monetary policy could be used to assist contractionary fiscal policy to put downward pressure on the price level. The risk then becomes a rising unemployment rate.

Are There Critics of Monetary Policy?

Some economists disagree with the effectiveness of monetary policy, particularly the expansionary policies that are designed to eliminate a recessionary gap. One group of economists, which has come to be known as the "monetarists," argues against active expansionary monetary policy on the grounds that such expansions of the money supply will not create more economic growth in the long run and will only create inflation. How would this happen?

Figure 11.13 shows an economy with a mild recessionary gap as real GDP (GDP_r) falls below full employment output (GDP_f). Suppose the central bank takes aggressive action to expand the money supply. With a lower interest rate, aggregate demand increases to AD_2, increasing real GDP beyond full employment. While the unemployment rate falls in the short run, the aggregate price level rises to PL_2 and inflation becomes a concern. As the economy, now with more money in circulation, adjusts to higher levels of spending, nominal wages and other factor prices rise, shifting the SRAS curve to the left to $SRAS_2$. When the economy fully adjusts, it is back at full employment, but the aggregate price level has now greatly risen to PL_3. Early monetarists such as Milton Friedman would therefore argue that such activist monetary policy doesn't "fix" the recession, it only creates inflation in the long run. The monetarists believe that the role of the central bank should be price stability, and the best way to accomplish this goal is to gradually and methodically increase the money supply by a fixed percentage each year.

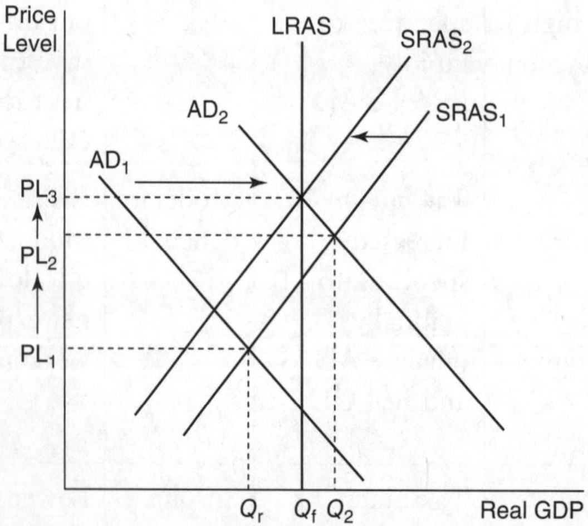

Figure 11.13

Another way to see the monetarist view of monetary policy is to examine the equation of exchange, the topic we turn to next.

Quantity Theory of Money

Fiscal policy directly puts money into, or takes money out of, the pockets of households and firms, but monetary policy depends on several cause-and-effect relationships. The critical link between monetary policy and real GDP is the relationship between changes in money supply, the real interest rate, and the level of private investment. After all, if the money supply increases and there is no increase in investment, expansionary monetary policy would have no effect on real GDP. As already noted, monetarists have become proponents of the **quantity theory of money**, which postulates that increasing the money supply has no effect on real GDP but only serves to increase the price level.

One way to view this theory is to use the **equation of exchange**. The equation says that nominal GDP ($P \times Q$) is equal to the quantity of money (M) multiplied by the number of times each dollar is spent in a year (V), the **velocity of money**. For example, if in a given year the money supply is \$100 and nominal GDP is \$1,000, then each dollar must be spent 10 times; $V = 10$.

$$MV = PQ, \text{ or } V = PQ/M$$

If the money supply (M) increases, this increase must be reflected in the other three variables. To accommodate an increase in money supply, the velocity of money must fall, the price level must rise, or the economy's output of goods and services must increase.

Historically, the velocity of money in the United States has been fairly constant and stable, so the increase in M must result in changes in either P or Q. Economists believe that the quantity of output produced in a given year is a function of technology and the supply of resources, rather than the quantity of money circulating in the economy. Therefore, the increased money supply is going to only create a higher price level—inflation.

- The quantity theory of money predicts that any increase in the money supply only causes an increase in the price level.

❯ Review Questions

1. Which function of money best defines \$1.25 as the price of a 20-ounce bottle of pop?

(A) Medium of exchange
(B) Unit of account
(C) Store of value
(D) Transfer of ownership
(E) Fiat money

2. If a bank has \$500 in checking deposits and the bank is required to reserve \$50, what is the reserve ratio? How much does the bank have in excess reserves?

(A) 10 percent, \$450 in excess reserves
(B) 90 percent, \$50 in excess reserves
(C) 90 percent, \$450 in excess reserves
(D) 10 percent, \$50 in excess reserves
(E) 10 percent, \$500 in excess reserves

3. A banking system has ample reserves and is experiencing a recessionary gap. Which of the following represents an appropriate response from the central bank?

(A) Buy government securities in an open market operation.
(B) Increase the interest rate that banks charge other banks for overnight loans.
(C) Decrease personal income tax rates.
(D) Sell government securities in an open market operation.
(E) Decrease the interest rate paid to banks that deposit reserves with the central bank.

4. If the money supply increases in a system with limited reserves, what happens in the money market (assuming money demand is downward sloping)?
(A) The nominal interest rates rises.
(B) The nominal interest rates falls.
(C) The nominal interest rate does not change.
(D) Transaction demand for money falls.
(E) Transaction demand for money rises.

5. To move the economy closer to full employment in a system with limited reserves, the central bank decides that the policy rate must be increased. The appropriate open market operation is to ______, which ______ the money supply, ______ aggregate demand, and fights ______.

	OMO	MONEY SUPPLY	AD	TO FIGHT
(A)	Buy bonds	Increases	Increase	Unemployment
(B)	Buy bonds	Increases	Increase	Inflation
(C)	Sell bonds	Decreases	Decrease	Unemployment
(D)	Sell bonds	Decreases	Increase	Inflation
(E)	Sell bonds	Decreases	Decrease	Inflation

6. Which of the following is a likely result of expansionary monetary policy in a recession?
(A) Aggregate demand decreases so that the price level falls.
(B) Aggregate demand increases, which increases real GDP and increases employment.
(C) Increases unemployment, but low prices negate this effect.
(D) It keeps interest rates high, which attracts foreign investment.
(E) It boosts the value of the dollar in foreign currency markets.

› Answers and Explanations

1. B—The price in this case measures the relative price (value) of the pop.

2. A—The reserve ratio = Required reserves/checking deposits = 0.1 = 10%. Excess reserves = (Checking deposits – Required reserves) = (\$500 – \$50) = \$450.

3. E—The central bank, when there are ample reserves, does not use open market operations to affect interest rates. If the interest rate paid to banks that deposit with the central bank is lowered, more bank reserves will be lent to borrowers, expanding aggregate demand.

4. B—If the demand for money is downward sloping, the nominal interest rate falls because the money supply curve has shifted rightward.

5. E—If the central bank has decided that moving to full employment requires an increase in the federal funds rate, it must sell bonds to decrease the money supply. The resulting increase in interest rates decreases AD and puts downward pressure on the price level.

6. B—Expansionary monetary policies decrease the interest rate, causing AD to increase, which increases GDP at equilibrium and increases employment.

› Rapid Review

Stock: A certificate that represents a claim to, or share of, the ownership of a firm.

Equity financing: The firm's method of raising funds for investment by issuing shares of stock to the public.

Bond: A certificate of indebtedness from the issuer to the bond holder.

Debt financing: A firm's way of raising investment funds by issuing bonds to the public.

Fiat money: Paper and coin money used to make transactions because the government declares it to be legal tender. Because it has no intrinsic value, it is backed by the public's trust that the government maintains its value.

Functions of money: Money serves three functions. It serves as a medium of exchange, a unit of account, and a store of value.

Money supply: The quantity of money in circulation as measured by the Federal Reserve (the Fed) as *M*1 and *M*2. Assumed to be fixed at a given point in time.

***M*1:** The most liquid of money definitions and the basis for all other more broadly defined measures of money. $M1 = \text{Cash} + \text{Coins} + \text{Checking deposits} + \text{Traveler's checks}$.

Liquidity: A measure of how easily an asset can be converted to cash. The more easily it can be converted to cash, the more liquid the asset.

Transaction demand: The amount of money held in order to make transactions. This is not related to the interest rate, but it increases as nominal GDP increases.

Asset demand: The amount of money demanded as an asset. As nominal interest rates rise, the opportunity cost of holding money begins to rise and you are more likely to lessen your asset demand for money.

Money demand: The demand for money is the sum of money demanded for transactions and money demanded as an asset. It is inversely related to the nominal interest rate.

Theory of liquidity preference: Keynes' theory that the interest rate adjusts to bring the money market into equilibrium.

Fractional (or limited) reserve banking: A system in which only a fraction of the total money deposited in banks is held in reserve as currency.

Reserve ratio (*rr*): The fraction of a bank's total deposits that are kept on reserve.

Reserve requirement: Regulation set by the central bank that states the minimum reserve ratio for banks. In a banking system with ample reserves there is essentially no reserve requirement.

Excess reserves: The cash reserves held by banks above and beyond the minimum reserve requirement.

T-account or balance sheet: A tabular way to show the assets and liabilities of a bank. Total assets must equal liabilities.

Asset of a bank: Anything owned by the bank or owed to the bank is an asset of the bank. Cash on reserve is an asset and so are loans made to citizens.

Liability of a bank: Anything owned by depositors or lenders is a liability to the bank. Checking deposits of citizens or loans made to the bank are liabilities to the bank.

Money multiplier: In a banking system with limited reserves, this measures the maximum amount of new checking deposits that can be created by a single dollar of excess reserves. $M = 1/(\text{reserve ratio}) = 1/rr$. The money multiplier is smaller if (a) at any stage the banks keep more than the required dollars in reserve, (b) at any stage borrowers do not redeposit funds into the bank and keep some as cash, and (c) customers are not willing to borrow.

Expansionary monetary policy: Designed to fix a recession by lowering interest rates to increase aggregate demand, lower the unemployment rate, and increase real GDP, which may increase the price level.

Contractionary monetary policy: Designed to avoid inflation by increasing interest rates to decrease aggregate demand, which lowers the price level and decreases real GDP back to full employment.

Open market operations (OMOs): A traditional tool of monetary policy, it involves the central bank's buying (or selling) of securities from (or to) commercial banks and the general public.

Federal funds rate: The interest rate paid on short-term loans made from one bank to another.

Discount rate: The interest rate commercial banks pay on short-term loans from the Fed.

Ample reserves regime: The current framework for the Federal Reserve's monetary policy. The banking system is provided enough cash reserves so that changes in the money supply do not cause a change in the federal funds rate.

Interest on reserves (IOR): The interest rate that is paid to banks that deposit excess reserves with the Fed. This is the primary tool of current monetary policy.

Overnight reverse repurchase agreement (ON RRP): The interest rate paid to a financial institution on an overnight transaction in which the Federal Reserve sells a U.S. government security to the financial institution while agreeing to buy the security back the next day. This is a secondary tool of current monetary policy.

Quantity theory of money: A theory that asserts that the quantity of money determines the price level and that the growth rate of money determines the rate of inflation.

Administered interest rates: In a banking system with ample reserves, these are the interest rates determined by the central bank and used to guide the policy rate to a target range. In the U.S., this is primarily the interest rate paid on reserve balances (IOR) deposited by banks in the Federal Reserve.

Policy rate: An interest rate that banks charge other banks for short-term lending. In the U.S., the policy rate is the federal funds rate. In a banking system with ample reserves, this is the rate that the central bank affects to conduct monetary policy.

Market for reserves: In a banking system with ample reserves, this is the model used to show how changes to the administered interest rates (like the IOR in the U.S.) affect the policy rate.

Equation of exchange: The equation says that nominal GDP ($P \times Q$) is equal to the quantity of money (M) multiplied by the number of times each dollar is spent in a year (V). $MV = PQ$.

Velocity of money: The average number of times that a dollar is spent in a year. V is defined as PQ/M.

International Trade

IN THIS CHAPTER

Summary: Economists agree on few things, but one of the few unifying themes in economics is that free and fair trade between two nations is mutually beneficial. Chapter 12 begins by reviewing the concept of comparative advantage and gains from trade and the difference between the domestic and world price of a good. This chapter also revisits the currency exchange markets to illustrate how trade between nations requires the trade of currency and the connection of monetary policy to foreign exchange rates. Finally, we look at the economic impact of trade barriers.

Key Ideas

- Comparative and Absolute Advantage
- Specialization and Gains from Trade
- Balance of Payments
- Foreign Exchange
- Trade Barriers

12.1 Comparative Advantage and Gains from Trade

Main Topics: *Comparative and Absolute Advantage; Gains from Trade; Exports, Imports, and the World Price*

Chapter 5 of this book introduces, albeit from the microeconomic perspective, the concept of production possibility curves. Comparative advantage and specialization at the microeconomic level explains why brain surgeons do not fly 747s and pilots do not analyze CAT scans. At the macroeconomic level, the **law of comparative advantage** says that nations can mutually benefit from trade so long as the relative production costs differ.

Comparative and Absolute Advantage

Our discussion of production possibilities illustrated the law of increasing costs. The more an economy produces of any one good, the more costly it becomes to produce the next unit. Rising costs of production lead to a search for less costly ways to produce and consume those goods. In many cases, this search leads to a potential trading partner who has **comparative advantage** in the production of a good. If Nation ABC can produce a good at lower opportunity cost than can Nation XYZ, it is said that Nation ABC has comparative advantage. An example can illustrate how this works between two states, but the same principle works between two nations.

Example:

Climate and topography have blessed Indiana with land extremely suitable for the cultivation of soybeans but there remains very little harvestable timber. Oregon's timber production is unmatched, but farmers find it difficult to produce soybean crops that can compare to those grown in Indiana. Table 12.1 summarizes the production possibilities of these two isolated economies. Because Oregon can produce more timber than Indiana, Oregon is said to have an **absolute advantage** over Indiana in timber production. Indiana has an absolute advantage over Oregon in soybean production. Trade does not rely on absolute advantages but on comparative advantages.

Table 12.1

INDIANA		OREGON	
Soybeans (tons)	**Timber (tons)**	**Soybeans (tons)**	**Timber (tons)**
0	6	0	10
9	3	5	5
18	0	10	0

Comparative Advantage and Specialization

In isolation, both states can produce soybeans and timber along their production possibility curves or frontiers (PPC or PPF), which are constrained by the available technology and resources. Suppose that without trade, they enjoy consuming at the midpoint of the PPC. But if there are differences in production costs, they can each gain from specialization and trade. The opportunity costs of each good can be found from the table and can be illustrated in a production possibility curve for each state:

Oregon:
Opportunity cost of timber is 1 soybean.
Opportunity cost of soybeans is 1 timber.

Indiana:
Opportunity cost of timber is 3 soybeans.
Opportunity cost of soybeans is ⅓ timber.

Since Indiana can produce soybeans at a cost that is lower than Oregon's cost of soybeans, Indiana has a comparative advantage in soybeans. Oregon can produce timber at a lower cost than Indiana's cost of timber, so Oregon has a comparative advantage in timber production. With these differences in cost, Indiana should specialize in soybean production (zero timber), while Oregon should specialize in timber production (zero soybeans). Then the two should trade. These specialization points are labeled in Figure 12.1.

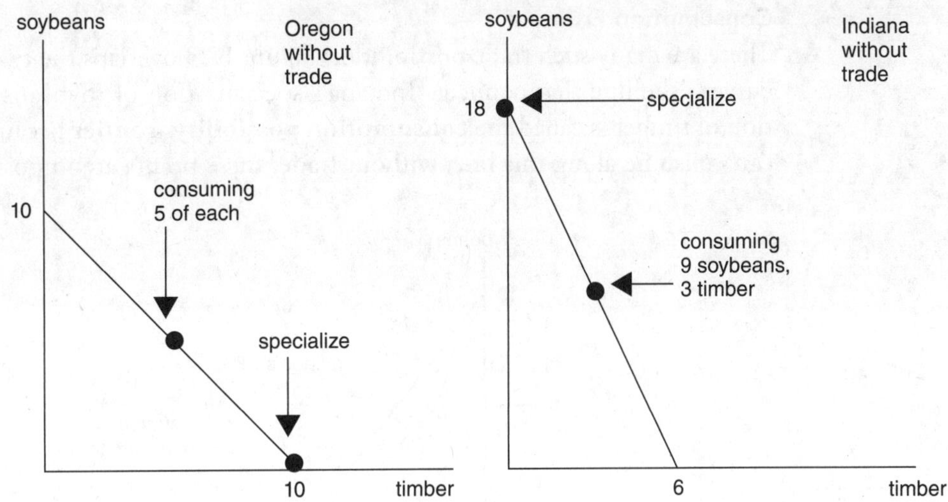

Figure 12.1

Gains from Trade

After each state specializes, suppose that each decides to keep half of its production and send the other half to the other state. See Figure 12.2.

Oregon:

Produce 10 timbers and send 5 to Indiana in exchange for 9 soybeans. The cost of a soybean before trade was 1 timber. Now we're getting 9 soybeans but only giving up 5 timbers. The cost of giving up 1 timber is now is 5/9, which is less than 1 timber. Great deal!

Indiana:

Produce 18 soybeans, and send 9 to Oregon in exchange for 5 timbers. The cost of a timber before trade was 3 soybeans. Now we're getting 5 timbers and only giving up 9 soybeans. The cost now is 9/5, which is less than 3 soybeans. Great deal!

Another look at the production possibility curves after the trade shows that each state has actually moved *beyond* the constraints of their technology and resources.

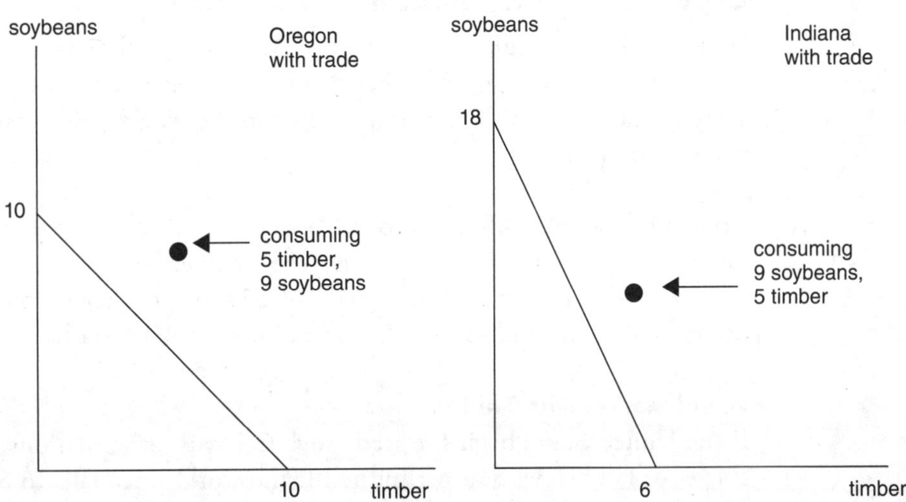

Figure 12.2

Consumption Frontier

There are many such trade possibilities. Figure 12.3 overlaps the two production possibility curves. The line that connects Indiana's specialization of soybeans to Oregon's specialization of timber is called the **consumption possibility frontier** because with trade, each state can consume along this line; without trade, these points are impossible to attain.

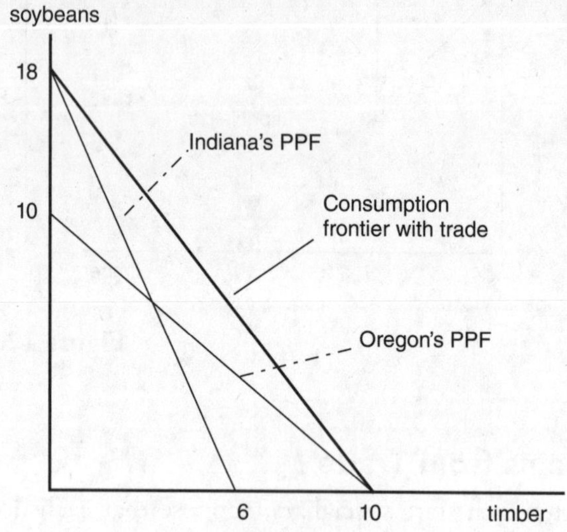

"Make sure to draw your graphs BIG on the test so they're easier to read."
—Sophia, AP Student

Figure 12.3

- If the opportunity costs of production are different, two economies find it mutually beneficial to specialize and trade.
- If you have comparative advantage in production of a good, specialize in production of that good and trade for the other.
- Specialization and trade allow nations to consume beyond the PPC.
- Free trade (i.e., without trade barriers) based on comparative advantage allows for a more efficient allocation of resources and greater prosperity for the trading partners than can be achieved without free trade.

Exports, Imports, and the World Price

In the market for a commodity like soybeans, many nations are both producers of soybeans and traders of soybeans. Whether or not a nation is a net exporter or a net importer of soybeans depends on the difference between the **world price** with trade and the **domestic price** without trade.

Domestic Market Without Trade

Figure 12.4 illustrates the competitive U.S. market for soybeans without trade. The (admittedly hypothetical) competitive price of $10 per bushel is found at the intersection of domestic demand and supply. At this point six million bushels are produced.

World Market with Trade

If the United States begins to trade soybeans with other nations, the world price may rise above, or fall below, $10 per bushel. If the world price falls to $8, there exists a shortage of soybeans in the U.S. market. Domestic producers supply only four million bushels, but domestic consumers demand eight million bushels. The United States must then import

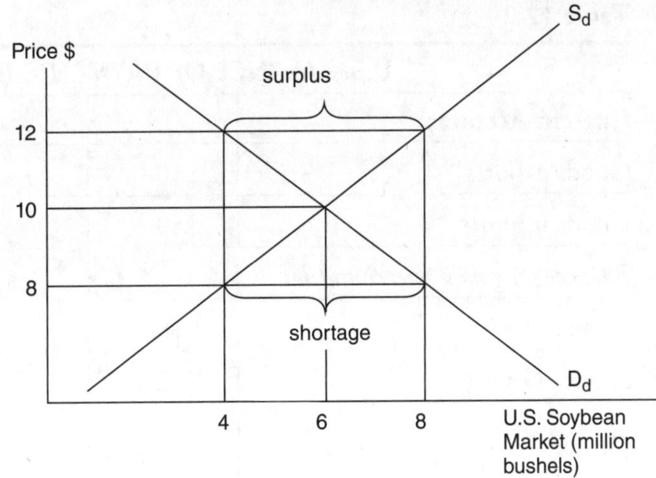

Figure 12.4

the difference of four million bushels. If the world price rises to $12, there exists a four-million bushel surplus in the U.S. market and the United States exports this surplus.

So, to reiterate:

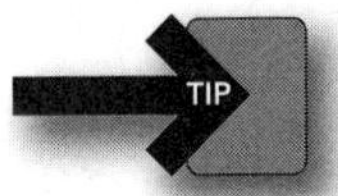

- If the world price of a good is *above* the domestic price, the nation becomes an exporter of that good.
- If the world price of a good is *below* the domestic price, the nation becomes an importer of that good.

12.2 Balance of Payments

Main Topic: *Balance of Payments Accounts*

If Japanese citizens wish to purchase U.S. soybeans, the Japanese must pay in dollars. If U.S. citizens wish to buy Spanish olives, the Americans must pay in euros. Before goods can be exchanged between foreign trading partners, the currency of the importing nation must first be converted to the currency of the exporting nation.

Balance of Payments Accounts

When American citizens and firms exchange goods and services with foreign consumers and firms, payments are sent back and forth through major banks around the world. The Bureau of Economic Analysis tracks the flow of goods and currency in the **balance of payments statement**. This statement summarizes the payments received by the United States from foreign countries and the payments sent by the United States to foreign countries. Table 12.2 summarizes the main components of a hypothetical balance of trade.

Current Account

The current account shows current import and export payments of both goods and services. It also reflects investment income sent to foreign investors and investment income received by U.S. citizens who invest abroad. For example, if a Canadian is receiving dividends from an American corporation or interest from a U.S. Treasury bill, these dollars would be sent out of the country. After accounting for all the payments sent to foreign countries and payments received from foreign countries, the hypothetical balance on the current account was –$26. A deficit balance such as this tells us that the United States sent more American dollars abroad than foreign currency received in current transactions.

Table 12.2

U.S. BALANCE OF PAYMENTS (HYPOTHETICAL)			
Current Account			
Goods exports	$30		
Goods imports	–$50		
Balance on goods (merchandise)		*–$20*	
Service exports	$18		
Service imports	–$12		
Balance on services		*$6*	
Balance on goods and service		*–$14*	Note: This negative balance indicates a trade deficit in goods and services.
Net investment income	–$5		
Net transfers	–$7		
Balance on current account		*–$26*	
Capital (or Financial) Account			
Inflow of foreign assets to U.S.	$35		
Outflow of U.S. assets abroad	–$20		
Balance on capital account		*$15*	
Official Reserves Account			
Official reserves		*$11*	
		$0	

Capital (or Financial) Account

When a corporation from one nation buys a foreign firm, or real estate or financial assets of another nation, it appears in the capital account. For example, if a Swedish firm buys a manufacturing facility in Idaho, or if a Mexican citizen buys a U.S. Treasury bond, it is recorded as an inflow of foreign capital assets into the United States. If an American firm buys a shipbuilding company in Turkey, it would be an outflow of assets to foreign nations. A surplus balance of $11 tells us that there was more foreign capital investment in the United States than there was U.S. investment abroad.

Official Reserves Account

The Federal Reserve holds quantities of foreign currency called **official reserves**. When adding the current account and the capital account, if the United States has sent more dollars out than foreign currency has come in, as in the earlier hypothetical example, there exists a **balance of payments deficit**. In this case the Fed credits the account so that it balances. This is similar to taking money from your savings account to make up for an overdrafted checking account. If the current and capital account balances are positive, more foreign currency was coming into the United States than American dollars flowed abroad.

With this **balance of payments surplus**, the Fed transfers the surplus currency back into official reserves.

A Circular Flow of Dollars

With the exception of some statistical discrepancies, the U.S. dollars that Americans send to foreigners are equal to the U.S. dollars that foreigners send to Americans. It is helpful to think of the global circulation of dollars as another example of the circular-flow model. When you buy an imported jacket made in Honduras, this appears in the U.S. current account as a negative entry, because those dollars are leaving the country. However, what will a Honduran jacket producer do with those dollars? American dollars in Honduras are not very useful unless they are being spent on either American-made goods and services or American assets. One way or another, either through the purchase of an American good (like a Ford) or the purchase of an American financial asset (like a share of Ford stock), those dollars will return as a positive entry in either the current or capital account. And while the Federal Reserve will make short-term adjustments to the official reserves account to balance the difference between the current account balance and the capital account balance, in the long term, dollars that leave the United States will eventually circle back into the United States. Thus, with all else equal, if Americans import more goods and services from abroad, the current account will move in the deficit direction but the capital/financial account will move in the surplus direction as those dollars return.

To summarize:

- U.S. imports require a demand for foreign currency and a supply of U.S. dollars.
- U.S. exports require a supply of foreign currency and a demand for U.S. dollars.
- If Current account balance + Capital account balance < 0, there is a balance of payments deficit.
- If Current account balance + Capital account balance > 0, there is a balance of payments surplus.

12.3 Foreign Exchange Rates

Main Topics: *Currency Markets, Appreciating and Depreciating Currency, Changes in Exchange Rates, Connection to Monetary Policy*

The previous section of the chapter discussed accounting for the flow of goods and services and currency between trading partners. The foreign exchange market, the topic of the following section, facilitates the importing and exporting of goods around the world.

Currency Markets

When nations trade goods and services, someone in the process is also trading currency. The rate of exchange between two currencies is determined in the foreign currency market. Some nations fix their exchange rates, while others are allowed to "float" with the forces of demand and supply. For example, in the flexible exchange market for euros pictured in Figure 12.5, the equilibrium 2-dollar price of a euro is at the intersection of the supply of euros and the demand. Likewise, in the market for dollars seen in Figure 12.6, the equilibrium euro price of one dollar is 0.50 euros. This floating exchange rate has an impact on the balance of payments of both the United States and the European Union.

So:

- The **exchange rate** between two currencies tells you how much of one currency you must give up to get one unit of the second currency.
- For example, if 2 dollars = 1 euro, 1 dollar = 0.5 euro.
- For example, if 1 dollar = 10 pesos, 10 cents = 1 peso.

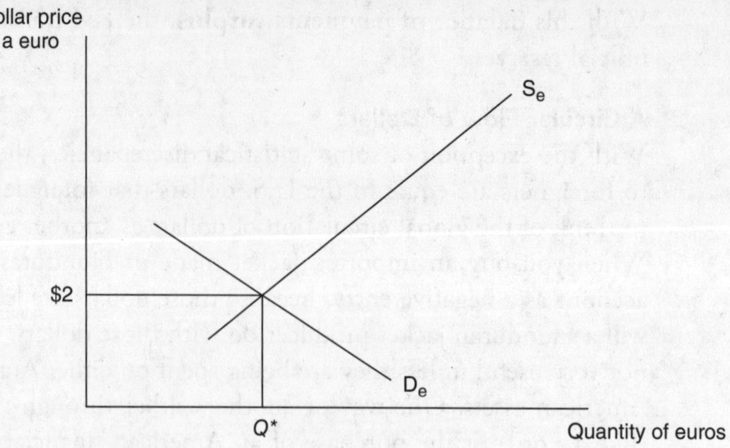

Figure 12.5

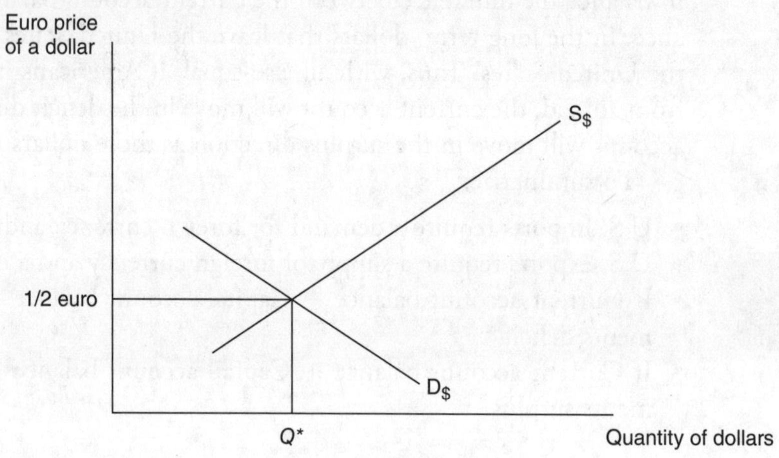

Figure 12.6

Appreciating and Depreciating Currency

If the U.S. economy is strong, Americans increase their demand for European goods and services. As American consumers increase their demand for the euro, they increase the supply of dollars in the foreign exchange market; the dollar price of a euro rises, and the euro price of a dollar falls. The euro as an asset is **appreciating** in value, and the dollar as an asset is **depreciating** in value. The changing value of euros and dollars is seen in Figures 12.7 and 12.8.

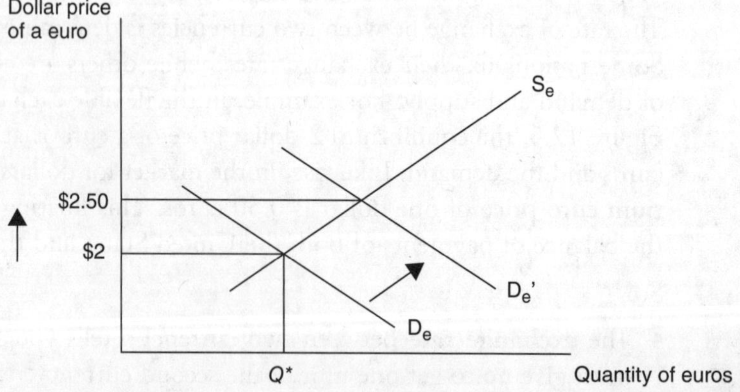

Figure 12.7

"Don't forget to label your axes."
—Timot,
AP Student

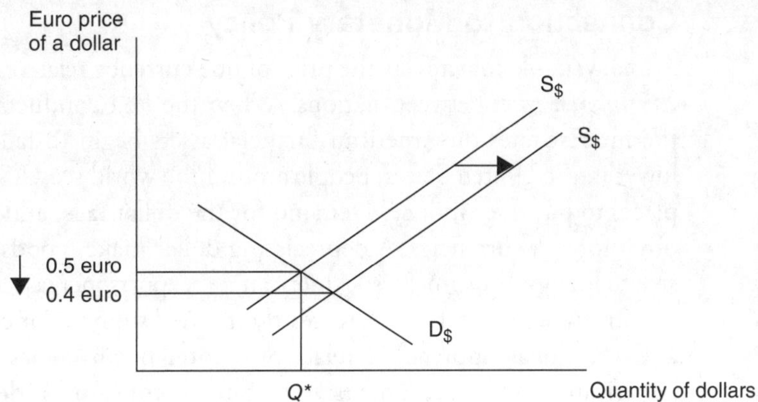

Figure 12.8

To summarize:

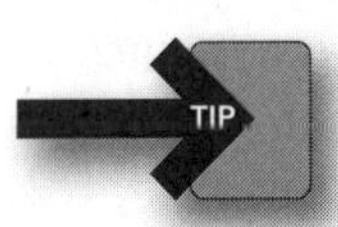

- When the price of a currency is rising, it is said to be *appreciating*, or "stronger." More dollars are needed to buy a euro.
- When the price of a currency is falling, it is said to be *depreciating*, or "weaker." Fewer euros are needed to buy a dollar.

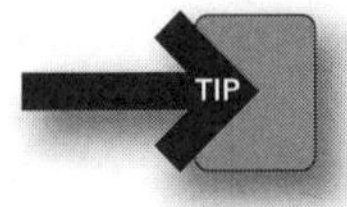

It is *very* important to label the axes correctly in a FRQ that asks you to draw the market for a currency. If the market is for the dollar, the *x*-axis should be labeled "Quantity of dollars." The label on the *y*-axis depends on how the dollar is being priced. If we are pricing dollars in terms of the number of euros it takes to purchase 1 dollar, then the correct label is "Euros per dollar" or "Euro price of a dollar" or even "€/$." You will *not* earn a graphing point if you call it simply "Price," "P," or "$."

Changes in Exchange Rates

The preceding example illustrates that market forces and changing macroeconomic variables have an impact on the rate of exchange between the dollar and the euro. There are several determinants that affect currency appreciation and depreciation.

Consumer Tastes. When domestic consumers build a stronger preference for foreign-produced goods and services, the demand for those currencies increases and the dollar depreciates. On the other hand, if foreign consumers increase their demand for U.S.-made goods, the dollar appreciates.

Relative Incomes. When one nation's macroeconomy is strong and incomes are rising, all else equal, they increase their demand for all goods, including those produced abroad. So if Europeans are enjoying economic growth and the United States is in a recession, the relative buying power of European citizens is growing. They increase their consumption of both domestic and U.S.-made goods, increasing demand for the dollar and appreciating its value.

Relative Inflation. If one nation's price level is rising faster than that of another nation, consumers seek the goods that are relatively less expensive. If European inflation is higher than inflation in the United States, U.S.-made goods are a relative bargain to German consumers and the dollar appreciates. This is another good reason for the Fed to keep inflationary pressure low.

Speculation. Because foreign currencies can be traded as assets, there are investors who seek to profit from buying currency at a low rate and selling it at a higher rate. For example, if it appears that future interest rates will fall in the United States relative to interest rates in Japan, the yen is looking like a good investment. Speculators would then increase their demand for Japanese financial assets, thus appreciating the yen and depreciating the dollar.

Connection to Monetary Policy

A final variable that affects the price of one currency relative to another is a difference in *relative interest rates* between nations. When the Fed conducts expansionary monetary policy, the interest rates on American financial assets begin to fall. If the interest rate is relatively lower in the United States, people around the world see U.S. financial assets as less attractive places to put their money. Demand for the dollar falls, and the dollar depreciates relative to other foreign currencies. A depreciating dollar makes goods in the United States less expensive to foreign consumers, so American net exports increase, which shifts the AD to the right.

Likewise, if the Fed decreases the money supply, American interest rates begin to rise and the dollar appreciates relative to foreign currencies. An appreciating dollar makes American goods more expensive to foreign consumers, decreasing American net exports, shifting AD to the left.

Be careful! When interest rates rise, we see a decrease in capital investments (machinery and other equipment) because it becomes more costly to borrow for those projects. But when interest rates rise, we see an increase in financial investments (bonds) because income earned on those bonds is rising.

Again:

- If the Fed ↓*i%*, ↓D$, Depreciates the $, ↑ U.S. Net Exports, ↑ AD.
- If the Fed ↑*i%*, ↑D$, Appreciates the $, ↓ U.S. Net Exports, ↓ AD.

Pay attention to the relationship between relative interest rates and exchange rates because it has made an appearance on several recent AP Macroeconomics exams.

All else equal, demand for the U.S. dollar increases and the dollar appreciates relative to the euro if:

- European taste for American-made goods is stronger.
- European relative incomes are rising, increasing demand for U.S. goods.
- The U.S. relative price level is falling, making U.S. goods relatively less expensive.
- Speculators are betting on the dollar to rise in value.
- The U.S. relative interest rate is higher, making the United States a relatively more attractive place for financial investments (i.e., bonds).

12.4 Trade Barriers

Main Topics: *Tariffs*, *Quotas*

The issue of free trade is hotly politicized. Proponents usually argue that free trade raises the standard of living in *both nations*, and most economists agree. Detractors argue that free trade, especially with nations that pay lower wages than those paid to domestic workers, costs domestic jobs in higher-wage nations. The evidence shows that in some industries, job losses have certainly occurred as free trade has become more prevalent. To protect domestic jobs, nations can impose trade barriers. Tariffs and quotas are among the most common of barriers. It should be noted that the topic of trade barriers does not fall neatly into a review of macroeconomics or microeconomics. A policy like a tariff on imported solar panels has a clear impact on the micro market for solar panels, but such a policy will also have an impact on the macroeconomy. Just to be on the safe side, take a quick review of this section in advance of your AP Macro exam.

Tariffs

In general, there are two types of tariffs. A **revenue tariff** is an excise tax levied on goods that are not produced in the domestic market. For example, the United States does not produce bananas. If a revenue tariff were levied on bananas, it would not be a serious impediment to trade, and it would raise a little revenue for the government. A **protective tariff** is an excise tax levied on a good that is produced in the domestic market. Though this tariff also raises revenue, the purpose of this tariff, as the name suggests, is to protect the domestic industry from global competition by increasing the price of foreign products.

Example:

The hypothetical domestic supply and demand for steel is pictured in Figure 12.9. The domestic price is $100 per ton and the equilibrium quantity of domestic steel is 10 million tons. Maybe other nations can produce steel at lower cost. As a result, in the competitive world market, the price is $80 per ton. At that price, the United States would demand 12 million tons but only produce eight million tons and so four million tons are **imported**. It is important to see that in the competitive (free trade) world market, consumer surplus is maximized and no deadweight loss exists. You can see the consumer surplus as the triangle below the demand curve and above the $80 world price.

If the steel industry is successful in getting a protective tariff passed through Congress, the world price rises by $10, increasing the quantity of domestic steel supplied, reducing the amount of steel imported from four million to two million tons. A higher price and lower consumption reduces the area of consumer surplus and creates deadweight loss.

Economic Effects of the Tariff

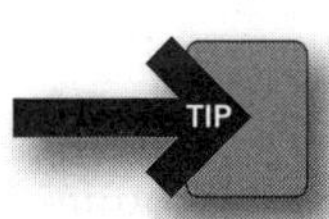

- *Consumers pay higher prices and consume less steel.* If you are building airplanes or door hinges, you have seen an increase in your costs.
- *Consumer surplus has been lost.*
- *Domestic producers increase output.* Domestic steel firms are not subject to the tariff, so they can sell more steel at the price of $90 than they could at $80.
- *Declining imports.* Fewer tons of imported steel arrive in the United States.

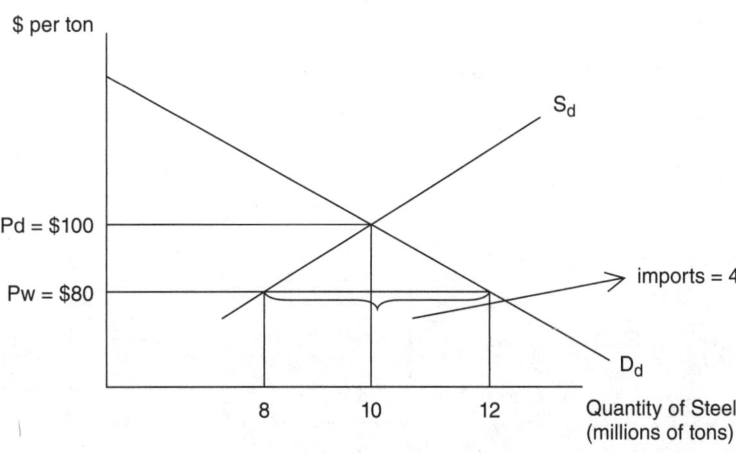

Figure 12.9

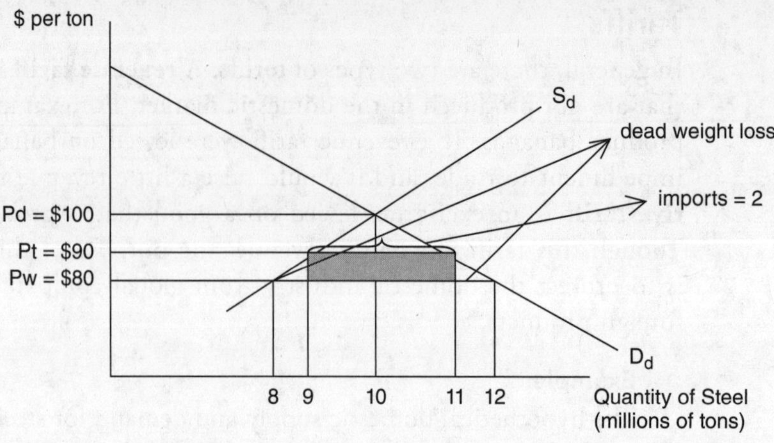

Figure 12.10

- *Tariff revenue.* The government collects $10 × 2 million = $20 million in tariff revenue, as seen in the shaded box in Figure 12.10. This is a transfer from consumers of steel to the government, not an increase in the total well-being of the nation. Note: The tariff is NOT paid by the nations that import steel into the US market, it is paid by American consumers of steel.
- *Inefficiency.* There was a reason the world price was lower than the domestic price. It was more efficient to produce steel abroad and export it to the United States. By taxing this efficiency, the United States promotes the less efficient domestic industry and stunts the efficient foreign sector. As a result, resources are diverted from the efficient to the inefficient sector.
- *Deadweight loss now exists.*

Quotas

Quotas work in much the same way as a tariff. An **import quota** is a maximum amount of a good that can be imported into the domestic market. With a quota, the government only allows two million tons to be imported. Figure 12.11 looks much like Figure 12.10, only without revenue collected by government. So the impact of the quota, with the exception of the revenue, is the same: higher consumer price and inefficient resource allocation.

"It is important to know the differences between tariffs and quotas."
—Lucas, AP Student

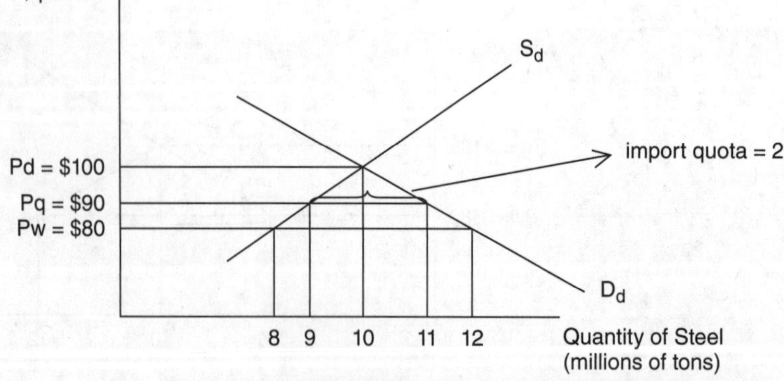

Figure 12.11

Tariffs and quotas share many of the same economic effects:

- Both hurt consumers with artificially high prices and lower consumer surplus.
- Both protect inefficient domestic producers at the expense of efficient foreign firms, creating deadweight loss.
- Both reallocate economic resources toward inefficient producers.
- Tariffs collect revenue for the government, while quotas do not.

❯ Review Questions

1. The United States produces rice in a competitive market. With free trade, the world price is lower than the domestic price. What must be true?

(A) The United States begins to import rice to make up for a domestic shortage.
(B) The United States begins to export rice to make up for a domestic shortage.
(C) The United States begins to import rice to eliminate a domestic surplus.
(D) The United States begins to export rice to eliminate a domestic surplus.
(E) There is no incentive to import or export rice.

2. If the U.S. dollar and Chinese yuan are traded in flexible currency markets, which of the following causes an appreciation of the dollar relative to the Chinese yuan?

(A) Lower interest rates in the United States relative to China
(B) Lower price levels in China relative to the United States
(C) Growing American preference to consume more Chinese-made goods
(D) Rising per capita GDP in China, increasing imports from the United States
(E) Speculation that the Chinese will decrease the money supply

3. You hear that the United States has a negative balance in the current account. With this information we conclude that

(A) there is a trade deficit.
(B) there is a capital account deficit.
(C) there is a capital account surplus.
(D) more U.S. dollars are being sent abroad than foreign currencies are being sent to the United States.
(E) there is a trade surplus.

4. Which of the following is a consequence of a protective tariff on imported steel?

(A) Net exports fall.
(B) Income is transferred from domestic steel consumers to domestic steel producers.
(C) Allocative efficiency is improved.
(D) Income is transferred from domestic steel producers to foreign steel producers.
(E) Aggregate supply increases.

5. If the Japanese economy suffers a deep, prolonged recession, in what ways would U.S. net exports and the values of the dollar and yen change?

	U.S. NET EXPORTS	VALUE OF DOLLAR	VALUE OF YEN
(A)	Decrease	Increase	Increase
(B)	Decrease	Decrease	Decrease
(C)	Decrease	Decrease	Increase
(D)	Increase	Decrease	Increase
(E)	Increase	Increase	Increase

6. When the United States places an import quota on imported sugar, we expect which of the following effects?

(A) Consumers seek substitutes for sugar and products that use sugar.
(B) Consumers consume more sugar and products that use sugar.
(C) The supply of sugar increases.
(D) Net exports in the United States fall.
(E) The government collects revenue on every ton of imported sugar.

› Answers and Explanations

1. **A**—If the world price is below the domestic price, a shortage exists in the domestic market. The importation of foreign rice fills this shortage.
2. **D**—Higher per capita income in trading nations increases demand for imported goods. The Chinese consumer increases demand for U.S. goods and services and for dollars.
3. **C**—When there is a negative balance in the current account, this does not always mean that there is a trade deficit. After all, there is more to the current account than the trade of goods and services. However, when there is a negative balance in the current account, there must be a positive balance (or surplus) in the capital account.
4. **B**—Protective tariffs increase the price of steel above the free-trade equilibrium. This higher price is a transfer of money from consumers to domestic producers of steel.
5. **C**—When the Japanese economy is suffering, demand for U.S. goods falls, decreasing U.S. net exports and demand for dollars. The dollar depreciates and the yen appreciates.
6. **A**—A quota increases the price of sugar so consumers seek substitutes. We may see rising demand for sugar-free gum or falling demand for rich desserts.

› Rapid Review

World price: The global equilibrium price of a good when nations engage in trade.

Domestic price: The equilibrium price of a good in a nation without trade.

Balance of payments statement: A summary of the payments received by the United States from foreign countries and the payments sent by the United States to foreign countries.

Current account: This account shows current import and export payments of both goods and services and investment income sent to foreign investors of United States and investment income received by U.S. citizens who invest abroad.

Capital (or financial) account: This account shows the flow of investment on real or financial assets between a nation and foreigners.

Official reserves account: The Fed's adjustment of a deficit or surplus in the current and capital account by the addition or subtraction of foreign currencies so that the balance of payments is zero.

Exchange rate: The price of one currency in terms of a second currency.

Appreciating (depreciating) currency: When the value of a currency is rising (falling) relative to another currency, it is said to be appreciating (depreciating).

Determinants of exchange rates: External factors that increase the price of one currency relative to another.

Revenue tariff: An excise tax levied on goods not produced in the domestic market.

Protective tariff: An excise tax levied on a good that is produced in the domestic market so that it may be protected from foreign competition.

Import quota: A limitation on the amount of a good that can be imported into the domestic market.

Build Your Test-Taking Confidence

AP Macroeconomics Practice Exam 1
AP Macroeconomics Practice Exam 2

AP Macroeconomics Practice Exam 1

SECTION I: Multiple-Choice Questions

ANSWER SHEET

1 Ⓐ Ⓑ Ⓒ Ⓓ Ⓔ	21 Ⓐ Ⓑ Ⓒ Ⓓ Ⓔ	41 Ⓐ Ⓑ Ⓒ Ⓓ Ⓔ
2 Ⓐ Ⓑ Ⓒ Ⓓ Ⓔ	22 Ⓐ Ⓑ Ⓒ Ⓓ Ⓔ	42 Ⓐ Ⓑ Ⓒ Ⓓ Ⓔ
3 Ⓐ Ⓑ Ⓒ Ⓓ Ⓔ	23 Ⓐ Ⓑ Ⓒ Ⓓ Ⓔ	43 Ⓐ Ⓑ Ⓒ Ⓓ Ⓔ
4 Ⓐ Ⓑ Ⓒ Ⓓ Ⓔ	24 Ⓐ Ⓑ Ⓒ Ⓓ Ⓔ	44 Ⓐ Ⓑ Ⓒ Ⓓ Ⓔ
5 Ⓐ Ⓑ Ⓒ Ⓓ Ⓔ	25 Ⓐ Ⓑ Ⓒ Ⓓ Ⓔ	45 Ⓐ Ⓑ Ⓒ Ⓓ Ⓔ
6 Ⓐ Ⓑ Ⓒ Ⓓ Ⓔ	26 Ⓐ Ⓑ Ⓒ Ⓓ Ⓔ	46 Ⓐ Ⓑ Ⓒ Ⓓ Ⓔ
7 Ⓐ Ⓑ Ⓒ Ⓓ Ⓔ	27 Ⓐ Ⓑ Ⓒ Ⓓ Ⓔ	47 Ⓐ Ⓑ Ⓒ Ⓓ Ⓔ
8 Ⓐ Ⓑ Ⓒ Ⓓ Ⓔ	28 Ⓐ Ⓑ Ⓒ Ⓓ Ⓔ	48 Ⓐ Ⓑ Ⓒ Ⓓ Ⓔ
9 Ⓐ Ⓑ Ⓒ Ⓓ Ⓔ	29 Ⓐ Ⓑ Ⓒ Ⓓ Ⓔ	49 Ⓐ Ⓑ Ⓒ Ⓓ Ⓔ
10 Ⓐ Ⓑ Ⓒ Ⓓ Ⓔ	30 Ⓐ Ⓑ Ⓒ Ⓓ Ⓔ	50 Ⓐ Ⓑ Ⓒ Ⓓ Ⓔ
11 Ⓐ Ⓑ Ⓒ Ⓓ Ⓔ	31 Ⓐ Ⓑ Ⓒ Ⓓ Ⓔ	51 Ⓐ Ⓑ Ⓒ Ⓓ Ⓔ
12 Ⓐ Ⓑ Ⓒ Ⓓ Ⓔ	32 Ⓐ Ⓑ Ⓒ Ⓓ Ⓔ	52 Ⓐ Ⓑ Ⓒ Ⓓ Ⓔ
13 Ⓐ Ⓑ Ⓒ Ⓓ Ⓔ	33 Ⓐ Ⓑ Ⓒ Ⓓ Ⓔ	53 Ⓐ Ⓑ Ⓒ Ⓓ Ⓔ
14 Ⓐ Ⓑ Ⓒ Ⓓ Ⓔ	34 Ⓐ Ⓑ Ⓒ Ⓓ Ⓔ	54 Ⓐ Ⓑ Ⓒ Ⓓ Ⓔ
15 Ⓐ Ⓑ Ⓒ Ⓓ Ⓔ	35 Ⓐ Ⓑ Ⓒ Ⓓ Ⓔ	55 Ⓐ Ⓑ Ⓒ Ⓓ Ⓔ
16 Ⓐ Ⓑ Ⓒ Ⓓ Ⓔ	36 Ⓐ Ⓑ Ⓒ Ⓓ Ⓔ	56 Ⓐ Ⓑ Ⓒ Ⓓ Ⓔ
17 Ⓐ Ⓑ Ⓒ Ⓓ Ⓔ	37 Ⓐ Ⓑ Ⓒ Ⓓ Ⓔ	57 Ⓐ Ⓑ Ⓒ Ⓓ Ⓔ
18 Ⓐ Ⓑ Ⓒ Ⓓ Ⓔ	38 Ⓐ Ⓑ Ⓒ Ⓓ Ⓔ	58 Ⓐ Ⓑ Ⓒ Ⓓ Ⓔ
19 Ⓐ Ⓑ Ⓒ Ⓓ Ⓔ	39 Ⓐ Ⓑ Ⓒ Ⓓ Ⓔ	59 Ⓐ Ⓑ Ⓒ Ⓓ Ⓔ
20 Ⓐ Ⓑ Ⓒ Ⓓ Ⓔ	40 Ⓐ Ⓑ Ⓒ Ⓓ Ⓔ	60 Ⓐ Ⓑ Ⓒ Ⓓ Ⓔ

AP Macroeconomics Practice Exam 1

SECTION I

Multiple-Choice Questions
Time—1 hour and 10 minutes
60 questions

For the multiple-choice questions that follow, select the best answer and fill in the appropriate letter on the answer sheet.

1. Which of the following statements is true of production possibility curves and trade between nations?

(A) Nations specialize and trade based on absolute advantage in production.
(B) Free trade allows each nation to consume beyond the production possibility curve.
(C) The flow of goods and services is based on the principle of absolute advantage.
(D) Nations can consume at points beyond the production possibility curve by protecting domestic industries from free trade.
(E) Tariffs and quotas divert resources from the inefficient producers of a good to the efficient producers of that good.

2. A nation is producing at a point inside of its production possibility curve. Which of the following is a possible explanation for this outcome?

(A) This nation has experienced a permanent decrease in its production capacity.
(B) This nation has experienced slower than usual technological progress.
(C) This nation has avoided free trade between other nations.
(D) This nation is experiencing an economic recession.
(E) This nation's economy is centrally planned.

3. How would fiscal and monetary policymakers combine spending, tax, and traditional monetary policy with limited reserves to fight a recessionary gap, while avoiding large budget deficits?

	SPENDING POLICY	TAX POLICY	MONETARY POLICY
(A)	Higher spending	Lower taxes	Sell Treasury securities
(B)	Lower spending	Higher taxes	Buy Treasury securities
(C)	Lower spending	Lower taxes	Increasing the reserve requirement
(D)	Higher spending	Higher taxes	Lowering the discount rate
(E)	Higher spending	Higher taxes	Sell Treasury securities

4. Corn is exchanged in a competitive market. Which of the following definitely increases the equilibrium price of corn?

(A) Both supply and demand shift rightward.
(B) Both supply and demand shift leftward.
(C) Supply shifts to the right; demand shifts to the left.
(D) Supply shifts to the left; demand shifts to the right.
(E) The government imposes an effective price ceiling in the corn market.

5. An increase in the consumer price index is commonly referred to as

(A) economic growth.
(B) inflation.
(C) unemployment.
(D) discouraged workers.
(E) deflation.

6. Which of the following is characteristic of a centrally planned economic system?

(A) Resources are allocated based on relative prices.
(B) The circular flow of goods and services minimizes the role of the federal government.
(C) Private ownership of resources is fundamental to economic growth.
(D) Government planners decide how best to produce goods and services.
(E) Efficiency is superior to the market economic system.

7. The government has just lowered personal income taxes. Which of the following best describes the effects that this policy has on the economy?

(A) Higher disposable income, higher consumption, higher real GDP, lower unemployment
(B) Higher disposable income, lower consumption, higher real GDP, lower unemployment
(C) Lower disposable income, higher consumption, higher real GDP, lower unemployment
(D) Lower disposable income, lower consumption, lower real GDP, higher unemployment
(E) Higher disposable income, higher consumption, higher real GDP, higher unemployment

8. Which of the following are harmed by unexpectedly high rates of inflation?

(A) Borrowers repaying a long-term loan at a fixed interest rate.
(B) Savers who have put their money in long-term assets that pay a fixed interest rate.
(C) Workers who have negotiated cost-of-living raises into their contracts.
(D) Renters of apartments who have signed a lease that holds rent constant for two years.
(E) Employers paying workers the minimum wage.

9. Which of the following statements is true?

(A) The velocity of money is equal to real GDP divided by the money supply.
(B) Dollars earned today have more purchasing power than dollars earned a year from today.
(C) The supply of loanable funds consists of investors.
(D) The demand for loanable funds consists of savers.
(E) Expansionary fiscal policy shifts the money supply curve to the right, lowering interest rates.

10. If your nominal income rises 4 percent and your real income falls 1 percent, by how much did the price level change?

(A) 5 percent decrease
(B) ¼ percent increase
(C) 3 percent increase
(D) 3 percent decrease
(E) 5 percent increase

11. The statistic used to measure the percentage of the population that is either working or seeking work is called the

(A) consumer price index
(B) real interest rate
(C) unemployment rate
(D) producer price index
(E) labor force participation rate

12. Which of the following lessens the impact of expansionary fiscal policy?

(A) An increase in the marginal propensity to consume.
(B) Lower interest rates that cause a decrease in net exports.
(C) Higher interest rates that cause an increase in net exports.
(D) Higher interest rates that decrease private investment.
(E) Falling price levels.

13. Suppose that the unemployment rate falls from 6 percent to 5 percent and the inflation rate falls from 3 percent to 2 percent. Which of the following best explains these trends?

(A) An increase in aggregate demand.
(B) A decrease in both aggregate demand and short-run aggregate supply.
(C) An increase in both aggregate demand and short-run aggregate supply.
(D) An increase in short-run aggregate supply.
(E) An increase in aggregate demand and a decrease in short-run aggregate supply.

14. A nation's economic growth can be seen as a(n)

(A) increase in the SRAS curve.
(B) increase in the AD curve.
(C) increase in the LRAS curve.
(D) decrease in the production possibility curve.
(E) increase in the short-run Phillips curve.

15. Some economists believe that when aggregate demand declines, prices are inflexible or "sticky" in the downward direction. This implies that the short-run aggregate supply curve is

(A) upward sloping at full employment.
(B) horizontal below full employment.
(C) vertical at full employment.
(D) vertical below full employment.
(E) vertical above full employment.

16. Which of the following policies best describes supply-side fiscal policy?

(A) An increase in the money supply
(B) Increased government spending
(C) Lower taxes on research and development of new technology
(D) Higher taxes on household income
(E) More extensive government social welfare programs

17. A likely cause of falling Treasury bond prices might be

(A) expansionary monetary policy.
(B) contractionary monetary policy.
(C) a depreciating dollar.
(D) fiscal policy designed to reduce the budget deficit.
(E) a decrease in the money demand.

18. The economy is currently operating at full employment. Assuming flexible wages and prices, how would a decline in aggregate demand affect GDP and the price level in the short run, and GDP and the price level in the long run?

	SHORT-RUN GDP	SHORT-RUN PRICE LEVEL	LONG-RUN GDP	LONG-RUN PRICE LEVEL
(A)	Falls	Falls	No change	Falls
(B)	Falls	Falls	Falls	Falls
(C)	No change	Falls	No change	No change
(D)	Falls	Falls	No change	No change
(E)	Falls	Falls	Falls	Falls

19. In the long run, aggregate supply is

(A) upward sloping at full employment.
(B) horizontal below full employment.
(C) vertical at full employment.
(D) vertical below full employment.
(E) vertical above full employment.

20. What does the presence of discouraged workers do to the measurement of the unemployment rate?

(A) Discouraged workers are counted as "out of the labor force"; thus, the unemployment rate is understated, making the economy look stronger than it is.
(B) Discouraged workers are counted as "out of the labor force"; thus, the unemployment rate is understated, making the economy look weaker than it is.
(C) Discouraged workers are not surveyed, so there is no impact on the unemployment rate.
(D) Discouraged workers are counted as "unemployed"; thus, the unemployment rate is understated, making the economy look stronger than it is.
(E) Discouraged workers are counted as "unemployed"; thus, the unemployment rate is overstated, making the economy look weaker than it is.

21. Which of the following is true of the complete circular flow model of an open economy?

(A) All goods and services flow through the government in exchange for resource payments.
(B) There is no role for the foreign sector.
(C) Households supply resources to producers in exchange for goods and services.
(D) Producers provide goods and services to households in exchange for the costs of production.
(E) The government collects taxes from firms and households in exchange for goods and services.

22. Which of the following most directly increases aggregate demand in the United States?

(A) An American entrepreneur founds and locates a software company in England.
(B) The U.S. military closes a military base in California.
(C) The Chinese government makes it increasingly difficult for American firms to export goods to China.
(D) A Mexican entrepreneur founds and locates a software company in the United States.
(E) The Canadian government cancels an order for airliners from a firm located in the United States.

23. When both short-run aggregate supply and aggregate demand increase, which of the following can be said for certain?

(A) The price level rises, but real GDP falls.
(B) Both the price level and real GDP rise.
(C) The price level rises, but the change in real GDP is uncertain.
(D) The price level falls, but real GDP rises.
(E) Real GDP rises, but the change in the price level is uncertain.

24. When nominal GDP is rising, we would expect money demand to

(A) increase as consumers demand more money as a financial asset, increasing the interest rate.
(B) increase as consumers demand more money for transactions, increasing the interest rate.
(C) decrease as the purchasing power of the dollar is falling, decreasing the interest rate.
(D) decrease as consumers demand more money for transactions, increasing the interest rate.
(E) increase as consumers demand more money as a financial asset, decreasing the interest rate.

25. Which of the following tends to increase the spending multiplier?

(A) An increase in the marginal propensity to consume
(B) A decreased velocity of money
(C) An increase in the marginal propensity to save
(D) An increase in the real interest rate
(E) An increase in the price level

26. Households demand more money as a financial asset when

(A) nominal GDP falls.
(B) the nominal interest rate falls.
(C) bond prices fall.
(D) the supply of money falls.
(E) nominal GDP increases.

27. Which of the following represents a combination of contractionary fiscal and expansionary monetary policy in a system with limited reserves?

	FISCAL POLICY	MONETARY POLICY
(A)	Higher taxes	Selling Treasury securities
(B)	Lower taxes	Buying Treasury securities
(C)	Lower government spending	Increasing the reserve requirement
(D)	Lower government spending	Increasing the discount rate
(E)	Higher taxes	Buying Treasury securities

28. Higher levels of government deficit spending would likely have which of the following changes in the market for loanable funds?

	MARKET FOR LOANABLE FUNDS	INTEREST RATE
(A)	Increase in supply	Rising
(B)	Increase in demand	Rising
(C)	Decrease in demand	Falling
(D)	Decrease in supply	Falling
(E)	Decrease in both demand and supply	Rising

29. Investment demand most likely increases when
   (A) real GDP decreases.
   (B) the cost of acquiring and maintaining capital equipment rises.
   (C) investor optimism improves.
   (D) the real rate of interest rises.
   (E) taxes on business investment rise.

30. At the peak of a typical business cycle, which of the following is likely the greatest threat to the macroeconomy?
   (A) Unemployment
   (B) Bankruptcy
   (C) Declining labor productivity
   (D) Falling real household income
   (E) Inflation

31. Suppose that households increase the demand for U.S. Treasury bonds as financial assets. Which of the following accurately describes changes in the price of Treasury bonds, the interest rate, and the value of the dollar in foreign currency markets?

	PRICE OF BONDS	INTEREST RATE	DOLLAR
(A)	Rising	Rising	Appreciates
(B)	Falling	Rising	Appreciates
(C)	Falling	Falling	Appreciates
(D)	Falling	Falling	Depreciates
(E)	Rising	Falling	Depreciates

32. If households are more optimistic about the future, how would the consumption function be affected?
   (A) The marginal propensity to consume would increase, increasing the slope of the consumption function.
   (B) The entire consumption function would shift downward.
   (C) The entire consumption function would shift upward.
   (D) The marginal propensity to consume would decrease, increasing the slope of the consumption function.
   (E) The marginal propensity to consume would increase, decreasing the slope of the consumption function.

33. U.S. real GDP most likely falls when
   (A) income taxes are lowered.
   (B) investment in human capital is high.
   (C) the money supply is increased.
   (D) there is a trade surplus in goods and services.
   (E) the value of the dollar, relative to foreign currencies, is high.

34. If current real GDP is $3,000 and full employment real GDP is at $4,000, which of the following combinations of policies is the most likely to return the economy to full employment? Assume the banking system has ample reserves.
   (A) A decrease in taxes and a lower policy rate
   (B) An increase in government spending and an increase in taxes
   (C) A decrease in taxes and a higher interest rate paid to banks that deposit reserves with the central bank.
   (D) An increase in government spending and open market purchases of government securities.
   (E) A decrease in taxes and a decrease in government spending

35. If a nation is operating at full employment, and the central bank with ample reserves decides to increase the administered interest rates, the nation can expect the mortgage interest rate, the purchases of new homes, and the unemployment rate to change in which of the following ways?

	MORTGAGE INTEREST RATES	NEW HOMES	UNEMPLOYMENT RATE
(A)	Decrease	Increase	Increase
(B)	Decrease	Decrease	Decrease
(C)	Increase	Decrease	Decrease
(D)	Increase	Decrease	Increase
(E)	Increase	Increase	Increase

36. In an economy with limited banking reserves, expansionary monetary policy is designed to

(A) decrease the interest rate, increase private investment, increase aggregate demand, and increase domestic output.
(B) decrease the interest rate, increase private investment, increase aggregate demand, and increase the unemployment rate.
(C) increase the interest rate, increase private investment, increase aggregate demand, and increase domestic output.
(D) increase the interest rate, decrease private investment, increase aggregate demand, and increase domestic output.
(E) increase the interest rate, decrease private investment, decrease aggregate demand, and decrease the price level.

37. If the economy is operating at full employment, which of the following policies will create the most inflation in the short run?

(A) An increase in government spending matched by an equal increase in taxes
(B) An increase in government spending with no change in taxes
(C) A decrease in government spending and a matching increase in taxes
(D) A decrease in taxes with no change in government spending
(E) A decrease in government spending matched by an equal decrease in taxes

38. Which of the following is a component of the *M*1 measure of money supply?

(A) Credit cards
(B) Gold bullion
(C) Cash and coins
(D) 30-year Treasury certificates
(E) 18-month certificates of deposits

39. Assuming that households save a proportion of disposable income, which of the following relationships between multipliers is correct?

(A) Tax multiplier > Spending multiplier > Balanced budget multiplier
(B) Spending multiplier = Tax multiplier > Balanced budget multiplier
(C) Spending multiplier > Tax multiplier = Balanced budget multiplier
(D) Spending multiplier > Tax multiplier > Balanced budget multiplier
(E) Tax multiplier > Spending multiplier = Balanced budget multiplier

40. The fractional reserve banking system's ability to create money is lessened if

(A) households that borrow redeposit the entire loan amounts back into the banks.
(B) banks hold excess reserves.
(C) banks lend all excess reserves to borrowing customers.
(D) households increase checking deposits in banks.
(E) the central bank lowers the reserve requirement.

41. All else equal, when the United States exports more goods and services,

(A) the value of the dollar falls as the supply of dollars increases.
(B) the value of the dollar rises as demand for dollars increases.
(C) the value of the dollar falls as demand for dollars decreases.
(D) the value of the dollar rises as the supply of dollars increases.
(E) the value of the dollar falls as demand for dollars increases.

42. If the reserve requirement is 10 percent in a system with limited reserves, and a new customer deposits $500, what is the maximum amount of money created?

(A) $500
(B) $4,500
(C) $5,000
(D) $50
(E) $5,500

43. Suppose today's headline is that private investment has decreased as a result of an action by the central bank operating with limited reserves. Which of the following choices is the most likely cause?

(A) Selling government securities to commercial banks
(B) Lowering of the discount rate
(C) Decreasing the reserve requirement
(D) Elimination of a corporate tax credit on investment
(E) A stronger stock market has increased investor optimism

44. If $1,000 is deposited into a checking account and excess reserves increase by $700, the reserve ratio must be

(A) 70%.
(B) 30%.
(C) 40%.
(D) 90%.
(E) 75%.

45. Suppose a nation is experiencing an annual budget surplus and uses some of this surplus to pay down part of the national debt. One potential side effect of this policy would be to

(A) increase interest rates and throw the economy into a recession.
(B) increase interest rates and depreciate the nation's currency.
(C) decrease interest rates and risk an inflationary period.
(D) decrease interest rates and throw the economy into a recession.
(E) decrease interest rates and appreciate the nation's currency.

46. Which of the following best describes a key difference between the short-run and long-run aggregate supply curve?

(A) Short-run aggregate supply is upward sloping as nominal wages quickly respond to price-level changes.
(B) Long-run aggregate supply is upward sloping as nominal wages quickly respond to price-level changes.
(C) Short-run aggregate supply is vertical as nominal wages quickly respond to price-level changes.
(D) Short-run aggregate supply is upward sloping as nominal wages do not quickly respond to price-level changes.
(E) Long-run aggregate supply is vertical as nominal wages do not quickly respond to price-level changes.

47. The "crowding-out" effect refers to which of the following?

(A) Lower interest rates that result from borrowing to conduct expansionary monetary policy
(B) Higher interest rates that result from borrowing to conduct contractionary fiscal policy
(C) Higher interest rates that result from borrowing to conduct expansionary fiscal policy
(D) Higher interest rates due to borrowing to conduct contractionary monetary policy
(E) Lower interest rates due to borrowing to conduct expansionary fiscal policy

48. Which of the following is a predictable consequence of import quotas?

(A) Increased competition and lower consumer prices
(B) Increased government tax revenue from imported goods
(C) Rising net exports and a rightward shift in aggregate supply
(D) An improved allocation of resources away from inefficient producers and lower consumer prices
(E) Higher consumer prices and a misallocation of resources away from efficient producers

49. If the central bank operates with ample reserves and is concerned about the "crowding-out" effect, they could engage in

(A) expansionary monetary policy by lowering the administered rate.
(B) expansionary monetary policy by selling government securities.
(C) contractionary monetary policy by raising the discount rate.
(D) contractionary monetary policy by lowering the home mortgage rate.
(E) expansionary monetary policy by purchasing government securities.

50. Which of the following would likely contribute to faster rates of economic growth?

(A) A more restrictive immigration policy
(B) Negative net investment
(C) Higher taxes on households and firms
(D) Higher government funding of research on clean energy supplies
(E) Protective trade policies

51. A nation that must consistently borrow to cover annual budget deficits risks

(A) a depreciation of the nation's currency as foreigners increase investment in the nation.
(B) a decline in net exports as the nation's goods become more expensive to foreign consumers.
(C) lower interest rates that discourage foreign investment in the nation.
(D) an appreciation of the nation's currency as foreigners decrease investment in the nation.
(E) lower interest rates that reduce private investment in productive capital.

52. Economic growth is best described as

(A) an increase in the production possibility curve and an increase in the natural rate of unemployment.
(B) an increase in the production possibility curve and a leftward shift in long-run aggregate supply.
(C) a decrease in the production possibility curve and a rightward shift in long-run aggregate supply.
(D) a decrease in the production possibility curve and a leftward shift in long-run aggregate supply.
(E) an increase in the production possibility curve and a rightward shift in long-run aggregate supply.

53. Which of the following is true of automatic fiscal policy stabilizers?

(A) For a given level of government spending, they produce a deficit during a recession and a surplus during an expansion.
(B) They serve to prolong recessionary and inflationary periods.
(C) The regressive tax system is a fundamental component of automatic stabilizers.
(D) For a given level of government spending, they produce a surplus during a recession and a surplus during an expansion.
(E) They lengthen the business cycle.

54. Which of the following is an example of expansionary monetary policy in a system of limited reserves for a central bank?

(A) Increasing the discount rate
(B) Increasing the reserve requirement
(C) Buying government securities from commercial banks
(D) Lowering income taxes
(E) Removal of import quotas

55. Labor productivity and long-term economic growth increase if

(A) a nation subsidizes education for all citizens.
(B) a nation imposes tariffs and quotas on imported goods.
(C) a nation removes penalties for firms that pollute natural resources.
(D) a nation ignores societal barriers like discrimination.
(E) a nation taxes income from interest on saving.

56. The short-run Phillips curve depicts the ____ relationship between ____ and ____.

(A) positive, price level, interest rate
(B) negative, interest rate, private investment
(C) negative, the inflation rate, the unemployment rate
(D) positive, price level, real GDP
(E) negative, interest rate, money demand

57. A negative, or contractionary, supply shock will

(A) shift the short-run Phillips curve to the left.
(B) shift the investment demand curve to the right.
(C) shift the money demand curve to the right.
(D) shift the money supply curve to the left.
(E) shift the short-run Phillips curve to the right.

58. When a nation is operating at the natural rate of unemployment,

(A) there is no cyclical unemployment.
(B) the inflation rate is zero.
(C) there is no structural unemployment.
(D) the nation is experiencing a recession.
(E) the unemployment rate is zero.

59. Which of the following likely results in a permanent increase in a nation's productive capacity?

(A) A decline in the birth rate
(B) Declining adult literacy rates
(C) Widespread relocation of manufacturing firms to low-wage nations
(D) National program of child immunization
(E) A global increase in the price of crude oil

60. Lower interest rates in the United States cause the value of the dollar and exports to change in which of the following ways?

	VALUE OF THE DOLLAR	U.S. EXPORTS
(A)	Increasing	Increasing
(B)	Increasing	Decreasing
(C)	Decreasing	Increasing
(D)	Decreasing	Unchanged
(E)	Increasing	Increasing

› Answers and Explanations

1. **B**—The gains from free trade are based on the principles of comparative, not absolute, advantage and specialization. Free trade allows nations to consume at points beyond their own PPC. In this way, free trade improves the economic well-being of trading nations. Tariffs inhibit the flow of free trade and promote inefficiency.

2. **D**—Points within the PPC imply unemployed resources, and this is indicative of a recession.

3. **D**—Balanced budget fiscal policy to eliminate a recession could increase spending and pay for that spending with higher taxes. Coordination of monetary policy requires some expansion of the money supply.

4. **D**—Combining a leftward supply shift with a rightward demand shift unambiguously raises the price.

5. **B**—Computing the change in the CPI is the most common way to measure price inflation.

6. **D**—A centrally planned economy decides which goods are needed and how best to provide them to the population. Resources are allocated and goods are distributed by the government, not the price system.

7. **A**—Lower taxes increase disposable income. Consumers spend most of this disposable income, which increases real GDP and lowers the unemployment rate.

8. **B**—Savers receive interest payments in "cheap" dollars and lose the purchasing power of their interest income due to rapid inflation.

9. **B**—Choice (A) is incorrect because the equation of exchange defines the velocity of money as nominal GDP divided by money supply. The supply of loanable funds includes savers, not investors. Fiscal policy shifts the AD curve, not the money supply curve.

10. **E**—The %Δ in real income is equal to the %Δ in nominal income less the rate of inflation.

11. **E**—The labor force participation rate is equal to (E + U)/Population and is used to measure engagement in the labor force. A falling LFPR indicates that a greater percentage of the population may be dropping out of the labor force.

12. **D**—Expansionary fiscal policy can be weakened if government borrowing drives up interest rates and diminishes private investment.

13. **D**—If the unemployment rate and inflation rate are both falling, they are likely the result of an increase in AS (either SRAS or LRAS).

14. **C**—An increase (or rightward shift) in the LRAS curve represents economic growth because this shows an increase in full employment real GDP.

15. **B**—If AD is falling and prices are not also falling, the AS curve must be horizontal. Keynesians believe that prices are sticky in the downward direction, but Classical economists believe prices are flexible. It is no surprise that the classical AS curve is vertical.

16. **C**—Supply-side fiscal policy tries to boost investment and productivity to increase LRAS and foster economic growth over time.

17. **B**—Falling bond prices correspond to rising interest rates, so look for the choice that increases interest rates. Lower money demand, one financial asset, creates rising demand for bonds, an alternative financial asset. Choice E therefore increases bond prices and lowers interest rates.

18. **A**—If prices and wages are flexible, the long-run economy readjusts to full employment. Falling AD lowers the price level and real GDP in the short run, but eventually lower wages shift the short-run AS curve to the right, further lowering the price level and moving long-run production back to full employment.

19. **C**—The short-run AS curve is upward sloping; the long-run AS is vertical at full employment.

20. **A**—The Bureau of Labor Statistics (BLS) only counts a worker as "unemployed" if they are actively seeking work. A discouraged worker is, by definition, not seeking work, and so the worker's omission from the unemployment rate understates this measure of economic health, making the economy look better than it is.

21. E—In the full circular flow model, the role of government is to collect taxes from firms and households in exchange for goods and services. Choice C is tempting, but households supply resources in exchange for wages, which they then use to purchase goods and services.

22. D—All production done in the United States is counted in U.S. GDP, regardless of the nationality of the entrepreneur.

23. E—Increased SRAS lowers the price level, but increased AD increases the price level. The change in the price level is uncertain, but real GDP rises.

24. B—The transaction demand for money rises with higher levels of nominal GDP. With a fixed supply of money, increased demand for money increases the interest rate as consumers sell financial assets (e.g., bonds), lowering the bond price and increasing the interest rate.

25. A—The spending multiplier $M = 1/(1 - \text{MPC}) = 1/\text{MPS}$, so an increase in the marginal propensity to consume increases the multiplier.

26. B—Asset demand for money is negatively related to the interest rate. Lower interest rates decrease the opportunity cost of holding money.

27. E—This is the only choice that combines contractionary fiscal and expansionary monetary policy.

28. B—Increased deficit spending will increase public borrowing, thus shifting the demand curve to the right and increasing the interest rate.

29. C—Increased optimism shifts investment demand to the right.

30. E—At the peak of the business cycle, the economy is very strong. Real GDP and incomes are high, unemployment is low, and the threat is a rapid increase in the price level.

31. E—An increase in demand for bonds as a financial asset increases the equilibrium price of bonds and lowers the interest rate paid to the bondholder. A lower interest rate in the U.S. makes the United States a less attractive place for foreign investors to place their money. This decreased demand for dollars depreciates the value of the dollar relative to foreign currencies.

32. C—Greater optimism shifts the consumption function upward. The MPC is unchanged.

33. E—If the value of the dollar is high, it makes American goods more expensive to foreign consumers. This decreases net exports and lowers U.S. real GDP. All other choices likely increase real GDP.

34. A—With the economy operating below full employment, look for a combination of expansionary policies. In a banking system with ample reserves, open market operations are not used to conduct monetary policy. The central bank increases or decreases the administered rates (in the United States, the interest rate on reserve balances) to influence the policy rate (federal funds rate).

35. D—Contractionary monetary policy increases interest rates. Higher interest rates decrease new home demand, investment spending, and AD, and increase the unemployment rate.

36. A—Expanding the money supply decreases the interest rate, increases investment, and stimulates AD.

37. B—Because the spending multiplier is larger than the tax multiplier, AD shifts farther to the right when spending is increased with no change in taxes. With the economy currently at full employment, this largest of rightward shifts in AD will be the most inflationary policy.

38. C—Because $M1$ is the most liquid measure of money, it begins with cash and coins.

39. D—For a given MPC, the spending multiplier exceeds the tax multiplier, which exceeds the balanced budget multiplier, which is always 1.

40. B—Money creation slows if banks do not lend all excess reserves.

41. B—More exports means an increased demand for the dollar. Stronger demand for the dollar increases the value of the dollar.

42. B—The money multiplier is $1/rr = 10$. So a \$500 deposit creates \$450 of new excess reserves, which can multiply to \$4,500 of newly created money. Note that the money multiplier is only relevant in a system with limited reserves and a reserve requirement.

43. A—Lower levels of investment are the result of higher interest rates, so look for the choice that describes a decrease in the money supply.

44. B—If \$700 of a \$1,000 deposit is in excess reserves, \$300 or 30 percent must have been reserved.

45. C—Reducing debt lowers interest rates, which increases private investment and risks inflation. Lower interest rates decrease foreign investment in the United States. Weaker demand for dollars depreciates the value of the dollar.

46. D—The short-run AS curve is upward sloping because when AD increases, the prices of goods and services rise faster than wages. This results in a profit opportunity for producers to increase output. In the long run, wages have time to fully respond to changes in the price level.

47. C—High levels of government borrowing increase the interest rate and squeeze private investors out of the investment market.

48. E—Quotas do not raise money for the domestic government, but they do increase prices and protect inefficient domestic producers, drawing resources away from efficient foreign producers.

49. A—To avoid "crowding out," a result of higher interest rates from deficit spending, the central bank should lower interest rates. With ample reserves, lower administered rates will push the policy rate lower, and other interest rates will follow.

50. D—Long-term investment in human capital and new technologies increases economic growth rates. Protection of a nation's natural resources and health of the citizens increases labor productivity.

51. B—Extensive borrowing increases the interest rate on U.S. securities. Foreign investors seek to buy dollars so that they can invest in these securities, but when the dollar appreciates, American exports become more expensive to foreign consumers, and so net exports fall.

52. E—When a nation's productive capacity increases, the PPC and long-run AS curves both shift rightward.

53. A—This choice describes exactly what automatic stabilizers do. By providing automatic fiscal stimulus during a recession, they also lessen the impact of a recession by shortening the business cycle.

54. C—Buying securities from commercial banks puts excess reserves in the banks, which begins the money creation process.

55. A—Subsidized public education is an investment in human capital and greatly increases labor productivity over time. This is one of the determinants of economic growth.

56. C—This choice describes the negative-sloping Phillips curve with the inflation rate on the *y*-axis and the unemployment rate on the *x*-axis.

57. E—If SRAS shifts to the left, both inflation and unemployment rise and result in a Phillips curve that is further to the right than before the supply shock.

58. A—At the natural rate of unemployment, there is frictional and structural unemployment but no cyclical job loss.

59. D—If more children are immunized against disease, the size of the adult workforce increases and higher levels of human capital and productivity are seen over time.

60. C—Lower interest rates decrease the demand for the dollar, which makes U.S.-made goods more affordable to foreign consumers, so exports from the United States increase.

AP Macroeconomics Practice Exam 1

SECTION II

Free-Response Questions
Planning time—10 minutes
Writing time—50 minutes

At the conclusion of the planning time, you have 50 minutes to respond to the following three questions. Approximately half of your time should be given to the first question, and the second half should be divided evenly between the remaining two questions. Be careful to clearly explain your reasoning and to provide clear labels to all graph axes and curves.

1. It is January 1, 2024, and the U.S. economy is operating at the level of real output that corresponds to full employment. The U.S. government is operating with a balanced budget and net exports are equal to zero:
   (A) Draw a correctly labeled graph of the long-run aggregate supply, short-run aggregate supply, and aggregate demand curves, and show each of the following.
      i. The current equilibrium real output and price level, labeled as Y1 and PL1, respectively
      ii. Full-employment output, labeled Yf
   (B) Suppose that by the end of 2024, Americans are importing more goods and services from other nations than they are exporting to other nations (a trade deficit) and there exists a deficit balance in the current account.
      i. How will this affect the balance of the capital/financial account? Explain.
      ii. On your graph from part (a), show how the trade deficit affects the U.S. economy, the level of real output, and the equilibrium price level.
   (C) Consider again the deficit balance in the current account.
      i. How will the deficit balance in the current account affect the demand for the dollar in the market for dollars?
      ii. Will the dollar appreciate or depreciate against other major foreign currencies?
   (D) Given your response to (B)(ii), how could the U.S. government engage in discretionary fiscal policy to return the economy to full employment output? Explain.

2. Assume that firms in Fundlandia become quite pessimistic about the state of the economy.
   (A) Using a correctly labeled graph of the loanable funds market, show how corporate pessimism will affect the equilibrium real interest rate.
   (B) Based only on the real interest rate change identified in part (A), what will happen to foreign purchases of Fundlandia's financial assets? Explain.
   (C) Fundlandia's currency, the Fundollar, has a floating exchange rate.
      i. What is the effect of the change in real interest rate indicated on your graph in part (A) on the exchange rate of the Fundollar? Explain.
      ii. Based on your answer to part C (i), would net exports in Fundlandia increase, decrease, or stay the same?

3. Ecuador and Paraguay use equal quantities of economic resources to produce consumption goods (C) and technological research (R). The table below shows the maximum possible consumption and research that can be attained by each nation.

NATION	ECUADOR		PARAGUAY		
Consumption units (C)	0	100	Consumption units (C)	0	50
Research units (R)	100	0	Research units (R)	150	0

(A) Draw a correctly labeled graph of the production possibilities curve for Ecuador. Place consumption (C) on the horizontal axis and research (R) on the vertical axis, and plot the relevant numerical values on each axis.

(B) On your graph in part (A), indicate the following.

i. A point that represents an unattainable level of production, labeled U.

ii. A point that represents an inefficient level of production, labeled I.

iii. A point that represents an efficient level of production, labeled E.

(C) Assume Ecuador moves from producing 60 units of consumption and 40 units of research to producing 50 units of consumption and 50 units of research. What will happen to economic growth in Ecuador in the future?

(D) Which nation has comparative advantage in technological research? Explain.

(E) Paraguay offers to trade 30 units of technological research for 20 units of consumption. Would Ecuador find this an acceptable term of trade? Explain.

› Free-Response Grading Rubric

Note: Based on my experience, these point allocations roughly approximate the weighting on similar questions on the AP examinations. Be aware that every year the point allocations differ and partial credit is awarded differently.

Question 1: (10 points)

Part (A): 2 points

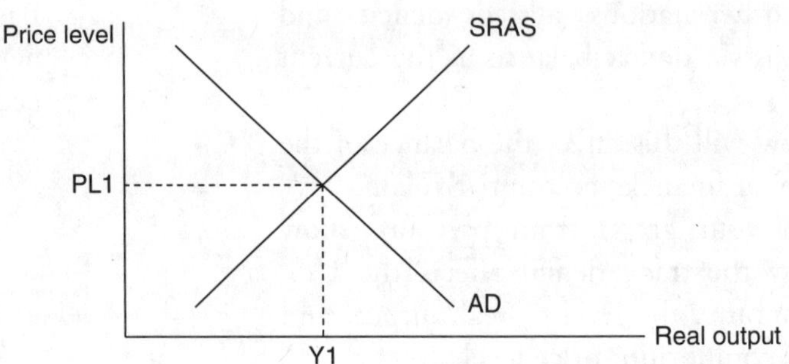

- One point is earned for drawing a correctly labeled graph showing a downward-sloping aggregate demand (AD) curve, an upward-sloping short-run aggregate supply (SRAS) curve, the equilibrium output level labeled Y1, and the equilibrium price level labeled PL1.

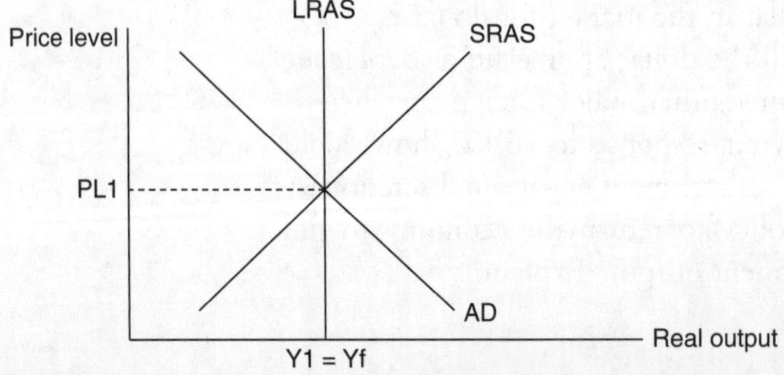

- One point is earned for drawing a correctly labeled vertical long-run aggregate supply (LRAS) curve with full employment output labeled Yf that is equal to the short-run equilibrium output level, Y1.

TIP 1: On graphing problems, you can lose a point for not indicating which variables lie on each graphical axis. In this case, it would be as simple as a PL and real output, or rGDP.

TIP 2: When asked to identify equilibrium price and quantity with specific labels, follow the instructions given to you.

Dashed lines from the intersection to the axes are enough to show that you understand exactly where equilibrium values lie on the axes.

TIP 3: Draw your graphs large enough for you to clearly identify the important components of the graph. If your graph is the size of a postage stamp, it becomes more difficult for you to identify all the relevant parts. It is also very tough for the reader to find all the points.

Part (B): 4 points

i. Two points. One point is earned for identifying "surplus" or "moves toward surplus." One point is earned for explaining that the existence of excess dollars from the trade deficit in the hands of foreign citizens leads to an increase in the purchase of U.S. financial assets by foreigners.

ii. Two points. One point is earned for adding a leftward shift of the AD curve in your graph. One point is earned for showing the new intersection with SRAS and indicating the decreased level of real output and the decreased price level.

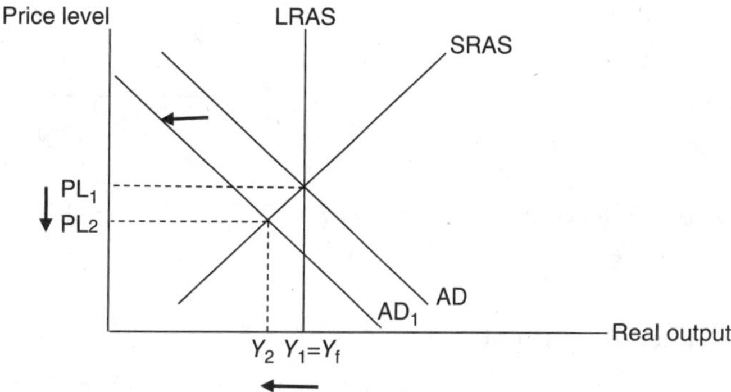

Part (C): 2 points

i. One point is earned for stating that there will be a decrease in the demand for dollars.

ii. One point is earned for indicating the dollar will depreciate in value relative to other foreign currencies.

Part (D): 2 points

i. One point is earned for stating either that the government could decrease taxes or increase government spending, and one point is earned for explaining that this policy would shift AD to the right, increasing real output.

What About Partial Credit?

Partial credit differs from year to year, so you do not want to bet your perfect 5 on the generosity of unknown readers. However, it is possible that you might receive some points for being consistent with an incorrect response. For example, suppose in (C)(i) you said that the demand for the dollar would increase. You would not receive the first point. However, if you said that the dollar would then appreciate, you could receive the second point for being consistent. Another opportunity for partial credit exists in (D). Suppose that in (B)(ii) you had shown the AD curve shift to the right. You would not receive any points in (B)(ii). However, in (D) you could describe a contractionary fiscal policy such as increasing taxes or decreasing government spending, and you could receive both points in (D).

Question 2: (5 points)

Part (A): 2 points

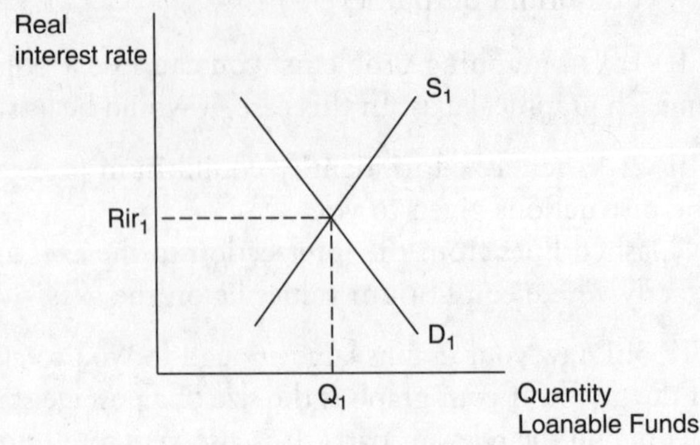

- One point is earned for drawing a correctly labeled graph of the loanable funds market and identifying the equilibrium real interest rate and quantity of loanable funds.

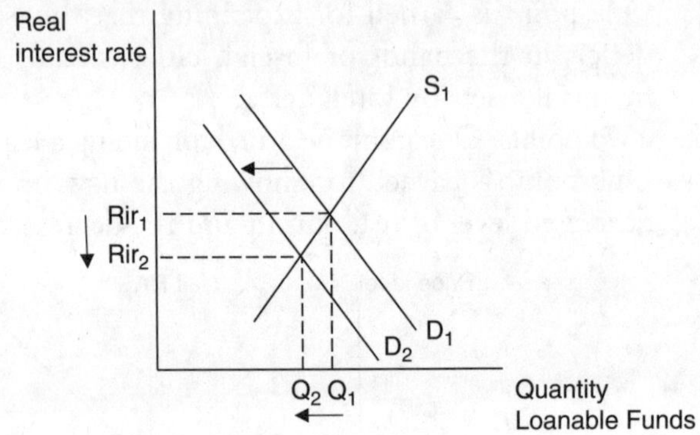

- One point is earned for showing a leftward shift of the demand curve and for showing a lower equilibrium real interest rate.

Part (B): 1 point

- One point is earned for stating that foreign purchases of Fundlandia's financial assets will decrease and for explaining that foreign investors, seeing lower real returns in Fundlandia, will invest elsewhere.

Part (C): 2 points

- One point is earned for stating that the exchange rate between the Fundollar and other currencies will depreciate (or the Fundollar will weaken in value) and for explaining that a lower real interest rate decreases demand for Fundlandian investments and thus decreases the demand for the Fundollar.
- One point is earned for stating that net exports in Fundlandia will increase.

What about partial credit?

As mentioned earlier, partial credit opportunities change from year to year, but there are likely to be a couple of ways where you could earn points on this question for being consistent. For example, suppose in part (A) that you showed the real interest rate increasing. You're not going to earn the second point. However, if in part (B) you state that foreign investors will increase purchases of Fundlandia's foreign assets (with a correct explanation), you could earn that point. You might also earn "consistency points" in part (C) if you stated that the Fundollar would appreciate and that next exports would decrease.

Question 3: (5 points)

Part (A): 1 point

One point is earned for drawing a correctly labeled production possibilities curve (PPC) for Ecuador with consumption (C) on the horizontal axis, technological research (R) on the vertical axis, and the relevant numerical values plotted.

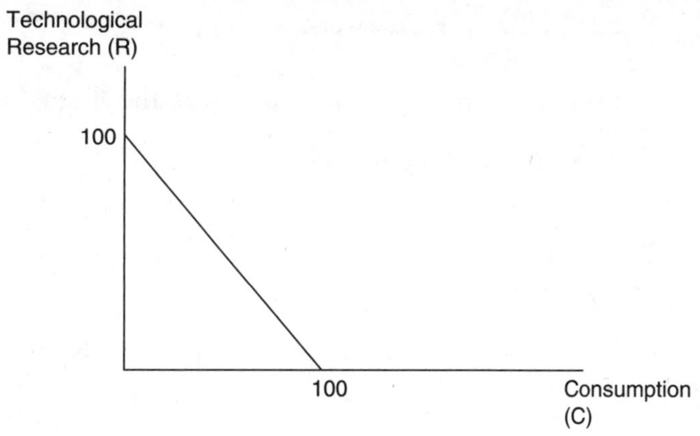

Part (B): 1 point

- One point is earned for showing point U outside the PPC, point E on the PPC, and point I inside the PPC.

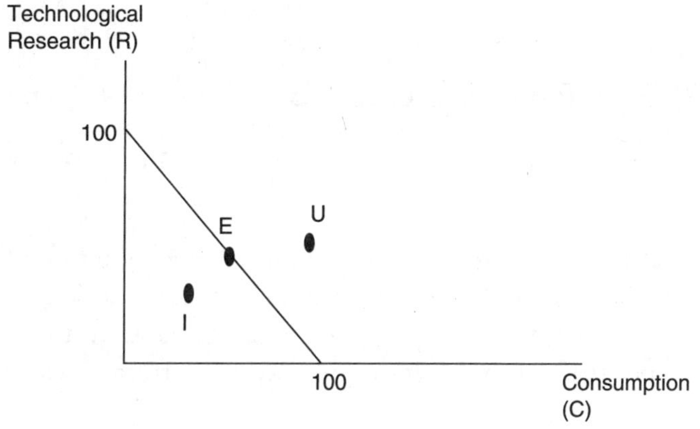

Part (C): 1 point

- One point is earned for stating that economic growth in Ecuador would increase, or accelerate.

Part (D): 1 point

- One point is earned for stating that Paraguay has comparative advantage in technological research and for explaining that one unit of research costs Paraguay 1/3 of a unit of consumption. Ecuador's opportunity cost of one unit of research is one unit of consumption.

Part (E): 1 point

- One point is earned for stating that Ecuador would agree to those terms and for explaining that Ecuador's internal cost of one unit of research is one unit of consumption and that with this deal they are receiving 1.5 units of research for every unit of consumption.

Scoring and Interpretation

AP Macroeconomics Practice Exam 1

Multiple-Choice Questions:

Number of correct answers: _____
Number of incorrect answers: _____
Number of blank answers: _____
Did you complete this part of the test in the allotted time? Yes/No

Free-Response Questions:

1. ____/10
2. ____/5
3. ____/5

Did you complete this part of the test in the allotted time? Yes/No

Calculate Your Score:

Multiple-Choice Questions:

________________ = ________________
(# right) MC raw score

Free-Response Questions:

Free-response raw score = (1.50 × Score #1) + (1.50 × Score #2) + (1.50 × Score #3) = _____

Add the raw scores from the multiple-choice and free-response sections to obtain your total raw score for the practice exam. Use the table that follows to determine your grade, remembering these are rough estimates using questions that are not actually from AP exams, so do not read too much into this conversion from raw score to AP score.

MACROECONOMICS #1	
RAW SCORE	APPROXIMATE AP GRADE
71–90	5
53–70	4
43–52	3
31–42	2
0–30	1

AP Macroeconomics Practice Exam 2

SECTION I: Multiple-Choice Questions

ANSWER SHEET

1 Ⓐ Ⓑ Ⓒ Ⓓ Ⓔ	21 Ⓐ Ⓑ Ⓒ Ⓓ Ⓔ	41 Ⓐ Ⓑ Ⓒ Ⓓ Ⓔ
2 Ⓐ Ⓑ Ⓒ Ⓓ Ⓔ	22 Ⓐ Ⓑ Ⓒ Ⓓ Ⓔ	42 Ⓐ Ⓑ Ⓒ Ⓓ Ⓔ
3 Ⓐ Ⓑ Ⓒ Ⓓ Ⓔ	23 Ⓐ Ⓑ Ⓒ Ⓓ Ⓔ	43 Ⓐ Ⓑ Ⓒ Ⓓ Ⓔ
4 Ⓐ Ⓑ Ⓒ Ⓓ Ⓔ	24 Ⓐ Ⓑ Ⓒ Ⓓ Ⓔ	44 Ⓐ Ⓑ Ⓒ Ⓓ Ⓔ
5 Ⓐ Ⓑ Ⓒ Ⓓ Ⓔ	25 Ⓐ Ⓑ Ⓒ Ⓓ Ⓔ	45 Ⓐ Ⓑ Ⓒ Ⓓ Ⓔ
6 Ⓐ Ⓑ Ⓒ Ⓓ Ⓔ	26 Ⓐ Ⓑ Ⓒ Ⓓ Ⓔ	46 Ⓐ Ⓑ Ⓒ Ⓓ Ⓔ
7 Ⓐ Ⓑ Ⓒ Ⓓ Ⓔ	27 Ⓐ Ⓑ Ⓒ Ⓓ Ⓔ	47 Ⓐ Ⓑ Ⓒ Ⓓ Ⓔ
8 Ⓐ Ⓑ Ⓒ Ⓓ Ⓔ	28 Ⓐ Ⓑ Ⓒ Ⓓ Ⓔ	48 Ⓐ Ⓑ Ⓒ Ⓓ Ⓔ
9 Ⓐ Ⓑ Ⓒ Ⓓ Ⓔ	29 Ⓐ Ⓑ Ⓒ Ⓓ Ⓔ	49 Ⓐ Ⓑ Ⓒ Ⓓ Ⓔ
10 Ⓐ Ⓑ Ⓒ Ⓓ Ⓔ	30 Ⓐ Ⓑ Ⓒ Ⓓ Ⓔ	50 Ⓐ Ⓑ Ⓒ Ⓓ Ⓔ
11 Ⓐ Ⓑ Ⓒ Ⓓ Ⓔ	31 Ⓐ Ⓑ Ⓒ Ⓓ Ⓔ	51 Ⓐ Ⓑ Ⓒ Ⓓ Ⓔ
12 Ⓐ Ⓑ Ⓒ Ⓓ Ⓔ	32 Ⓐ Ⓑ Ⓒ Ⓓ Ⓔ	52 Ⓐ Ⓑ Ⓒ Ⓓ Ⓔ
13 Ⓐ Ⓑ Ⓒ Ⓓ Ⓔ	33 Ⓐ Ⓑ Ⓒ Ⓓ Ⓔ	53 Ⓐ Ⓑ Ⓒ Ⓓ Ⓔ
14 Ⓐ Ⓑ Ⓒ Ⓓ Ⓔ	34 Ⓐ Ⓑ Ⓒ Ⓓ Ⓔ	54 Ⓐ Ⓑ Ⓒ Ⓓ Ⓔ
15 Ⓐ Ⓑ Ⓒ Ⓓ Ⓔ	35 Ⓐ Ⓑ Ⓒ Ⓓ Ⓔ	55 Ⓐ Ⓑ Ⓒ Ⓓ Ⓔ
16 Ⓐ Ⓑ Ⓒ Ⓓ Ⓔ	36 Ⓐ Ⓑ Ⓒ Ⓓ Ⓔ	56 Ⓐ Ⓑ Ⓒ Ⓓ Ⓔ
17 Ⓐ Ⓑ Ⓒ Ⓓ Ⓔ	37 Ⓐ Ⓑ Ⓒ Ⓓ Ⓔ	57 Ⓐ Ⓑ Ⓒ Ⓓ Ⓔ
18 Ⓐ Ⓑ Ⓒ Ⓓ Ⓔ	38 Ⓐ Ⓑ Ⓒ Ⓓ Ⓔ	58 Ⓐ Ⓑ Ⓒ Ⓓ Ⓔ
19 Ⓐ Ⓑ Ⓒ Ⓓ Ⓔ	39 Ⓐ Ⓑ Ⓒ Ⓓ Ⓔ	59 Ⓐ Ⓑ Ⓒ Ⓓ Ⓔ
20 Ⓐ Ⓑ Ⓒ Ⓓ Ⓔ	40 Ⓐ Ⓑ Ⓒ Ⓓ Ⓔ	60 Ⓐ Ⓑ Ⓒ Ⓓ Ⓔ

AP Macroeconomics Practice Exam 2

SECTION I

Multiple-Choice Questions
Time—1 hour and 10 minutes
60 questions

For the multiple-choice questions that follow, select the best answer and fill in the appropriate letter on the answer sheet.

Questions 1 and 2 refer to the figure below.

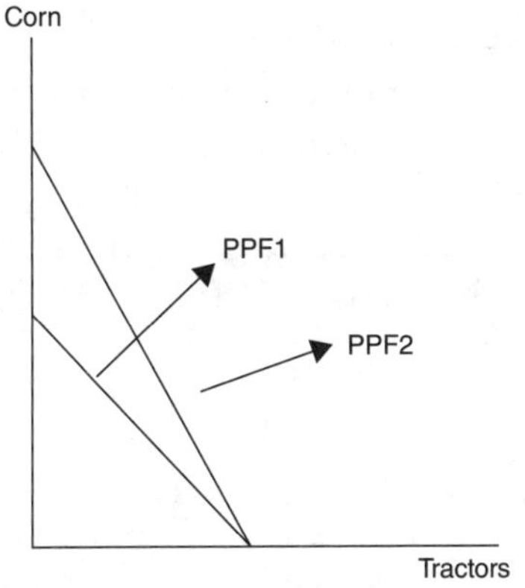

1. Suppose that the production possibility frontier (PPF) of this nation moves from PPF1 to PPF2. Which of the following could be the cause of this movement?
   (A) Technological improvements in the production of tractors
   (B) A long-lasting and destructive drought
   (C) A more efficient use of steel, an important raw material in the production of tractors
   (D) An economy-wide improvement in the productivity of the labor force
   (E) More effective pesticides used to protect crops from insect damage

2. Assume that the economy was once operating on PPF1 but is now operating on PPF2. What has happened to the opportunity cost of producing these goods?
   (A) The opportunity cost of producing tractors has decreased, while the opportunity cost of producing corn has increased.
   (B) The opportunity cost of producing tractors has increased, while the opportunity cost of producing corn has decreased.
   (C) The opportunity costs of producing tractors and corn have both decreased.
   (D) There has been no change in the opportunity cost of producing tractors and corn.
   (E) The opportunity costs of producing tractors and corn have both increased.

3. The price of gasoline has recently increased, while at the same time gasoline consumption has also increased. What is happening in the gasoline market?
   (A) This is evidence that contradicts the law of demand.
   (B) The price of crude oil has fallen, shifting the supply of gasoline to the right.
   (C) A price ceiling has been imposed in the market for gasoline.
   (D) The price of gasoline has decreased, shifting the demand for gasoline to the right.
   (E) Consumers prefer larger automobiles, shifting the demand for gasoline to the right.

4. If Nation A can produce a good at lower opportunity cost than Nation B can produce the same good, it is said that
   (A) Nation A has comparative advantage in the production of that good.
   (B) Nation B has comparative advantage in the production of that good.
   (C) Nation A has absolute advantage in the production of that good.
   (D) Nation B has absolute advantage in the production of that good.
   (E) Nation A has economic growth in the production of that good.

5. Which of the following is a consequence of removal of a protective tariff on imported steel?
   (A) Imports fall.
   (B) Income is transferred from steel consumers to domestic steel producers.
   (C) Income is transferred from foreign steel producers to domestic steel producers.
   (D) Allocative efficiency is improved.
   (E) Aggregate supply is decreased.

6. In the last 30 years, firms that produce cameras have begun to produce very few 35-mm cameras that use rolls of film and more digital cameras. This trend is an example of

(A) how central planners dictate which cameras are produced.
(B) the market system answering the question of "how" cameras should be produced.
(C) the market system answering the question of "what" cameras should be produced.
(D) the market system answering the question of "who" should consume the cameras that are produced.
(E) how firms fail to respond to improvements in technology and changes in consumer tastes.

7. Which of the following transactions would be included in the official computation of gross domestic product this year?

(A) Josh buys a new pair of running shoes.
(B) Nancy offers to babysit her granddaughter.
(C) Max buys his dad's used car.
(D) Eli cannot go to a concert, so he resells his ticket to a friend.
(E) Melanie rakes the leaves in her own yard.

8. Theo loses his job at the public swimming pool when the pool closes for the winter. This is an example of

(A) cyclical unemployment.
(B) discouraged worker.
(C) seasonal unemployment.
(D) frictional unemployment.
(E) structural unemployment.

9. Which of the following is *not* a scarce economic resource?

(A) Labor
(B) Capital
(C) Human wants
(D) Land
(E) Natural resources

10. How does an increasing national debt impact the market for U.S. dollars and the value of the dollar with respect to other currencies?

	MARKET FOR THE DOLLAR	VALUE OF THE DOLLAR
(A)	Increased demand	Appreciating
(B)	Increased supply	Appreciating
(C)	Decreased supply	Depreciating
(D)	Decreased demand	Depreciating
(E)	Increased demand	Depreciating

11. Suppose the price level in the United States has risen in the past year, but the production of goods and services has remained constant. Based on this information, which of the following is true?

	NOMINAL GDP	REAL GDP
(A)	Increased	Increased
(B)	No change	Decreased
(C)	Decreased	Decreased
(D)	Increased	Decreased
(E)	No change	No change

12. Which of the following is not an addition to national income?

(A) Wages
(B) Salaries
(C) Interest
(D) Depreciation of physical capital
(E) Profits

13. Which choice produces a faster rate of long-term economic growth for the United States?

(A) Institution of higher tariffs on imported goods
(B) More investment in capital infrastructure and less consumption of nondurable goods and services
(C) Elimination of mandatory school attendance laws
(D) Annual limits on the number of foreigners immigrating into the United States
(E) More investment in the military and less investment in higher education

YEAR	ADULT POPULATION	EMPLOYED	UN-EMPLOYED
2023	1000	600	200
2024	1200	800	200

14. The table above summarizes the local labor market. Based on this information, which of the following is an accurate statement?

(A) The number of discouraged workers has fallen from 2023 to 2024.
(B) Although the population has grown, the labor force has remained constant from 2023 to 2024.
(C) The unemployment rate fell from 33 percent in 2023 to 25 percent in 2024.
(D) The economic recession in 2023 worsened in 2024.
(E) The unemployment rate fell from 25 percent in 2023 to 20 percent in 2024.

15. Which of the following is true of money and financial markets?

(A) As the demand for bonds increases, the interest rate increases.
(B) For a given money supply, if nominal GDP increases, the velocity of money decreases.
(C) When demand for stocks and bonds increases, the asset demand for money falls.
(D) A macroeconomic recession increases the demand for loanable funds.
(E) Equilibrium in the money market occurs where the transaction demand for money equals the supply of money.

16. Which of the following would increase the aggregate demand?

(A) Higher levels of imported goods
(B) Lower levels of consumer wealth
(C) A higher real interest rate
(D) Lower taxes on personal income
(E) Lower levels of exported goods

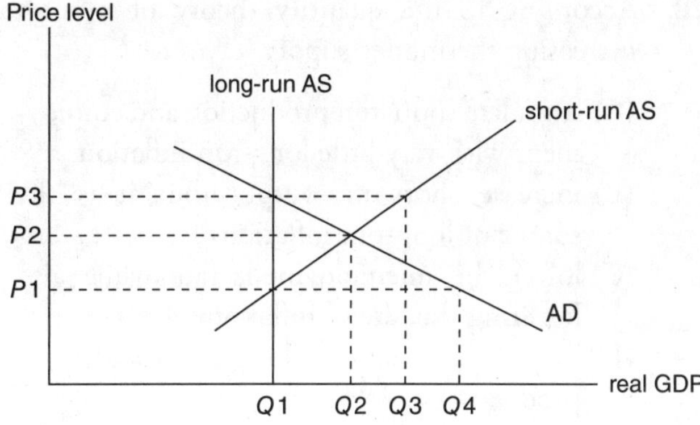

17. The figure above shows aggregate demand (AD) and supply (AS) for the economy. Assuming that aggregate demand remains constant, which of the following best predicts the short-run price level, the long-run price level, and the long-run level of output?

	SHORT-RUN PRICE LEVEL	LONG-RUN PRICE LEVEL	LONG-RUN OUTPUT
(A)	*P*2	*P*3	*Q*4
(B)	*P*2	*P*2	*Q*1
(C)	*P*2	*P*3	*Q*1
(D)	*P*1	*P*2	*Q*3
(E)	*P*3	*P*2	*Q*2

18. Which of the following transactions would be recorded as an addition to the U.S. financial account?

(A) An American farm sells a ton of wheat to a firm in Canada.
(B) A Canadian firm sells a condominium to a buyer from the United States.
(C) A Brazilian buys a bond issued by the American government.
(D) An American attorney sells an hour of legal advice to a Canadian firm.
(E) A Japanese firm sells electronics to an American retailer.

19. A policy supported by supply-side economists would be

(A) higher taxes on corporate profits.
(B) lower tax rates on interest earned from savings.
(C) removal of investment tax credits.
(D) a longer duration of unemployment benefits.
(E) higher marginal income tax rates to fund social welfare programs.

20. According to the quantity theory of money, increasing the money supply serves to

(A) stimulate short-run production and employment with very little long-run inflation.
(B) increase short-run output, but it is the source of long-run inflation.
(C) lower the unemployment rate while also lowering the rate of inflation.
(D) increase the nation's long-run capacity to produce.
(E) decrease short-run real GDP but increase real GDP in the long run.

21. Of the following choices, the most direct exchange in the circular flow model of a private closed economy is when

(A) households provide goods to firms in exchange for wage payments.
(B) households provide resources to firms in exchange for goods.
(C) households provide revenues to firms in exchange for wage payments.
(D) firms supply goods to households in exchange for revenues.
(E) firms supply resources to households in exchange for costs of production.

22. Suppose that the federal government reclassified the purchase of a new home as consumption spending rather than investment spending. This decision would

(A) increase aggregate demand and decrease real GDP.
(B) decrease aggregate demand and decrease real GDP.
(C) decrease aggregate demand and increase real GDP.
(D) increase aggregate demand and increase real GDP.
(E) have no impact on aggregate demand and real GDP.

23. Suppose that current disposable income is \$10,000 and consumption spending is \$8,000. For every \$100 increase in disposable income, saving increases \$10. Given this information,

(A) the marginal propensity to consume is 0.80.
(B) the marginal propensity to save is 0.20.
(C) the marginal propensity to save is 0.10.
(D) the marginal propensity to save is 0.90.
(E) the marginal propensity to consume is 0.10.

24. When we observe an unplanned decrease in inventories, we can expect

(A) prices to begin to fall.
(B) output to begin to rise.
(C) saving to begin to fall.
(D) output to begin to fall.
(E) planned investment to begin to rise.

25. Stagflation is the result of

(A) a leftward shift in the short-run aggregate supply curve.
(B) a leftward shift in the aggregate demand curve.
(C) a leftward shift in both the short-run aggregate supply and aggregate demand curves.
(D) a rightward shift in the short-run aggregate supply curve.
(E) a rightward shift in the aggregate demand curve.

26. If the short-run aggregate supply curve is horizontal, it is because

(A) there exist many unemployed resources so that output can be increased without increasing wages and prices.
(B) any increase in output requires a corresponding increase in wages and prices.
(C) increases in output cause prices to increase, but wages adjust much less quickly.
(D) falling interest rates increase the demand for goods and services, putting upward pressure on prices.
(E) resources are fully employed so that output can be increased but only if the price level also increases.

27. In a private closed economy, which of the following statements is true?

(A) Household saving can never be negative.
(B) Investment is always greater than savings.
(C) The economy is in equilibrium when consumption equals saving.
(D) Saving is equal to zero when consumption equals disposable income.
(E) Government is the only source of spending and investment.

28. Which of the following is true of a typical contraction of the business cycle?

(A) Consumption is falling, but household wealth is rising.
(B) Consumption is increasing.
(C) Private investment is rising.
(D) Employment and inflation are low.
(E) Private saving rates are rising.

29. Which of the following is most likely to produce stronger economic growth over time?

(A) More rapid consumption of natural resources.
(B) Higher adult illiteracy rates.
(C) A falling stock of capital goods.
(D) Investment tax credits.
(E) Higher taxes on foreign capital investment.

30. If \$100 of new autonomous private investment were added to an economy with a marginal propensity to consume of 0.90, by how much would aggregate demand shift to the right?

(A) \$190
(B) \$900
(C) \$1,000
(D) \$1,900
(E) \$90

31. The U.S. has a banking system with ample reserves. Which of the following serves as the upper limit on the policy rate for the Federal Reserve?

(A) Federal funds rate
(B) Discount rate
(C) Interest on reserve balances rate
(D) Overnight reverse repurchase agreement rate
(E) Mortgage rate

32. Which of the following increases the size of the tax multiplier?

(A) An increase in the marginal propensity to consume.
(B) An increase in the reserve ratio.
(C) An increase in the marginal propensity to save.
(D) A decrease in the spending multiplier.
(E) A decrease in the velocity of money.

33. Which of the following might worsen a nation's trade deficit?

(A) Lower wages relative to other nations.
(B) Lower taxes on corporate profits relative to other nations.
(C) A higher interest rate on financial assets relative to other nations.
(D) A higher rate of inflation relative to other nations.
(E) Other nations remove tariffs and quotas on foreign imports.

34. If the economy is suffering from extremely high rates of inflation, which of the following fiscal policies would be an appropriate strategy for the economy?

(A) Increase government spending and decrease taxes.
(B) Decrease government spending and increase taxes.
(C) Increase government spending with no change in taxes.
(D) The central bank increases interest rates.
(E) Decrease taxes with no change in government spending.

35. Which of the following is an example of an expansionary supply shock?

(A) Rapid increasing wages
(B) A greatly depreciated currency
(C) Declining labor productivity
(D) Lower than expected agricultural harvests
(E) Lower factor prices in major industries

36. Which of the following fiscal policy combinations would be most likely to slowly increase real GDP without putting tremendous upward pressure on the price level?

(A) Increase government spending with a matching decrease in taxes.
(B) Decrease government spending with a matching increase in taxes.
(C) Increase government spending with no change in taxes.
(D) The central bank lowers the reserve ratio.
(E) Increase taxes with a matching increase in government spending.

37. Which of the following is an example of traditional contractionary monetary policy in a system with limited reserves?

(A) The central bank lowers the reserve ratio.
(B) The central bank lowers the discount rate.
(C) The central bank increases taxes on household income.
(D) The central bank decreases spending on welfare programs.
(E) The central bank sells government securities to commercial banks.

38. An economy with ample reserves in the banking system finds itself in a deep recession. The central bank should:

(A) Increase the interest rate that banks charge other banks for overnight loans.
(B) Decrease the administrative rate to lower the policy rate.
(C) Use open market operations to buy government bonds.
(D) Use open market operations to sell government bonds.
(E) Decrease the personal income tax.

39. Auntie Morebucks withdraws $1 million from her savings account and puts the cash in her refrigerator. This affects *M*1 and *M*2 in which of the following ways?

	M1	M2
(A)	Rises	Rises
(B)	No change	No change
(C)	Falls	Falls
(D)	Rises	Falls
(E)	Rises	No change

40. What is the difference between how the short-run and long-run Phillips curves are drawn?

(A) The short-run Phillips curve is downward sloping, and the long-run Phillips curve is upward sloping.
(B) The short-run Phillips curve is upward sloping, and the long-run Phillips curve is vertical.
(C) The short-run Phillips curve is horizontal, and the long-run Phillips curve is upward sloping.
(D) The short-run Phillips curve is downward sloping, and the long-run Phillips curve is vertical.
(E) The short-run Phillips curve is vertical, and the long-run Phillips curve is upward sloping.

41. Which of the following ensures the value of the U.S. dollar?

(A) The euro and other foreign currencies held by the Federal Reserve
(B) Gold bars in secure locations like Fort Knox
(C) The promise of the U.S. government to maintain its value
(D) The value of the actual paper on which it is printed
(E) An equal amount of physical capital, land, and natural resources

42. The reserve ratio is 0.10, and Mommy Morebucks withdraws $1 million from her checking account and keeps it as cash in her refrigerator. In a banking system with limited reserves, how does this withdrawal potentially impact money in circulation?

(A) Decreases it by $9 million
(B) Decreases it by $1 million
(C) Decreases it by $100,000
(D) Increases it by $1 million
(E) Decreases it by $10 million

43. If the economy were experiencing a recessionary gap, choose the option below that would be an appropriate fiscal policy to eliminate the gap, and the predicted impact of the policy on real GDP and unemployment.

	FISCAL POLICY	REAL GDP	UNEMPLOYMENT
(A)	Increase taxes.	Increase	Decrease
(B)	Decrease spending.	Decrease	Increase
(C)	Decrease taxes.	Increase	Increase
(D)	Increase money supply.	Increase	Decrease
(E)	Decrease taxes.	Increase	Decrease

44. Traditional monetary tools of the Federal Reserve do *not* include which of the following choices?

(A) Buying Treasury securities from commercial banks
(B) Changing tariffs and quotas on imported goods
(C) Changing the reserve ratio
(D) Changing the discount rate
(E) Selling Treasury securities to commercial banks

45. Of the following choices, which combination of fiscal and monetary policy would most likely reduce a recessionary gap in an economy with ample banking reserves?

	FISCAL POLICY	MONETARY POLICY
(A)	Increase taxes.	Increase the reserve requirement.
(B)	Decrease spending.	Sell government securities.
(C)	Decrease taxes.	Lower the interest rate on reserve balances.
(D)	Increase spending.	Increase the policy rate.
(E)	Decrease taxes.	Increase the administered interest rates.

46. For a given level of government spending, the federal government usually experiences a budget____during economic____and a budget ______during economic_______.

(A) deficit, recession, surplus, expansion
(B) surplus, recession, deficit, expansion
(C) deficit, expansion, surplus, recession
(D) surplus, recession, surplus, expansion
(E) deficit, recession, deficit, expansion

47. Suppose that elected officials and the central bank agree to combine fiscal and monetary policies to lessen the threat of inflation. Which of the following combinations would likely accomplish this goal? Assume the economy operates with limited banking reserves.

	FISCAL POLICY	MONETARY POLICY
(A)	Decrease taxes	Increase the reserve requirement.
(B)	Decrease spending	Buy government securities
(C)	Decrease taxes	Sell government securities
(D)	Decrease spending	Decrease the reserve requirement
(E)	Increase taxes	Increase the discount rate

48. As chair of the central bank in a system with ample reserves, how would you reduce the "crowding-out" effect from deficit spending, and what macroeconomic problem might your policy exacerbate?

(A) Increase the administered rate, risking the devaluation of the dollar
(B) Sell government securities, risking inflation
(C) Buy government securities, risking a recessionary gap
(D) Lower the administered rate, risking inflation
(E) Lower the interest on reserve balances rate, risking cyclical unemployment

49. Which of the following is likely to shift the long-run aggregate supply curve to the right?

(A) A nation that devotes more resources to nondurable consumption goods, rather than durable capital goods
(B) Research that improves the productivity of labor and capital
(C) More restrictive trade policies
(D) Annual limits to immigration of foreign citizens
(E) A permanent increase in the price of energy

50. Holding all else equal, which of the following monetary policies would be used to boost a nation's exports? Assume the nation has limited reserves and the same monetary tools as the Federal Reserve.

(A) Increasing the discount rate
(B) Increasing the reserve requirement
(C) Buying government securities
(D) Lowering tariffs
(E) Removing import quotas

51. Which of the following could limit the ability of a central bank to conduct expansionary monetary policy in a banking system with limited reserves?

(A) Money demand is nearly perfectly elastic.
(B) Investment demand is nearly perfectly elastic.
(C) Banks make loans with all excess reserves.
(D) Households carry very little cash, holding their money in checking and saving deposits.
(E) Money supply is nearly perfectly inelastic.

52. Which of the following is a predictable outcome of expansionary monetary policy in a recession?

(A) It decreases aggregate demand so that the price level falls, which increases demand for the dollar.
(B) It increases investment, which increases aggregate demand and increases employment.
(C) It increases aggregate demand, which increases real GDP and increases the unemployment rate.
(D) It keeps interest rates high, which attracts foreign investment.
(E) It decreases the interest rate, which attracts foreign investment in U.S. financial assets.

53. Suppose the economy is in long-run equilibrium when an expansionary supply shock is felt in the economy. This changes the short-run Phillips curve, the short-run unemployment rate, and the long-run unemployment rate in which of the following ways?

	SHORT-RUN PHILLIPS CURVE	SHORT-RUN UN-EMPLOYMENT	LONG-RUN UN-EMPLOYMENT
(A)	Shifts down	Falls	Rises
(B)	Shifts up	Rises	Falls
(C)	Shifts down	Falls	Falls
(D)	Shifts up	Rises	Rises
(E)	Shifts down	Rises	Falls

54. As the Japanese economy expands, in what ways do U.S. net exports and the values of the dollar and the yen change?

	U.S. NET EXPORTS	VALUE OF DOLLAR	VALUE OF YEN
(A)	Decrease	Increase	Increase
(B)	Increase	Decrease	Increase
(C)	Decrease	Decrease	Increase
(D)	Increase	Increase	Decrease
(E)	Increase	Increase	Increase

55. Suppose the president plans to cut taxes for consumers and also plans to increase spending on the military. How does this affect real GDP and the price level?

(A) GDP increases and the price level decreases.
(B) GDP decreases and the price level increases.
(C) GDP stays the same and the price level increases.
(D) GDP decreases and the price level decreases.
(E) GDP increases and the price level increases.

56. U.S. dollars and the European Union's (EU's) euros are exchanged in global currency markets. Which of the following is true?

(A) If inflation is high in the EU and the price level in the United States is stable, the value of the dollar appreciates.
(B) If the Fed decreases the money supply, the value of the dollar depreciates.
(C) If EU consumers are less inclined to purchase American goods, the dollar appreciates.
(D) If U.S. income levels are rising relative to incomes in the EU, the euro depreciates.
(E) If the European central bank expands the money supply, the euro appreciates.

57. If in a given year the government collects more money in net taxes than it spends, there would exist

(A) a current account deficit.
(B) a budget surplus.
(C) a trade surplus.
(D) a budget deficit.
(E) a trade deficit.

58. Which component of a nation's balance of payments recognizes the purchase and sale of physical and financial assets between nations?

(A) The capital account
(B) The official reserves account
(C) The current account
(D) The trade deficit account
(E) The trade surplus account

59. An import quota on foreign automobiles is expected to

(A) increase domestic efficiency and protect domestic producers at the expense of foreign producers.
(B) decrease the price of automobiles and protect domestic consumers at the expense of foreign producers.
(C) increase the price of automobiles and protect domestic producers at the expense of consumers.
(D) increase the price of automobiles and protect domestic consumers at the expense of domestic producers.
(E) decrease domestic efficiency and protect domestic producers at the expense of domestic autoworkers.

60. When a large increase in aggregate demand has an even greater increase in real GDP, economists refer to this as

(A) the balanced budget multiplier.
(B) the money multiplier.
(C) the foreign substitution effect.
(D) the wealth effect.
(E) the spending multiplier.

› Answers and Explanations

1. E—The capacity to produce corn has increased, but the capacity for tractor production is the same. More effective pesticides do not improve the ability to produce tractors but improve the ability to harvest corn.
2. B—When the slope of the PPF increases, the opportunity cost of producing the *x*-axis good rises, while the opportunity cost of producing the *y*-axis good falls.
3. E—Rising prices and rising quantities does not disprove the law of demand; it simply reflects a rightward shift in demand with a constant supply curve.
4. A—Defines comparative advantage.
5. D—Tariffs create inefficiency in the world steel market.
6. C—The free market responds to changes in consumer tastes, technology, and prices to produce "what" is most wanted by society.
7. A—Household production is not included in GDP calculations. Secondhand sales are counted the first time the good was produced.
8. C—Know the difference between types of unemployment.
9. C—Human wants are neither scarce nor are they economic resources.
10. A—Rising national debt increases interest rates and attracts foreign investment in U.S. financial assets. Greater demand for dollars appreciates the dollar.
11. D—Nominal GDP rises with the price level. If output increases at a slower rate than increases in the price level, real GDP falls.
12. D—National income includes all sources of income and depreciation is not a source of income.
13. B—Know the factors critical to long-term economic growth.
14. E—UR = U/LF and LF = (E + U).
15. C—Stocks, bonds, and money are all financial assets. All else equal, rising demand for stocks and bonds lowers the asset demand for money.
16. D—Lower taxes on personal income increase consumption and AD.
17. C—Short-run equilibrium is where short-run AS intersects AD, in this case, above full employment. In the long run, wages increase, shifting SRAS leftward until settling at full employment Q_1 and higher price P_3.
18. C—The financial account summarizes international purchases and sales of real or financial assets, so an addition would be created when a foreign entity buys an asset in the United States.
19. B—Supply-side economists prefer lower taxes on saving to encourage saving. More saving increases investment and, over time, increases LRAS.
20. B—The equation of exchange says $MV = PQ$, and it is assumed that Q and V are fairly constant. Any increase in money supply (M) might initially boost output, but it eventually results in a higher price level (P).
21. D—Know the circular flow model.
22. E—This reclassification would not affect AD or tabulation of GDP.
23. C—If income increases $100 and saving increases by $10, the MPS = 0.10 and the MPC = 0.90.
24. B—If inventories unexpectedly fall, consumption exceeds production, so expect production to begin rising.
25. A—Stagflation is inflation with high unemployment, and this occurs when SRAS shifts to the left.
26. A—The horizontal range of SRAS occurs when resources are unemployed. If output rises, wages do not rise and prices are constant.
27. D—Consumption spending is equal to disposable income minus saving: $C = \text{DI} - S$.
28. D—Weak AD (contraction) causes job loss and low inflation rates.
29. D—Investment tax credits provide incentives for firms to invest in capital equipment and new factory construction. This policy stimulates economic growth and productivity.
30. C—With an MPC = 0.90, $M = 10$, so increased investment shifts AD $1,000 to the right.
31. B—The Fed uses the federal funds rate as the policy rate. The federal funds rate is the rate that banks charge each other for overnight lending. The discount rate is the rate that the Fed charges banks that borrow from the Fed. Since banks will always prefer to pay lower interest rates, they would never pay more to borrow from the Fed

than they can pay to borrow from each other. So, the Fed uses the discount rate as an upper bound (or ceiling) interest rate for the policy rate.

32. A—$Tm = M \times MPC$. A larger MPC increases the size of Tm.

33. D—Higher inflation than other nations causes goods to be more expensive relative to those produced abroad, causing a drop in net exports.

34. B—High inflation rates require a decrease in AD, and this is the only contractionary fiscal policy. Fed policy is not fiscal; it is monetary.

35. E—Lower factor prices in major industries represent decreased costs of production, and this creates an increased SRAS.

36. E—This balanced budget policy increases real GDP at a slower rate than the other expansionary options.

37. E—Selling securities pulls excess reserves out of the banking system, decreasing the money supply.

38. B—When banks have ample reserves, purchasing government bonds will not lower interest rates. Instead, the central bank lowers the administrated rates, which lowers the policy rate. This should increase aggregate demand to get the economy out of the recession.

39. B—Savings is already part of *M*1, so converting it to cash doesn't affect *M*1. And since *M*1 is included in *M*2, there will also be no change in *M*2.

40. D—The short-run Phillips curve portrays the inverse relationship between inflation and unemployment rates. In the long run, it is vertical at the natural rate of unemployment.

41. C—The U.S. dollar is not "backed" by any physical asset or commodity.

42. A—The money multiplier is 10, so withdrawing $1 million leads you to conclude that money in circulation falls by $10 million, but the original $1 million is still in circulation, so money falls by $9 million.

43. E—Know how fiscal policy affects real GDP and unemployment.

44. B—The Fed does not make changes in tariff and quota policy.

45. C—Have a strong knowledge of fiscal and monetary policies.

46. A—Budget deficits emerge during a recession because net taxes fall when incomes fall. The trend is reversed during expansion.

47. E—Know all combinations of fiscal and monetary policy.

48. D—The central bank wants to lower interest rates and offset the higher rates from deficit spending. Combine the expansionary fiscal with the lower policy rate, and the bank risks inflation.

49. B—Long-run AS rises if the productive capacity of the economy rises and more productive labor and capital resources have this effect.

50. C—Lower interest rates decrease foreign demand for the nation's government securities, depreciating the currency. "Cheap" domestic currency make the nation's exports more affordable to foreigners, increasing exports.

51. A—A horizontal money demand curve implies that increasing the money supply does not lower the interest rate. Investment is constant, and AD does not increase.

52. B—Know how monetary policy affects investment, AD, and employment.

53. A—If short-run AS shifts rightward, the short-run Phillips curve shifts down or leftward. The short-run unemployment rate falls below the natural rate but eventually rises back to the natural rate and a lower rate of inflation, as expectations readjust to the new AS.

54. D—Higher Japanese incomes increase net exports in the United States, increasing the value of the dollar versus the yen, decreasing the value of the yen versus the dollar.

55. E—Know how fiscal policy affects AD, real GDP, and the price level.

56. A—A difference in relative prices affects the exchange rate between the dollar and the euro. European customers will see U.S. goods as relatively less expensive and increase their purchases from the United States, thus appreciating the dollar and depreciating the euro.

57. B—This defines a budget surplus.

58. A—In the balance of payments statement, the capital account shows the flow of currency in physical and financial assets.

59. C—Import quotas protect domestic producers at the expense of the higher price paid by consumers.

60. E—Because an injection of dollars into the circular flow goes through the economy several times, the impact on real GDP is multiplied.

AP Macroeconomics Practice Exam 2

SECTION II

Free-Response Questions
Planning time—10 minutes
Writing time—50 minutes

At the conclusion of the planning time, you have 50 minutes to respond to the following three questions. Approximately half of your time should be given to the first question, and the second half should be divided evenly between the remaining two questions. Be careful to clearly explain your reasoning and to provide clear labels to all graph axes and curves.

1. The U.S. economy is experiencing a severe recession, the banking system has ample reserves, and the budget is currently balanced.

(A) One policy analyst advocates expansionary tax cuts, while another advocates expansionary government spending. Which of these policies will have the greatest impact on real domestic output? Explain how you know.

(B) Choose one of the two proposed policies in part (A).
   i. Based on this policy, will the federal budget be in a deficit, in a surplus, or be balanced?
   ii. Based on your response to (B)(i), state what happens to interest rates in the market for loanable funds. Explain.

(C) Assuming that the economy has still not recovered from the recession, what monetary policy could the Federal Reserve use to stimulate the economy?

(D) Using a correctly labeled graph of the reserve market, show how the Fed policy identified in part (C) would affect the policy rate in the short run.

(E) Based on the interest rate change from part (D), will real output increase, decrease, or remain the same in the short run? Explain.

2. Assume that the European Union (EU) has experienced lower real interest rates, while real interest rates in the United States have remained relatively high. Explain how these lower real interest rates will affect each of the following:

(A) The purchase of EU financial assets by American investors

(B) The international value of the euro (EU currency)

(C) EU exports of goods and services to the United States

(D) EU imports of goods and services from the United States

(E) Unemployment rates in the European Union

3. Assume the expected inflation rate in a country is 2%, the current unemployment rate is 3%, and the natural rate of unemployment is 4%.

(A) Draw a correctly labeled graph of the short-run and long-run Phillips curves. Label the current short-run equilibrium as point W and plot the numerical values above on the graph.

(B) Is the actual inflation rate greater than, less than, or equal to the expected inflation rate of 2%?

(C) Assume loans were made taking into account the expected inflation rate of 2%. Will borrowers be better off or worse off after they realize the actual inflation rate identified in part (B)? Explain.

(D) Based on the relationship between the actual and the expected inflation rates identified in part (A), what will happen to the natural rate of unemployment in the long run? Explain.

› Free-Response Grading Rubric

Note: Based on my experience, these point allocations roughly approximate the weighting on similar questions on the AP examinations. Be aware that every year the point allocations differ and partial credit is awarded differently.

Question 1: (10 points)

Part (A): 2 points

One point is earned for stating that the spending policy will increase real GDP more than the tax cut policy.

One point is earned for explaining that the spending multiplier is greater than the tax multiplier. Tax cuts increase disposable income and some of that is saved, not spent, so the multiplier effect is smaller.

Part (B): 3 points

i. One point is earned for stating that regardless of policy, the budget will be in deficit.

ii. One point is earned for stating that interest rates will rise.
One point is earned for the explanation that the government borrowing causes demand for loanable funds to shift to the right (or the supply of loanable funds to shift to the left).

Part (C): 1 point

One point is earned for stating that the Federal Reserve should lower the policy rate (or federal funds rate) by lowering the interest on reserve balances rate or by lowering the administered rates.

Part (D): 3 points

These are graphing points.

One point is earned for a correctly drawn reserve market graph with the vertical axis labeled as policy rate and the horizontal axis labeled as quantity of reserves.

One point is earned for showing a vertical supply of reserves curve and a demand for reserves curve with the three ranges and the equilibrium policy rate on the vertical axis.

One point is earned for showing a downward movement of the demand for reserves and a lower policy rate.

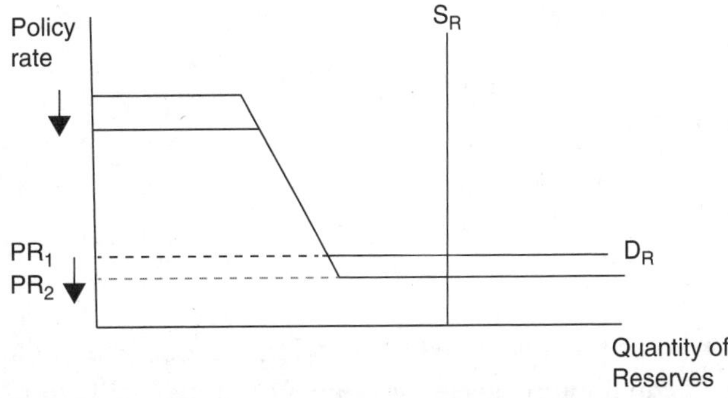

Part (E): 1 point

One point is earned for stating that real output would increase and for explaining that lower interest rates increase investment spending and would shift AD to the right.

Question 2: (5 points)

Part (A): One point is earned for stating that lower interest rates make EU financial assets less attractive to American investors, so fewer EU financial assets will be purchased.

Part (B): One point is earned for stating that decreased demand for the euro depreciates the euro versus the dollar and appreciates the dollar against the euro.

Part (C): One point is earned for stating that a depreciating euro makes EU goods look like a bargain to American consumers, increasing the demand for EU goods and services. The EU exports more goods to the United States.

Part (D): One point is earned for stating that an appreciating dollar makes American goods look more expensive to EU consumers, decreasing demand for U.S. goods and services. The EU imports fewer U.S. goods.

Part (E): One point is earned for stating that rising net exports in the EU would increase AD and lower unemployment rates.

Question 3: (5 points)

Part (A): 2 points

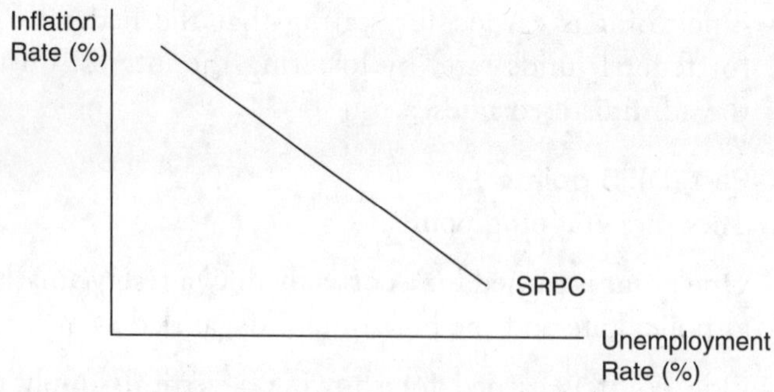

- One point is earned for drawing a correctly labeled graph showing the short-run Phillips curve (SRPC).

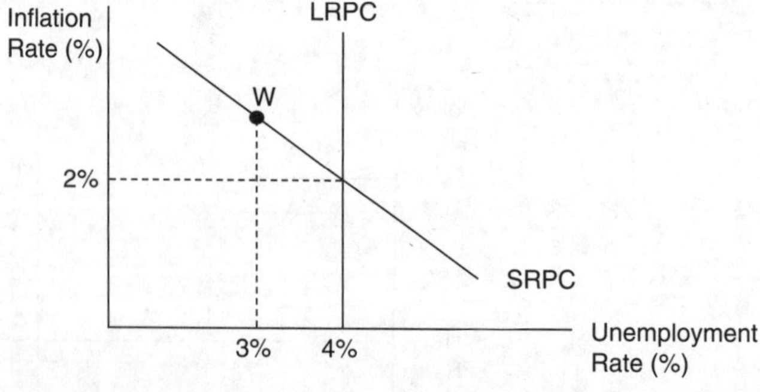

- One point is earned for drawing the long-run Phillips curve (LRPC) showing the short-run equilibrium, labeled as point W, on the SRPC to the left of the LRPC, and for plotting the numbers in the correct places on the graph.

Part (B): 1 point

- One point is earned for stating that the current inflation rate is higher than expected inflation.

Part (C): 1 point

- One point is earned for stating that borrowers are better off and for explaining that loans are being repaid with lower real values to the lender.

Note: If in part (B) you had stated that the current inflation rate was lower than the expected inflation rate, you might be able to earn a "consistency point" here by stating that borrowers are worse off, with a correct explanation.

Part (D): 1 point

- One point is earned for stating that, in the long run, the natural rate of unemployment does not change and for explaining that expectations will adjust to the higher actual rate of inflation and the economy returns to long run equilibrium.

Scoring and Interpretation

AP Macroeconomics Practice Exam 2

Multiple-Choice Questions:

Number of correct answers: _____
Number of incorrect answers: _____
Number of blank answers: _____

Did you complete this part of the test in the allotted time? Yes/No

Free-Response Questions:

1. _____/10
2. _____/5
3. _____/5

Did you complete this part of the test in the allotted time? Yes/No

Calculate Your Score:

Multiple-Choice Questions:

__________ = __________
(# right)   MC raw score

Free-Response Questions:

Free-Response Raw Score = (1.5 × Score #1) + (1.50 × Score #2) + (1.50 × Score #3) = _____

Add the raw scores from the multiple-choice and free-response sections to obtain your total raw score for the practice exam. Use the table that follows to determine your grade, remembering these are rough estimates using questions that are not actually from AP exams, so do not read too much into this conversion from raw score to AP score.

MACROECONOMICS #2	
RAW SCORE	APPROXIMATE AP GRADE
71–90	5
53–70	4
43–52	3
31–42	2
0–30	1

Appendixes

FURTHER READING

Dodge, Eric, and Melanie Fox. *Economics Demystified.* New York: McGraw-Hill, 2012.

Krugman, Paul, and Robin Wells. *Macroeconomics,* 6th ed. New York: Worth Publishers, 2020.

Mankiw, N. Gregory. *Principles of Economics,* 9th ed. Boston, MA: Cengage Publishing, 2021.

McConnell, Campbell L., Stanley L. Brue, and Sean Flynn. *Macroeconomics: Principles, Problems, and Policies,* 23rd ed. New York: McGraw-Hill/Irwin, 2023.

Stevenson, Betsey, and Justin Wolfers. *Principles of Economics.* New York: Worth Publishers, 2nd ed. 2023.

WEBSITES

Here is a list of websites that you might find useful in your preparation for the AP Macroeconomics exam:

https://apstudent.collegeboard.org/

https://www.economist.com/economics-a-to-z

www.councilforeconed.org

https://www.stlouisfed.org/education

GLOSSARY

absolute advantage The ability to produce more of a good than all other producers.

absolute (or money) prices The price of a good measured in units of currency.

administered interest rates In a banking system with ample reserves, these are the interest rates determined by the central bank and used to guide the policy rate to a target range. In the U.S., this is primarily the interest rate paid on reserve balances (IOR) deposited by banks in the Federal Reserve.

aggregate demand curve The negative relationship between all spending on domestic output and the aggregate price level of that output.

aggregate income The sum of all income earned by suppliers of resources in the economy.

aggregate spending (GDP) The sum of all spending from four sectors of the economy.

aggregation The process of summing the microeconomic activity of households and firms into a macroeconomic measure of economic activity.

all else equal The assumption that all other variables are held constant so that we can predict how a change in one variable affects a second. Also known as the "ceteris paribus" assumption.

ample reserves regime The current framework for the Federal Reserve's monetary policy. The banking system is provided enough cash reserves so that changes in the money supply do not cause a change in the federal funds rate.

appreciating currency An increase in the price of one currency relative to another currency.

asset demand for money The amount of money demanded as an asset is inversely related to the real interest rate.

assets of a bank Anything owned by the bank or owed to the bank.

automatic stabilizers Fiscal policy mechanisms that automatically regulate, or stabilize, the macroeconomy as it moves through the business cycle.

autonomous consumption The amount of consumption that occurs no matter the level of disposable income.

autonomous investment The level of investment determined by investment demand and independent of GDP.

autonomous saving The amount of saving that occurs no matter the level of disposable income.

balance of payments statement A summary of the payments received by the United States from foreign countries and the payments sent by the United States to foreign countries.

balance sheet or T-account A tabular way to show a bank's assets and liabilities.

balanced-budget multiplier A change in government spending offset by an equal change in taxes results in a multiplier effect equal to one.

base (or reference) year The year that serves as a reference point for constructing a price index and comparing real values over time.

bond A certificate of indebtedness from the issuer to the bond holder.

budget deficit Exists if government spending exceeds the tax revenue collected.

budget surplus Exists if tax revenue collected exceeds government spending.

business cycle The periodic rise and fall in economic activity around its long-term growth trend.

capital (or financial) account This account shows the flow of investment on real or financial assets between a nation and foreigners.

capitalist market system (capitalism) An economic system based on the fundamentals of private property, freedom, self-interest, and prices.

circular flow of economic activity (or circular flow of goods and services) A model that shows how households and firms circulate resources, goods, and incomes through the economy. This basic model is expanded to include the government and the foreign sector.

Classical school A macroeconomic model that explains how the economy naturally tends to come to full employment in the long run.

closed economy A model assuming no foreign sector (imports and exports).

comparative advantage The ability to produce a good at lower opportunity cost than all other producers.

complementary goods Two goods that provide more utility when consumed together than when consumed separately.

consumer price index (CPI) The price index that measures the average price level of the items in the base year market basket. The change in the CPI is the main measure of consumer inflation.

consumption and saving schedules Tables that show the direct relationships between disposable income and consumption and saving.

consumption function A positive relationship between disposable income and consumption.

consumption possibility frontier The line that illustrates all possible combinations of goods that two nations can consume with specialization and trade.

contraction A period where real GDP is falling.

contractionary fiscal policy Lower government spending or higher net taxes to shift AD to the left to full employment and reduce inflationary pressures.

contractionary monetary policy Decreases in the money supply to increase real interest rates, shift AD to the left to full employment, and reduce inflationary pressures.

cost of living adjustment An annual adjustment to a salary (or pension) so that the purchasing power of that income remains constant. This adjustment is typically based on the change in the consumer price index.

crowding-out effect Typically the result of government borrowing to fund deficit spending, this is the decline in spending in one sector due to an increase in spending from another sector.

current account This account shows current import and export payments of both goods and services and investment income sent to foreign investors and investment income received by U.S. citizens who invest abroad.

debt financing A firm's way of raising investment funds by issuing bonds to the public.

decision to invest A firm invests in projects if the expected rate of return is at least as great as the real interest rate.

deflation A decline in the overall price level.

demand curve Shows the quantity of a good demanded at all prices.

demand-pull inflation Inflation that results from stronger AD as it increases in the upward-sloping range of AS.

demand schedule A table showing quantity demanded for a good at all prices.

depreciating currency A decrease in the price of one currency relative to another currency.

depression A prolonged, deep trough in the business cycle.

determinants of demand The external factors that shift demand to the left or right.

determinants of supply The external factors that influence supply. When these variables change, the entire supply curve shifts to the left or right.

discount rate The interest rate commercial banks pay on short-term loans from the Fed.

discouraged workers Citizens who have been without work for so long that they become tired of looking for work and drop out of the labor force. Because these citizens are not counted in the ranks of the unemployed, the reported unemployment rate is understated.

disequilibrium Any price where the quantity demanded does not equal the quantity supplied.

disposable income (DI) The income a consumer has to spend or save once they have paid out net taxes.

dissaving Another way of saying that saving is less than zero.

domestic price The equilibrium price of a good in a nation without trade.

double counting The mistake of including the value of intermediate stages of production in GDP on top of the value of the final good.

economic growth The increase in an economy's production possibilities curve, or long-run AS curve, over time.

economics The study of how society allocates scarce resources.

equation of exchange The equation says that nominal GDP ($P \times Q$) is equal to the quantity of money (M) multiplied by the number of times each dollar is spent in a year (V).

equilibrium GDP The level of real GDP where real domestic production is equal to real domestic spending.

equity financing The firm's method of raising funds for investment by issuing shares of stock to the public.

excess demand The difference between quantity demanded and quantity supplied. A shortage.

excess reserves The portion of a bank deposit that may be loaned to borrowers.

excess supply The difference between quantity supplied and quantity demanded. A surplus.

exchange rate The amount of one currency you must give up to get one unit of the second currency.

expansion A period where real GDP is growing.

expansionary fiscal policy Increases in government spending or lower net taxes meant to shift AD to the right toward full employment and lower the unemployment rate.

expansionary monetary policy Increases in the money supply meant to decrease real interest rates shift AD to the right toward full employment and reduce the unemployment rate.

expected rate of return The rate of profit the firm anticipates receiving on investment expenditures.

exports Goods and services produced domestically but sold abroad.

factors of production Inputs or resources that go into the production function to produce goods and services.

fiat money Paper and coin money with no intrinsic value but used to make transactions because the government declares it to be legal tender.

final goods Goods that are ready for their final use by consumers and firms.

financial account See *capital account.*

the firm An organization that employs factors of production to produce a good or service that it hopes to profitably sell.

fiscal policy Deliberate changes in government spending and net tax collection to affect economic output, unemployment, and the price level.

foreign sector substitution effect The process of domestic consumers looking for foreign goods when the domestic price level rises, thus reducing the quantity of domestic output consumed.

fractional reserve banking A system in which only a fraction of the total money deposited in banks is held in reserve.

full employment Exists when the economy is experiencing no cyclical unemployment.

functions of money Money serves as a medium of exchange, a unit of account, and a store of value.

GDP price deflator The price index that measures the average price level of goods and services that make up GDP.

gross domestic product (GDP) The market value of the final goods and services produced within a nation in a given period.

human capital The amount of knowledge and skills that labor can apply to the work that they do.

imports Goods produced abroad but consumed domestically.

income effect Due to a higher price, the change in quantity demanded that results from a change in the consumer's purchasing power (or real income).

inferior goods A good for which demand decreases with an increase in consumer income.

inflation An increase in the overall price level.

inflation rate The percentage change in the price level from one year to the next.

inflationary gap The amount by which equilibrium real GDP exceeds full employment GDP.

interest on reserves (IOR) The interest rate that is paid to banks that deposit excess reserves with the Fed. This is the primary tool of current monetary policy.

interest rate effect The process of reduced domestic consumption due to a higher price level, causing an increase in the real interest rate.

intermediate goods Goods that require further modification before they are ready for their final use.

investment demand The negative relationship between the real interest rate and the cumulative dollars invested.

investment spending Spending on physical capital, inventories, and new construction.

investment tax credit A reduction in taxes for firms that invest in new capital like a factory or piece of equipment.

Keynesian school A macroeconomic model that believes the economy is unstable and does not naturally move to full employment in the long run.

labor force The sum of all individuals 16 years and older who are either currently employed (E) or unemployed (U). $LF = E + U$.

law of comparative advantage Nations can mutually benefit from trade so long as the relative production costs differ.

law of demand All else equal, when the price of a good rises, the quantity demanded of that good falls.

law of diminishing marginal returns As successive units of a variable input are added to a fixed input, beyond some point the marginal product declines.

law of increasing costs As more of a good is produced, the greater is its opportunity (or marginal) cost.

law of increasing marginal cost As a producer produces more of a good, the marginal cost rises. This is very similar to the idea of increasing opportunity costs in Chapter 5.

law of supply All else equal, when the price of a good rises, the quantity supplied of that good rises.

liability of a bank Anything owned by depositors or lenders to the bank.

liquidity A measure of how easily an asset can be converted to cash.

loanable funds market A hypothetical market where borrowers (investors) demand more funds at a lower real interest rate and lenders (savers) supply more funds at a higher real interest rate.

long run A period long enough for the firm to alter all production inputs, including the plant size.

long-run aggregate supply A vertical curve drawn at full-employment real GDP. In the long run it is believed that all prices and input costs will adjust to any short-run shock, thus bringing the economy back to long-run equilibrium.

***M*1** The most liquid measure of money supply, including cash, checking deposits, and savings deposits.

***M*2** *M*1 plus time deposits, and money market and mutual funds balances.

macroeconomic long run A period long enough for input prices to have fully adjusted to market forces, all input and output markets are in equilibrium, and the economy is operating at full employment (GDP_f).

macroeconomic short run A period during which the prices of goods and services are changing in their respective markets but the input prices have not yet adjusted to those changes in the product markets.

marginal The next unit, or increment of, an action.

marginal analysis Making decisions based on weighing the marginal benefits and costs of that action. The rational decision maker chooses an action if $MB \geq MC$.

marginal benefit (MB) The additional benefit received from the consumption of the next unit of a good or service.

marginal cost (MC) The additional cost of producing one more unit of output.

marginal propensity to consume (MPC) The change in consumption caused by a change in disposable income. The slope of the consumption function.

marginal propensity to save (MPS) The change in saving caused by a change in disposable income. The slope of the saving function.

marginal tax rate The rate paid on the last dollar earned, calculated by taking the ratio of the change in taxes divided by the change in income.

market A group with buyers and sellers of a good or service.

market basket A collection of goods and services used to represent what is consumed in the economy.

market economy An economic system in which resources are allocated through the decentralized decisions of firms and consumers.

market equilibrium Exists at the only price where the quantity supplied equals the quantity demanded. Or, it is the only quantity where the price consumers are willing to pay is exactly the price producers are willing to accept.

market failure A market outcome for which the quantity produced is not allocatively efficient ($MSB \neq MSC$) and either too many or too few units are produced.

market for reserves In a banking system with ample reserves, this is the model used to show how changes to the administered interest rates (like the IOR in the U.S.) affect the policy rate.

money demand The negative relationship between the nominal interest rate and the quantity of money demanded as an asset plus the quantity of money demanded for transactions.

money market The interaction of money demand and money supply determines the "price" of money, the nominal interest rate.

money multiplier Equal to one over the reserve ratio; this measures the maximum amount of new checking deposits that can be created by a single dollar of excess reserves.

money supply The fixed quantity of money in circulation at a given point in time as measured by the central bank.

multiplier effect The idea that a change in any component of aggregate demand creates a larger change in GDP.

national debt The accumulation of all annual budget deficits.

natural rate of unemployment The unemployment rate associated with full employment, somewhere between 4 to 6 percent in the United States.

net exports The value of a nation's total exports minus total imports.

net export effect The process of how expansionary fiscal policy decreases net exports due to rising interest rates. Another form of crowding out.

nominal GDP The value of current production at the current prices.

nominal interest rate The interest rate unadjusted for inflation. The opportunity cost of holding money in the money market.

nonmarket transactions Household work or do-it-yourself jobs that are missed by GDP accounting.

nonrenewable resources Natural resources that cannot replenish themselves.

normal goods A good for which demand increases with an increase in consumer income.

official reserves account The Fed's adjustment of a deficit or surplus in the current and capital account by the addition or subtraction of foreign currencies so that the balance of payments is zero.

open market operation (OMO) A tool of monetary policy, it involves the Fed's buying (or selling) of Treasury bonds from (or to) commercial banks and the general public.

opportunity cost The value of the sacrifice made to pursue a course of action.

overnight reverse repurchase agreement (ON RPP) The interest rate paid to a financial institution on an overnight transaction in which the Federal Reserve sells a U.S. government security to the financial institution while agreeing to buy the security back the next day. This is a secondary tool of current monetary policy.

peak The top of the business cycle where an expansion has ended and is about to turn down.

policy rate An interest rate that banks charge other banks for short-term lending. In the U.S., the policy rate is the federal funds rate. In a banking system with ample reserves, this is the rate that the central bank affects to conduct monetary policy.

price index A measure of the average level of prices in a market basket for a given year, when compared to the prices in a reference (or base) year.

production possibilities The different quantities of goods that an economy can produce with a given amount of scarce resources.

production possibility curve or frontier (PPC or PPF) A graphical device that shows the combination of two goods that a nation can efficiently produce with available resources and technology.

productivity The quantity of output that can be produced per worker in a given amount of time.

protective tariff An excise tax levied on an imported good that is produced in the domestic market so that it may be protected from foreign competition.

quantity theory of money The theory that an increase in the money supply will not affect real output and will only result in higher prices.

quota A maximum amount of a good that can be imported into the domestic market.

real GDP The value of current production, but using prices from a fixed point in time.

real rate of interest The cost of borrowing to fund an investment and equal to the nominal interest rate minus the expected rate of inflation.

recession A macroeconomic downturn, often described unofficially as two or more consecutive quarters of falling real GDP.

recessionary gap The amount by which full employment GDP exceeds equilibrium real GDP.

relative prices The price of one unit of good X measured not in currency, but in the number of units of good Y that must be sacrificed to acquire good X.

renewable resources Natural resources that can replenish themselves if they are not overharvested.

required reserves The minimum amount of deposits that must be held at the bank for withdrawals.

reserve requirement The fraction of total deposits that must be kept on reserve.

resources Also called *factors of production,* these are commonly grouped into the four categories of labor, physical capital, land or natural resources, and entrepreneurial ability.

revenue tariff An excise tax levied on goods that are not produced in the domestic market.

saving function A positive relationship between disposable income and saving.

scarcity The imbalance between limited productive resources and unlimited human wants.

secondhand sales Final goods and services that are resold.

shortage A situation in which, at the going market price, the quantity demanded exceeds the quantity supplied.

short-run aggregate supply curve The positive relationship between the level of domestic output produced and the aggregate price level of that output.

specialization Production of goods, or performance of tasks, based on comparative advantage.

spending multiplier The amount by which real GDP changes due to a change in spending.

stagflation A situation seen in the macroeconomy when inflation and the unemployment rate are both increasing. Also called *cost-push inflation.*

sticky prices The case when price levels do not change, especially downward, with changes in AD.

stock A certificate that represents a claim to, or share of, the ownership of a firm.

substitute goods Two goods are consumer substitutes if they provide essentially the same utility to the consumer.

substitution effect The change in quantity demanded resulting from a change in the price of one good relative to the price of other goods.

supply curve Shows the quantity of a good supplied at all prices.

supply schedule A table showing quantity supplied for a good at various prices.

supply shock An economy-wide phenomenon that affects the costs of firms and results in a shifting AS curve.

supply-side fiscal policy Fiscal policy centered on incentives to save and invest to prompt economic growth with very little inflation.

surplus A situation in which, at the going market price, the quantity supplied exceeds the quantity demanded.

tax multiplier The magnitude of the effect that a change in lump sum taxes has on real GDP.

technology A nation's knowledge of how to produce goods in the best possible way.

theory of liquidity preference Keynes's theory that the interest rate adjusts to bring the money market into equilibrium.

trade-offs The reality of scarce resources implies that individuals, firms, and governments are constantly faced with difficult choices that involve benefits and costs.

transaction demand The amount of money held in order to make transactions.

trough The bottom of the business cycle where a contraction has stopped and is about to turn up.

underground economy The unreported or illegal activity, bartering, or informal exchange of cash for goods and services that are not reported in official tabulations of GDP.

velocity of money The average number of times that a dollar is spent in a year.

world price The global equilibrium price of a good when nations engage in trade.

IMPORTANT FORMULAS AND CONDITIONS

Chapter 5

1. Optimal decision making: MB = MC
2. Opportunity cost from a production possibility curve or frontier (PPC or PPF):

   Good X: The slope of the PPC

   Good Y: The inverse of the slope of the PPC

Chapter 6

1. Market equilibrium:

   $Q_d = Q_s$
2. Shortage:

   $Q_d - Q_s$
3. Surplus:

   $Q_s - Q_d$

Chapter 7

1. Nominal GDP:

   = Current year production × Current year prices
2. Real GDP:

   $= 100 \times \dfrac{\text{(Nominal GDP)}}{\text{(GDP deflator)}}$
3. Aggregate spending (GDP):

   $= C + I + G + (X - M)$
4. Disposable income (DI):

   = Gross income − Net taxes
5. Net taxes:

   = Taxes paid − Transfers received
6. %Δ real GDP:

   = %Δ nominal GDP – %Δ price index
7. Price index current year:

   = 100 × (Spending current year)/(Spending base year)
8. Consumer inflation rate:

   $= 100 \times (CPI_{New} - CPI_{Old})/CPI_{Old}$
9. Real Income:

   = (Nominal income)/CPI (in hundredths)
10. Nominal interest rate:

    = Real interest rate + Expected inflation
11. Labor force:

    = Employed + Unemployed
12. Unemployment rate:

    = 100 × (Unemployed/Labor force)

Chapter 8

1. Consumption function:

   C = Autonomous consumption + MPC(DI)
2. Saving function:

   S = Autonomous savings + MPS(DI)
3. Marginal propensity to consume (MPC):

   $= \Delta C/\Delta \text{DI}$ = Slope of consumption function
4. Marginal propensity to save (MPS):

   $= \Delta S/\Delta DI$ = Slope of saving function
5. MPC + MPS = 1
6. Net exports $(X - M)$:

   = Exports – Imports
7. Equilibrium in the loanable funds market:

   $S = I$

8. Spending multiplier:

 = 1/(1 − MPC) = 1/MPS

 = (Δ GDP)/(Δ spending)

9. Tax multiplier (Tm):

 = MPC × (Spending multiplier) = MPC/MPS

 = (Δ GDP)/(Δ taxes)

10. Balanced-budget multiplier = 1

Chapter 9

1. Macroeconomic short-run equilibrium

 AD = SRAS

2. Macroeconomic long-run equilibrium

 AD = SRAS = LRAS

3. Recessionary gap:

 = Full employment GDP – Current GDP

4. Inflationary gap:

 = Current GDP – Full employment GDP

Chapter 10

1. Budget deficit:

 = Government spending – Net taxes

2. Budget Surplus:

 = Net taxes – Government spending

Chapter 11

1. *M*1 measure of money:
 = Cash + Coins + Checking Deposits + Traveler's checks

2. *M*2 measure of money:
 = *M*1 + Savings deposits + Small (e.g., under $100,000 CDs) time deposits + Money market deposits + Money market mutual funds

3. Money demand:

 = Transaction demand + Asset demand

4. Equilibrium in the money market:

 MS = MD

5. Reserve ratio (*rr*)

 = Required reserves/Total deposits

6. Simple money multiplier:

 = 1/*rr*

Chapter 12

1. Equilibrium in the currency ($) market:

 Q_d for the $ = Q_s of the $

2. Revenue from a tariff:

 = Per unit tariff × Units imported

NOTES

NOTES

NOTES

NOTES

NOTES

NOTES